ENVIRONMENTALLY AND SOCIALLY SUSTAINABLE DEVELOPMENT

CORAL REEFS

Challenges and Opportunities for Sustainable Management

Proceedings of an Associated Event of the
Fifth Annual World Bank Conference on
Environmentally and Socially Sustainable Development

*Cosponsored by the World Bank and the International
Center for Living and Aquatic Resources Management*

*Held at the World Bank, Washington, D.C.
October 9-11, 1997*

Marea E. Hatziolos, Anthony J. Hooten, and Martin Fodor, Editors

*The World Bank
Washington, D.C.*

This report has been prepared by the staff of the World Bank. The judgments expressed do not necessarily reflect the views of the Board of Executive Directors or the government they represent.

Cover design by Beni Chibber-Rao.
Composite cover photograph by Jan C. Post and Anthony J. Hooten.
Photograph of Jacques-Yves Cousteau by Francine Cousteau, courtesy of Phillip Dustan.

Library of Congress Cataloging-in-Publication Data

International Conference on Environmentally Sustainable Development
  (5th ; 1997 ; World Bank)
    Coral reefs : challenges and opportunities for sustainable
management : proceedings of an associated event of the fifth annual
World Bank Conference on Environmentally and Socially Sustainable
Development/Marea E. Hatziolos, Anthony J. Hooten, Martin Fodor,
editors.
    p. cm. -- (Environmentally and socially sustainable
development series. Environment)
    "Sponsored by the World Bank and the International Center for
Living and Aquatic Resources Management (ICLARM), held at the World
Bank, Washington, D.C., October 9, 10, 11, 1997."
    Includes bibliographical references.
    ISBN 0-8213-4235-5
    1. Coral reef conservation--Congresses. 2. Coral reefs and
islands--Economic aspects--Congresses. 3. Endangered ecosystems-
-Congresses. 4. Ecosystem management--Congresses. I. Hatziolos,
Marea Eleni. II. Hooten, Anthony J. III. Fodor, Martin, 1968- .
IV. World Bank. V. International Center for Living and Aquatic
Resources Management. VI. Title. VII. Series.
QH75.A1I54 1997
333.95′5316--dc21
                                                          98-19384
                                                          CIP

 The text and cover are printed on recycled paper, with a flood aqueous coating on the cover.

In Memoriam

It is my fondest wish that the world below, hidden in the deeps, may become as well known to future generations as the continents are to us today. For this to occur, it is necessary above all that the world survive...the gold-flecked madreporarians, the translucent alcyonaceans, the gorgeous sea fans—all these things, and many more, are threatened by the side effects of our civilization....

I have spoken often about the decline of coral....This decline, if it continues, will mark the end of one of the great beauties of creation and the end of a great hope—that of discovering life forms hitherto unknown on Earth....If our grandchildren never have the opportunity to see living coral—it will be to the everlasting shame of our age....Let us not forget that we are responsible to posterity for the preservation of the beauties of the sea as well as for those on land....We have a moral obligation toward our descendants. We must not pass on to them a legacy of empty oceans and dead reefs.

We must no longer think of the sea as "mysterious"....There are no longer "mysteries"; there are only problems to which we must find the answers....We are entering a new era of research and exploration. We must learn how to make use of the biological and mineral resources of the oceans....But we must also learn how to preserve the integrity and the equilibrium of that world which is so inextricably bound to our own. Soon, perhaps, we will realize that the sea is but an immense extension of our human world, a province of our universe, a patrimony that we must protect if we ourselves are to survive.

Captain Jacques-Yves Cousteau
Excerpts from *Life and Death in a Coral Sea,*
1971

An Emperor angelfish, *Pomacanthus emperator*, surrounded by small fishes, *Anthias squamipinnis*, in the northern Red Sea. Photograph by Jan C. Post.

Contents

Acknowledgments

The Coral Reef Conference and this proceedings are the product of many partnerships. First and foremost, we thank the International Center for Living and Aquatic Resources Management (ICLARM), our cosponsor, without whose financial and logistical support neither the conference nor these proceedings would have been possible. Meryl Williams, John McManus, Sheila Vergara, Rosenne Funk, and James McMahon were instrumental in bringing these efforts to fruition. We would also like to acknowledge the Great Barrier Reef Marine Park Authority, the Smithsonian Institution, and The World Conservation Union (IUCN) for their support in program development. We thank all panelists and session chairs, who contributed their time and energy. Special thanks also go to Joan Martin-Brown, adviser to the Environmental and Socially Sustainable Development vice presidency, for making the Coral Reef Conference a major element of the Fifth Annual World Bank Conference on Environmentally and Socially Sustainable Development (ESSD5).

In addition, we are grateful to the following individuals for their support in planning and logistics: Jane Ballentine, Razmik Bazikian, Barbara Best, Jennifer Bossard, Beni Chibber-Rao, Reza Firuzabadi, Catherine Golitzen-Jones, Yusri Harun, Gita Hemple, Alicia Hetzner, Virginia Hitchcock, Bonnie Howell, Irani Huda, Seyda Kocer, Matthew Manfreda, and Jonathan Miller.

Finally, we express our appreciation to Ismail Serageldin, vice president, Environmentally and Socially Sustainable Development, for his continued commitment and unflagging support to coral reef conservation and the World Bank's role in this effort.

These proceedings are contributions to both the International Coral Reef Initiative and the International Year of the Reef, 1997.

Foreword

As the International Year of the Reef draws to a close, it is clear that the challenges to conservation of the world's coral reefs have, if anything, intensified. The global picture, gleaned from monitoring efforts such as Reef Check 97 and ReefBase, is one of general reef decline amidst the still rich beauty of coral reefs along the Red Sea coast or the far reaches of the Chagos Archipelago. But even here, the notion of pristine is no longer valid. Not surprisingly, increased pressures on reefs brought about by spectacular demographic growth in the coastal zone, expanding tourism, changes in agricultural practices, destructive fishing, and the influence of climate change phenomena such as El Niño have left us swimming against the tide in a race against time.

Our mandate is to see that we win the race and reverse the decline. We have made important strides, educating the public and policymakers about the silent crisis unfolding beneath the world's seas and building constituencies for coral reef conservation around the globe. Since Elliott Norse's strategic vision for conserving global marine biological diversity was published in 1993, several initiatives have been launched with support from the World Bank and others. In 1995, the International Coral Reef Initiative was launched in the Philippines and has now been endorsed by more than 70 countries. Recognizing the importance of establishing and maintaining marine protected areas (MPAs) as essential elements of any strategy for marine

conservation, the Bank and its partners, The World Conservation Union (IUCN) and the Great Barrier Reef Marine Park Authority, supported a priority-setting exercise to establish and maintain key protected sites around the world. The results, published in the four-volume report "A Global Representative System of Marine Protected Areas," were presented two-and-one-half years ago at the Bank's first international conference on coral reefs, which explored sustainable financing for coral reef conservation.

Now, in this follow-up event on coral reefs, organized as part of the Bank's Fifth Annual Conference on Environmentally and Socially Sustainable Development, attention has focused on addressing some of the most urgent threats facing coral reefs today. These include reef-destructive practices exemplified by the growing use of cyanide fishing in some of the richest reefs of the world, unsustainable trade in reef products, and constraints to effective establishment and management of marine protected areas. This proceedings volume stresses the need for strengthening the policy environment while adopting economic incentives and improved resource valuation techniques, informing management decisions through targeted research and monitoring, and rallying public support through environmental education and the media.

Strategic partnerships have a vital role to play. As the cover of these proceedings suggests, such partnerships often emerge from the least likely corners. The power of new alliances between the public and private sectors and inclusion of market-based incentives must be explored if we are to move the conservation agenda forward. Turning the tide toward effective conservation will require sustained new commitments and a willingness to take on major tasks in reforming policies, identifying alternative—sustainable— technologies, and creating the right incentives for their adoption. In the name of the late Captain Jacques-Yves Cousteau and the underwater world he so eloquently represented, let us rededicate ourselves to meeting the challenges ahead for preserving life on earth in 1998, the International Year of the Oceans, and well beyond into the next millennium.

Ismail Serageldin

OPENING SESSION

Keynote Address

Coral Reef Conservation: Science, Economics, and Law

Ismail Serageldin
World Bank

This is the International Year of the Reef, in which we celebrate the unique splendors of the most amazing habitats on earth. The richness and diversity of coral reefs defy the imagination. All shapes and colors are represented in a dazzling array of species that coexist in a delicate balance around and within. This "fragile symphony of inner space," to use Cousteau's words, harbors some of the most biologically diverse and productive systems on earth. Coral reefs are, by conservative estimates, home to hundreds of thousands of species of plants and animals, less than 1/10 of which have been discovered or described.

At the phyletic level, coral reefs are more diverse than rain forests, including unique life forms and body plans known only in the marine realm. Reefs are also life support systems for the millions of human beings who derive their livelihoods from them, benefiting from the multiple services that reefs provide in shoreline protection, nutrient cycling, recreation and tourism and human inspiration.

Reefs themselves are the largest organic structures built by living creatures, tiny polyps that actually create barriers hundreds of kilometers long, atolls, lagoons, and many unusual structures. Corals also coexist with tiny creatures of the plant kingdom known as zooxanthellae, in a unique symbiotic bond.

We have, in the last five years from the time of the Earth Summit in Rio, learned much about the need to modify our behavior and to respect the ecosystems on which we depend for air, water, food, and livelihoods. From issues such as climate change to biodiversity to rain forests, the public has been educated about the need to change human behavior if we are to act as true stewards of the earth.

While the need for change is finally manifesting itself in our practices on land, the challenge is infinitely greater for the magnificent but increasingly threatened communities under the sea. Not only are coral reefs obscured from sight, but the damage that occurs to them is usually the result of many different forces, some of which are from actions taken on land and often miles away, resulting from agriculture, industry, or simple habitation. Externalities associated with these often distant actions can devastate the delicate balance of reef communities. Sometimes it is by our more direct actions, from improper fishing to anchoring to overharvesting the bounty of the reefs, that destruction occurs. Today, more and more reefs are showing the signs of severe degradation, transformed from lush communities teaming with life to desolate wastelands within the space of a decade. It is therefore fitting that in this fifth year, this year of Rio+5, that we should also be observing the International Year of the Reef, an occasion to focus public attention on the inherent splendor of reefs—and their plight—as we enter a critical phase in their future on this earth.

The themes of this year's Fifth Annual World Bank Conference on Environmentally and

Socially Sustainable Development (ESSD5) Conference, "Partnerships for Global Ecosystems: Science, Economics, and Law," have much to teach us about finding solutions to the myriad problems confronting us as we struggle to conserve these magnificent legacies of the last 10,000 years. The interactions between environmental degradation and coral reef decline are often complex. While the basic ingredients are well known—overpopulation, poverty, and the growing disparity between rich and poor, political disenfranchisement, and unregulated economic growth, we rely on the physical, biological, and social sciences to elucidate the cause and effect relationships between the human condition and environmental change. While science and technology may show us a way out, we cannot get there without the right incentives and sufficient resources. Economic and social policies, legal frameworks, and education are essential to creating these conditions. So too, are ethics and spirituality, fueled by a greater awareness of our impact on this earth and our place in the universe.

Solutions require that we address these different components as pillars of effective action. Therefore, let me speak briefly to each of the above themes of this year's ESSD conference in the context of coral reefs.

Science

What do we know? The scientific community tells us there is now a global crisis in the health and productivity of coral reefs. For example, the results of the first global survey of human impact on coral reefs, ReefCheck 97, involved 250 coral reefs in 30 countries around the world. And the findings are alarming: the surveys revealed no pristine reefs; in almost every case there were visible signs of human impacts, including the complete absence of high-valued target species in many areas of Southeast Asia. Even remote reefs were heavily fished of sharks, lobster, giant clam, and grouper, with evidence of cyanide and blast fishing, pollution and overharvesting. These and other recent reports of growing incidence of disease and pathologies being documented in both hard and soft corals indicate that the phenomenon of reef decline is indeed global.

The human sources of this degradation are well documented in many cases, while others, such as the recent outbreaks of disease, require further study. Other forms of stress, such as global warming and rises in sea surface temperatures, and changes in precipitation and storm frequency (including those anticipated with the current El Niño event), are likely being accelerated by human activities, and contribute to the cumulative stress being heaped on coral reefs.

Climate change, which has been the topic of recent major conferences held at the White House, by the World Bank, and many others, is in fact a serious issue for many small island states and could be affected by rising sea level. Some of the flatter islands could disappear completely. The global warming of sea surface temperature has been among the highest on record and is leading to increased bleaching on coral reefs worldwide.

What can science give us to improve our understanding of the cause and effect relationships from these threats?

Research and monitoring, such as that just completed under ReefCheck, and more comprehensive surveys underway in programs like the Global Coral Reef Monitoring Network (GCRMN), ReefBase, CoralBase, and remote sensing, are essential in helping us understand the nature of cause-effect relationships and assessing the extent of coral reef degradation. It is important that we monitor and understand what is going on, just as we've been doing with the rain forests. In fact, one of my campaigns is to ensure that coral reefs receive as much attention and public awareness as rain forests have received. However, we need to also be able to predict and quantify ecosystem change at a mid temporal scale. Aside from our need to understand global climate change as a long-term process, events such as the current El Niño have climatological effects that are predictable within a one- to three-year time frame, and this has major impacts that we should factor into our policymaking.

Yet we need more from the scientific community than simply monitoring and reporting what is happening on coral reefs—we need research to inform management decisions and alternatives to unsustainable use patterns as well. What is the carrying capacity of visitors to a particular reef? Do we know how far one can harvest sustainably? There is the need for scientists to offer solutions through alternative forms of production and harvest, to promote resource enhancement and habitat restoration. Science and technology can contribute to identifying solutions to these problems, such as carrying capacity studies, alternative production and harvesting techniques, mariculture, marine bioprospecting, resource enhancement, and habitat restoration, many of which will be reviewed in this conference.

Economics

Solutions will also require the integration of economics. By internalizing the environmental and social costs of resource use, we can create the price signal that will move people in the right direction. We need to create enabling frameworks for the smallholders, small fishers, and local communities to participate in that economic solution. We want to introduce best practices in production that use market-based incentives, and we want to lower the costs of "going green" through concessional financing, through risk capital, so that entrepreneurs can find a way of doing things in an environmentally friendly fashion, and not find the effort too costly.

There are millions of poor fishers whose livelihood depend on coral reefs. Coral reefs provide up to 25 percent of all the fisheries harvested in developing countries and 90 percent of animal protein consumed in the South Pacific. Thus, coral reefs are not an insignificant aspect of the livelihoods and social welfare of communities— a facade only for tourism. They are an integral part of the economy of many, often poor, coastal communities. Preservation and conservation strategies have to incorporate such realities.

Finding new ways to enhance the livelihoods of reef-dependent communities and to increase the benefits derived from the productivity of coral reefs while not undermining the functional integrity of these ecosystems is a major challenge that we must meet. It is a big challenge to capture the profits for conservation and development for the poorest communities concerned. It is important that indigenous communities, in fact, receive continuous benefits from well-managed coastal ecosystems so that they have an interest and stake in protecting the coral reefs. Other ways of generating additional income are marine-based tourism, aquaculture, and bioprospecting of coral reef and related ecosystems for the natural products and pharmaceuticals industry.

Tourism holds out tremendous prospects for income generation based on the health and productivity of coral reefs. The Caribbean boasts an annual revenue in excess of US$10 billion dollars. For the reef-studded island states that populate this region, tourism—most of it coastal—is the principal engine of economic growth. In other regions, popular tourist destinations like the Seychelles—where work has been initiated on behalf of environmental sensitivity—70 percent of foreign exchange and 20 percent of the gross domestic product come from tourism.

But success stories are not always the case. In Indonesia, for example, in economic terms, reef loss from destructive practices and degradation is substantial. The value of coral reefs along Indonesia's coast has been estimated at more than US$120,000 per square kilometer in a recent Bank study. When one considers the number of square kilometers among 17,000 islands spread over an area larger than the United States, coral reef loss becomes a major issue. The value of the live fish trade exceeds one billion dollars. The challenge is to replace destructive fishing practices, including the use of cyanide and dynamite, with sustainable production. But it is important to know how to design and ensure the adoption of sustainable production technologies. We need to create incentives for these by first getting the price of resources right. We need to green national accounts, measuring the intrinsic (not just the productive) value of natural resources and functioning ecosystems to the national economy. Equally important, we need to internalize the environmental and social costs to society of destructive actions that benefit only a few. Costs and benefits need to be seen in the proper light so that tradeoffs can be understood and decisions about resource allocation made in a transparent, rational way. Finally, we need to remove harmful subsidies, quite possibly the single worst enemy of biodiversity on earth.

Environmental economics and natural resource valuation have much to offer but even more to achieve along this frontier. Effective communication is an important element of the challenge. Information must be interpreted and effectively communicated to decisionmakers and to the public. Public education campaigns will be essential in identifying the impacts of various use options and tradeoffs to be considered, and in shaping human behavior. In everything that we do the central question should continue to be: Who pays, and who benefits?

Law

We need to incorporate the principles of integrated coastal zone management and recognize the linkages upstream and downstream, and across sectors. Unfortunately, the fragmentation of decisionmaking prevents policymakers from "seeing" that coastal zones are precisely the interface between human beings, their economic activity and the sea, and that is where the primary impacts take place. Many people look at municipal development, agriculture, and other sectors, but fail to see them as an integrated system.

We need to introduce much more systematic environmental impact assessment and zoning, licensing agreements as appropriate, and we need to regulate access to certain parts of the coastal zone, to ensure the maintenance of environmental quality.

In our policies we need to invoke the polluter-pays principle and systematically enforce the regulations we adopt. For example, we now have cyanide detection tests—small field test kits that enable detection of cyanide use in fish for export. Examples such as this begin to put in place mechanisms that identify destructive practices. While economic incentives are important to compliance, these must be backed up by the threat of legal prosecution of violators. The Bank is placing new emphasis on transparency and combating corruption in the enforcement of policies related to its projects. The Coral Reef Rehabilitation and Management Project (COREMAP), set for implementation in Indonesia early next spring, has a strong enforcement component to complement the technical management interventions.

Marine Protected Areas and Fisheries Reserves An essential task before us is the establishment of functional marine protected areas (MPAs). Over 1,300 MPAs were identified and mapped in the four volume study, A Global Representative System of Marine Protected Areas, launched here more than two years ago in a similar symposium. But those MPAs that are properly managed are relatively few—under 200. The rest are poorly managed or lack any kind of management information. Many of these protected areas are really paper parks, and simply having them on a map does not safeguard their protection.

Building Social Capital

Ultimately, there is no solution that can be successful from the top down. We must build social capital at the grass roots—empowering communities by building on the indigenous knowledge that exists—and helping with enforcement, education and information, access to credit, markets and new technologies. We must also learn to listen. This is not an easy task, but it is an essential task. Reaching out to the local community, listening to its wisdom and adding to its knowledge is what the discourse between indigenous culture and the modern sciences should be.

Summary

This synthetic approach, which brings together science, economics and law will cost very little relative to how much will be saved in the future; it is the evidence of almost every case dealing with environmental issues that small investments now bring huge dividends later and for the world at large. To make such approaches work, we need to build partnerships across the world as well as across sectors—public and private, formal and informal, international and national, and local.

The International Coral Reef Initiative (ICRI) is such a partnership, and the World Bank is pleased to be a partner in this global effort. Many things have happened under ICRI's aegis—six regional workshops have been held around the world to prioritize issues and actions at the regional level; the GCRMN, in six regions and with more than 15 nodes has recently been launched and its findings reported elsewhere in these proceedings. Recapitulating many of the themes endorsed by these initiatives, the International Year of the Reef (IYOR) has placed enormous efforts on environmental education and deployment of rapid reef assessment, such as ReefCheck.

These efforts underscore the need for cooperation through partnerships. For only through partnerships do I believe that we will be able to move forward to protect the magnificence of the creatures that live on the reef. And it will require breaking new ground. Just as some of the relationships found within a coral reef may seem extraordinary or counterintuitive to us humans, new partnerships may not always appear to be symbiotic—and one wonders whether the big multinational corporations and the small, local communities can actually work together. But we should be inspired by the reef itself, for there is where complementarity and symbiosis abound, and it is up to us to use our imagination to make this happen.

In conclusion, decisive action in the few years ahead is essential if we are not to irretrievably destroy or diminish one of the earth's most wonderful treasures. To act responsibly now, to find the solutions that allow for the sustainable use of these precious resources, that find adequate livelihood for the poor who are sometimes caught into being the unwitting agents and victims of these destructive practices, to expand our awareness to encompass these magnificent habitats and all that they imply, that is the challenge before us. It is to this task that we are gathered here, and I am hopeful that our deliberations will be more than a descriptive litany of all that is going wrong. Our deliberations must result in a series of specific actions to which we must pledge ourselves. For only by action now will we be acting as true stewards of the earth. This earth that we did not inherit from our parents, this earth that we borrowed from our children.

Objectives of the Conference

Marea E. Hatziolos
World Bank

This conference has multiple objectives. Principal among them, however, is to mobilize *action* in support of coral reef conservation and management. The best available information on the status of coral reefs worldwide tells us that reefs are in decline or threatened over a large part of their distribution. While there are many factors associated with coral reef degradation, the focus of this conference is on a growing set of unsustainable practices, which, by their very nature and accelerated growth, are resulting in severe and potentially irreversible impacts on coral reefs. These practices, from the destructive harvest and trade of live reef organisms to the rapid growth of unregulated tourism in coastal areas—along with measures to counteract them—are the central themes of this conference. Understanding the nature and underlying causes of these impacts is essential to identifying options and sustainable solutions. A key objective of this conference, therefore, is to bring to bear the wealth of experience and the range of disciplines and institutional affiliations represented here, to shed more light on the problems and open the way to possible solutions.

Major Issues and Conference Themes

The conference revolves around three major themes dealing with destructive use of coral reef resources. These include reef-destructive fishing, such as blast fishing, *muro ami*, cyanide and other poison fishing used in the live aquarium and food fish trades. These methods destroy not only coral reef habitat but a host of nontarget species as well in the process of extraction. Destructive practices such as these are increasing around the world, but most alarmingly in Southeast Asia—the global epicenter of marine biodiversity.

Related to the live reef fish trade is the unsustainable and often illegal trade in reef products, including a variety of corals, sea horses, mollusks, and sponges, as well as sea turtles and dugongs. This has resulted in the endangerment of several species through the economic and biological extinction of local populations.

Finally, there is the exponential growth of marine-based tourism. This is manifest in the explosive growth of beachfront resorts and related infrastructure, and the rapid expansion of the cruise ship industry. The direct impacts of these industries through the conversion and loss of habitat for resort and port construction, the physical damage to reefs from trampling by tourists, anchoring or grounding of vessels, and the eutrophic effects of effluent discharges are major sources of stress on coral reef systems. Other, indirect impacts of tourism include those associated with overfishing and overharvesting in the coral reef ornamentals trade as local demand for these products increases, thus undermining the value of these reefs to tourism and other productive industries in the future.

Why do such practices persist? A number of factors conspire to keep them going. While the proximate causes and impacts of such behavior are clear, the root causes of many of these issues are complex. Lack of information and knowledge are likely to be key factors. These include a failure by actors or decisionmakers to comprehend the longer-term implications of selective or destructive fishing practices on reef recovery and biodiversity, or the impacts of "non extractive" but polluting industries like tourism on reef productivity. Educated as we scientists and managers are, we, too, have failed to appreciate that by our very presence we are creating an impact, as documented recently in the sobering results from ReefCheck 97.

Ignorance is only part of the problem. Perverse incentives also play a role. Often in place is an incentive structure that favors quick profits for a few at the expense of many. Subsidies across sectors—in fisheries, water, and agriculture, totalling hundreds of billions of dollars a year—have distorted markets, with devastating results for coastal and marine resources. Analyzing these perverse incentives and their failure to internalize the environmental and social costs of reef resource use, emphasizing instead the financial gain, is the subject of a special plenary session on economic valuation. Last, but by no means least, are the problems of weak regulatory regimes and policy frameworks. There are few laws protecting coral reef ecosystems and their resources. What laws exist are generally not enforced, and when they are, there is often a lack of transparency or consistency in how they are applied. Shifting these incentives, through the introduction of market-based mechanisms and a level playing field, will form the basis of discussion in each of the conference theme plenary sessions

The challenge, of course, lies in identifying viable alternatives to current tradeoffs between long-term sustainability and short-term gains in the management and use of reef resources. Among the options that will be examined are reef-based mariculture of grouper and other high-value species, bioprospecting and opportunities for certification and trade in sustainably produced goods and services derived from coral reefs, and initiatives that create synergies in the design of marine ecotourism with the establishment of marine protected areas and no-take fishery reserves—that is, operations that are mutually reinforcing and self-sustaining.

Identifying Solutions

To be sustainable, management solutions must be informed by science, stimulated by economics and reinforced by laws. These income-generating alternatives will also have to be sensitive to environmental and social equity concerns. We know that there are many studies under way that speak to these concerns. Some of these pilot studies have been field-tested; others require further research to determine their feasibility and replicability. A major contribution of this forum will be to document these approaches in the context of the conference themes, assess their effectiveness, and identify means to develop them further with a view to incorporating the more successful ones into the design of Bank projects. In addition to the policy and regulatory framework necessary to introduce these alternatives, we will take a look at the incentive structures required, and how these may be brought about through environmental education, public awareness, and the creation of greener markets. Equally essential will be the need to continually monitor our efforts— to make sure that what we are doing is resulting in positive impact. If not, how can we redesign our efforts to create value rather than destroy it in the context of managing coral reefs? This is where science must come in—not only with respect to research and development, but in the monitoring and evaluation of interventions, and in the redesign of activities consistent with our criteria for sustainability and best practice. Targeted research and global monitoring will be essential elements of any solutions to problems surrounding the sustainable management of coral reef ecosystems.

As the theme of this year's Environmentally and Socially Sustainable Development Conference suggests, partnerships play a major role in these solutions. Building on the ideas and alliances that emerged from a related conference organized here two years ago on sustainable financing for coral reef conservation, this event should bring us several steps closer to realizing strategic partnerships on the ground. Since June 1995, a number of initiatives are now under way—within the Bank and elsewhere. Adding value to these initiatives by identifying potential collaborators and resources, and facilitating networks to disseminate results, is another important objective of this conference.

In the course of our discussions, we will try to identify and pair specific actions with key stakeholder groups. For each of the five conference themes then, our objectives will be to distill some key conclusions and recommendations that can be offered for follow-up. The bottom line is **action**. At the end of the day our goal is to have identified concrete actions and a strategy to implement them—over the short, medium, and long terms—with benchmarks to measure our progress along the way. If we can take it upon ourselves to advance this agenda, by entering into new partnerships, leveraging resources, and sustaining our commitments, this conference will have been a great success.

Status of the International Coral Reef Initiative

Richard Kenchington
Great Barrier Reef Marine Park Authority

The background to the International Coral Reef Initiative (ICRI), as it stands, stems from the colloquium organized in 1993 in Miami, Florida, under the driving force of Dr. Robert Ginsburg. That colloquium considered the range of evidence about the deterioration of reefs and reached the conclusion that despite many years of identifying the problems with reefs, there was still depressingly little action toward their conservation.

Since the 1993 meeting, there have been a number of actions. The first of these was through the high-level meeting of the Small Island Developing States (SIDS), held in Barbados, as a follow-up of the United Nations Commission on Environment and Development in Rio de Janeiro. The SIDS expressed that they, more than anyone else, had concerns and vital interests in their coral reefs. After all, if the coral reef represents a very significant part of a given SIDS country's natural resource base, its continuing productivity in the face of the pressures of developing a modern economy is an overwhelming challenge. This challenge presents three particular dimensions that we may seek to manage.

The first is pollution—the tendency of humankind to physically put things into coastal systems and coral reefs that did not exist before. Whether we are considering chemical, thermal, or biological introductions—they all add things that the receiving system is not ecologically pre-adapted to operate.

The second is removing things that occur naturally on or around coral reefs. The particular issue is the quest for sustainable fishing. It seems almost inevitable that we have to address the vicious spiral through overfishing to destructive fishing. In short, as the catch goes down, the desperation among fishers goes up, and the means of catching for subsistence or in pursuit of development is increasingly likely to lead to destructive fishing practices.

The third dimension is something I prefer to call "alienation." It is converting coral reefs to something else—it is turning a coral reef into a harbor, a sewage system, an air strip, land for building hotels or condominiums, land for agriculture or factory sites—into anything other than a coral reef. We use weasel words, such as "reclamation." Reclamation implies salvation, redemption, improvement to serve a higher purpose. The reality is that for every square kilometer of coral reef that we alienate or damage so that it is no longer productive, we must generate the equivalent of US$120,000 per year forever (see Cesar, pages 163–74). Alternatively, we have deprived our coastal communities of the rights or the means to feed 40 to 80 families forever, without recourse to other economic resources.

In 1994, the U.S. Coral Reef Initiative was started, and as a linked activity, the International Coral Reef Initiative was established. For both, the driving force was the urgency to protect coral reefs and related ecosystems. Both reflected that there had been many previous calls, that the problems had been well known at the academic and community levels for several decades, but there has been depressingly little action. I prefer to use an analogy of a patient visiting his doctors and being told through increasingly sophisticated diagnosis that the condition is bad and getting worse, without any treatment procedures being implemented.

Based on this background, what is the ICRI? It is a strange association—a free and informal partnership of governments, international development banks, nongovernmental organizations, scientific groups, and the private sector—brought together to focus on the need for action to manage and save the world's coral reefs. ICRI is sparked and spirited by the active involvement of decisionmakers, particularly economic and social decisionmakers, to an extent that was not achieved in many of the earlier attempts to catalyze actions on behalf of coral reefs.

Originally eight government partners signed on to ICRI in the context of the SIDS meeting in Barbados. The United States and Japan started the process through a joint agreement, and rapidly welcomed aboard Australia, France, Jamaica, Philippines, Sweden, and the United Kingdom. The World Bank, UNEP, UNDP, Coral Reef Alliance, UNESCO, IUCN and many others became involved. Presently, it is difficult to identify the total membership, but officers of over 80 governments have participated in ICRI activities. Most of the relevant United Nations agencies have been exposed to ICRI activity. Nevertheless, ICRI is not a part of the international bureaucratic structure. It sits to one side as a vehicle for like-minded governments and groups to identify and promote action. The word "action" comes up with great frequency in the agendas of ICRI; it is almost a mantra.

ICRI is there to identify and promote action within the scope of the widest possible range of international programs. ICRI gets raised in the context of such things as the Conference of Parties for the biodiversity convention, the Land-Based Sources of Marine Pollution discussion, the Global Environment Facility, the UNEP Council, UNDP, and others. ICRI has not yet partnered as closely to the food and agricultural

organizations as we might wish, and there is scope for going further with such organizations.

ICRI Progress

The first phase in ICRI was led by the United States. It consisted primarily of thorough preparations for and immediate follow-up of the global workshop held in Dumaguete City, Philippines, in 1995. The workshop was attended by delegations from more than 40 countries. Donor partners sponsored the attendance of government delegations from the regions. The essential part of ICRI is getting people from the regions, particularly managers and decisionmakers whose work affects coral reefs, to participate and play a substantial role in developing an understanding of the issues and solutions to the problems. ICRI started from a top-down approach, but with the deliberate objective of becoming a bottom-up organization as quickly as possible.

The mantra of action—the whole purpose of the Dumaguete City meeting—was to provide the basis for an action-based approach. The documents which emerged were a call to action—a brief, pithy statement of many parenthood values, couched in terms for decisionmakers. The call to action basically states to decisionmakers that coral reefs are not just an important part of the world's heritage, they are an important part of the world's health—economic as well as environmental.

The second document was a framework for action, couched at the global level, identifying the issues and the types of actions needed if the deterioration of coral reefs is to be slowed, halted and eventually reversed. The framework for action sorts out what we can now call "assured sustainability." It identifies four major themes:

1. Integrated Coastal Zone Management Framework: Coordinating policies, management concerns, development objectives and stakeholders interests across the different landscapes of the coastal zone.

2. Capacity Building: Building the capacity for communities, governments, nongovernmental organizations—everyone involved with coral reef areas and resources—to understand the needs and the options for managing coral reefs and the whole range of human activities that affect them.

3. Research and Monitoring: Systematic gathering of socioeconomic and biophysical information that relates to the scales of time and space necessary to design and sustain measures to manage coral reefs.

4. Review: In the early phase of ICRI, there was a considerable amount of skepticism as to the probability of any detectable action on coral reefs or among coastal communities, and previous calls to action and the subsequent lack of progress. There was a general feeling, which I detected at Dumagete City, that said: We have now signed up for a call to action—a promise to address the plight of deteriorating coral reefs around the world Let us ensure that we deliver this time by putting something in place that will enable us to demonstrate how well or badly we perform in delivering on that promise. That is this review process—systematically collecting information that enables us to assess the extent to which we are successful in meeting the goals of management to ensure the continuing survival, health, and productivity of coral reefs and related ecosystems.

Regional Workshops

Flowing from Dumaguete City, there has been a series of six regional ICRI workshops—in the Caribbean, Pacific, East Asian Seas, South Asian Seas, East Africa and the Western Indian Ocean, and, most recently, in the Middle East, held in Aqaba, Jordan. The purpose of the workshops was to turn the global framework for action into an agenda for action for each region, that addresses the ecological, economic, and social and political realities, taking into account the resources ICRI has, is likely to get, and the pace at which we can work.

The purpose of the regional workshops was to identify the issues, the priorities in the region, the actions required to address those issues, a schedule of activities to implement those actions, and those important performance criteria, so that we can improve management.

The different regional characteristics reflect the different past, present, and likely future of biophysical factors and socioeconomic settings.

Regional Activities

In the Caribbean the priorities have been community action and activities related to developing sustainable tourism—using the economic motor of tourism and the parallel economic motor of sustainable aquaculture, to provide an underpinning for valuing coral reefs and their conservation, linked with the CARICOMP monitoring network system.

In the Pacific the major priority has been community education. In particular, the Pacific has invested substantially—in the last 18 months—in the International Year of the Reef education programs ranging from primary schools to regional communities. They have fought in promoting the "Pacific Way," which links conservation terminology of the present with customary ownership and customary practices of management—to stress to communities the importance of conservation in a system, where in many of the cases a breakdown in community management can be directly linked to the failure of coral reefs in some areas.

In the East Asian seas one of the driving priorities has been destructive fishing, particularly cyanide fishing, but to a large extent explosive fishing, linked to management capacity building and the development of a monitoring system from an existing information base.

Major priorities in South Asian seas are baseline inventory and monitoring of the condition of reefs and related ecosystems, with a parallel effort in regional capacity development

In East Africa and the Western Indian Ocean the priority has been community- and village-level education and action, covering both management activity and methods whereby the local people can be part of monitoring reef conditions and therefore understand the linkage between good-quality reefs and good-quality outcomes.

The workshop in the Middle East is so recently completed that we cannot identify any major themes, but the exciting achievement is that the Middle Eastern partners have come together to discuss a network.

Other Activities Linked to ICRI

The Global Coral Reef Monitoring Network (GCRMN), which is discussed elsewhere in these proceedings, is linked with ReefBase (from ICLARM). The GCRMN is jointly sponsored by the International Oceanographic Commission of UNESCO, UNEP, and the World Conservation Union. The linkage between the GCRMN and ReefBase is essential; it is part of an effort enabling us to establish an accessible global biophysical baseline as to the ecological status of coral reefs.

The International Year of the Reef (IYOR) 1997, originally was scheduled for 1995 but slipped to late 1996 when it was launched during the International Coral Reef Symposium in Panama. IYOR has two themes—one is public education, with literally hundreds of coral reef education products presently around the world, and the other is the promotion of research and monitoring.

The International Year of the Ocean is an official United Nations international function and is designated for the calendar year 1998. At the suggestion of the ICRI Coordinating Planning IOC, we agreed to recognize November 1998 as the coral reef month of the International Year of the Ocean.

Underlying is the principle of ICRI serving and seeking to capitalize and encourage action on a broad range of fronts. ICRI is not a funding organization; it is not an implementer of activities at the field or local community level. ICRI is there to encourage such activity, to urge and facilitate its members—both coral reef nations and donors—in establishing projects and programs for such actions and to review and report on performance against the objectives of the call to action.

ICRI is a vehicle for underpinning the development and implementation of policy for ecologically sustainable use and development and conservation of coral reefs and associated ecosystems. There are two themes that I believe we will see develop. The first is the economic theme, whereby we eventually reverse the onus of proof for use of coral reef resources. Now the onus is on those who would keep a reef in its natural and productive state to prove publicly that to do so is preferable to a proposed change or development, or that the costs of activity to remove or reduce impacts should be built into the costs of the proposed development and not simply borne through environmental degradation. This is very difficult to do, because normally the opportunity to prove comes too late in an economically and politically charged process to alter the development. Thus, the idea is to reverse the proof and ask those who are trying to develop coral reefs to look at the long term to see whether the benefits of the development and the activity are going to be worth it against the recurrent $US120,000 per square kilometer per year free goods from the reef.

Linked to this is the issue of implementing a much more sophisticated approach to identifying and managing risks, and to assigning costs and liabilities, perhaps using insurance and director's professional liabilities, particularly with international companies. It may be possible to make those liabilities accountable against the development beneficiaries and to remove ourselves gradually from the tradition of privatizing benefits and socializing natural resource and environmental losses.

Summary

Where should ICRI go from here? Phase One established the alert and the need in the meeting in Dumaguete City, Philippines. Phase Two consisted of the regional workshops. During Phase Two the coordination of ICRI passed from the United States to Australia. In the preparation for that passage the management changed from an executive planning committee to a coordinating planning committee, with a strong emphasis on regional capacity development, with the aspiration that sooner or later the international coordination role can be phased down as the regional coordination capacity is built up.

Phase Three: The next major activity on the ICRI calendar will be the first review meeting. The International Tropical Marine Ecosystems

Management Symposium (ITMEMS) reflects a desire to extend beyond coral reefs, but also to tropical marine systems generally, because those systems are linked. The object of the conference, which will be held in Townsville, Australia, at the end of 1998 will be to review activity against the regional action strategies, and as necessary to revise those strategies.

In the meantime, we are continuing work within the ICRI secretariat on increasing communication between regions through use of the Internet, and in three to four weeks we hope to be on-line with an interactive ICRI home page cross-linked to the GCRMN and a whole range of coral reef web pages.

We see a need for a continuation of the Coordinating Planning Committee (CPC) on a policy discussion and coordinating basis, feeding into its partners at government, nongovernment, and agency levels. We see a continuing need for the secretariat and the CPC to develop briefs to partners for performance in a number of international forums. We conclude again that ICRI was set up as a catalyst for urgent action in coral reefs. It has produced a framework for action; it is both top-down and bottom-up.

ICRI has drawn on the fact that there is a strong correlation among coral reefs, scuba diving, and decisionmakers. Many of the world's decisionmakers either dive or see the attractive images from coral reefs. This is a very fortuitous overlap, because what we are seeking to do with ICRI and with coral reef conservation has an even broader significance. Coral reefs are perhaps the easiest part of the vitally important shallow marine environment with which to engage the attention of the world's decisionmakers. We are helping communities, governments, nongovernmental organizations, donors, and others identify priorities and performance in relation to coral reefs and other marine systems, and much rests on our success through his strange hybrid, ICRI, in making sure that we do indeed achieve action.

The Global Coral Reef Monitoring Network: Reversing the Decline of the World's Reefs

Clive Wilkinson
Global Coral Reef Monitoring Network

Bernard Salvat
GCRMN Scientific and Technical Advisory Committee

There are certainly problems with the status and health of many coral reefs around the world. However, the problems are not specifically *global*, but a coincidence of related problems, occurring simultaneously at many locations.

Global Status of Coral Reefs

Coral reefs, often termed *fragile* ecosystems because of high biodiversity and the apparent fragility of corals, are actually *robust* and have existed for about 35 million years. Current reefs are about 8,000 years old after they grew back when sea levels rose over 100 meters as the glaciers melted. Coral reefs have recovered over short and long time scales after large climate changes, meteorites, volcanic activity, and other catastrophic events. There is now clear evidence that reefs and human populations are not co-existing well, with clear evidence of reef decline. It was predicted in 1992 that 10 percent of the world's reefs were irreparably damaged and 30 percent of the reefs would suffer significant damage within 10 to 20 years if remedial action was not implemented; another 30 percent could also be similarly damaged in 20 to 40 years if human populations continued to grow and apply pressures similar to current levels.

Serious reef decline was confirmed in 1993 at a meeting organized by Professor Bob Ginsburg in Miami. However, the predictions could not be quantified because of insufficient data.

The Global Coral Reef Monitoring Network (GCRMN) has been established to provide these data to determine whether reefs are declining or recovering.

The status of the world's reefs reported at the Eighth International Coral Reef Symposium in Panama in 1996, was:

- Reefs in the Red Sea and Middle East were generally healthy with few significant pressures.
- Many East African reefs were being severely affected by sediment runoff from increased agriculture and deforestation, nutrient pollution, and major overfishing, including some damaging practices.
- Most Indian Ocean reefs and banks are near pristine, but there is distinct degradation around the well-populated islands (Comoros, Madagascar, Mauritius).
- South Asian reefs vary, with the major island chains (Andamans, Chagos, Maldives, and Nicobars) being very healthy, whereas reefs off India and Sri Lanka have been severely damaged by over-exploitation of fisheries, sand and rock, and large-scale pollution.
- Southeast Asian reefs vary, with reefs on shallow continental shelves near large populations being overfished, including extensive damage from shallow water trawling, blast, cyanide and *muro ami* fishing, and from sediment and nutrient pollution. Many reefs surrounded by deep water have

been damaged during fishing, but have high recovery potential if damaging practices are minimized. Most remote reefs are being damaged by roving bands of fishers, including the Spratly Islands.

- East Asian reefs are affected by overfishing and pollution. Reefs off China are severely damaged, and Japanese reefs have been affected by unwise development (building of seawalls and harbors), pollution, and overfishing.
- Remote Pacific reefs are in good health, but some are showing signs of overfishing, including the use of cyanide and localized extinctions of animals like giant clams and bêche-de-mer.
- The Great Barrier Reef is well managed, with minor impacts from sediment and nutrient runoff from overgrazed land, along with some fishing impacts.
- Reefs in the wider Caribbean are heavily affected by overfishing and pollution, with coral diseases increasing. Tourism is bringing long-term benefits to communities and reducing reef damage. Some reefs, like Jamaica, have effectively collapsed, whereas others, like those in Belize and Bahamas, are still healthy.

Coral reefs will not become extinct, but we will witness the effective loss of many reefs and their economic benefits around large human populations in East Africa; South, Southeast, and East Asia; and parts of the Caribbean and tropical Americas. These pressures will increase, as populations in many tropical countries will double in the next 20 to 30 years, and rapid economic growth will increase sediment and nutrient pollution and the demand for coral reef products.

Many coral reef species are threatened with regional extinction, like the commercially important bêche-de-mer, giant clams, trochus, some reef sharks, the humphead wrasse, coral trout, and the Nassau and other grouper. Many are already endangered species as listed by IUCN.

What Causes Reef Decline?

Reefs generally recover in 10 to 20 years from severe natural stresses such as cyclones, hurri-

canes, and typhoons; earthquakes and volcanoes; extreme low tides; very high rainfall and floods. Recovery from quasi-natural impacts is less certain: global climate change and ENSO events; global sea level rise; ultraviolet radiation increases; crown-of-thorns starfish and other predators; and diseases of corals and other organisms. There is growing evidence that these may be linked to human alteration of the global environment, but solutions lie with international forums and agencies, like the United Nations and World Bank.

The GCRMN will focus on local anthropogenic or human impacts that are causing steady reef decline. Most human stresses are chronic, persistent, and have relatively minor to moderate immediate impacts (with the exception of catastrophic impacts, like nuclear blasts and shipwrecks), but the persistence leads to steady reef decline. Resource users and management agencies can reduce or eliminate these by controlling damaging activities on the coast and in the watershed.

The major anthropogenic stresses causing damage are sediment pollution, nutrient pollution, and overfishing, including destructive fishing. A range of lesser anthropogenic stresses—pesticides and complex chemicals, heavy metals and other toxins, and oil spills—are causing either relatively minor or localized damage to coral reefs, or are undocumented. Minimizing these will be difficult, but many will be alleviated if other sources of pollution are reduced.

Global Coral Reef Monitoring Network

GCRMN is a key component of the International Coral Reef Initiative (ICRI) in that it will produce the necessary data for effective reef management, provide training to many people involved in resource management, raise awareness in communities of the problems facing reefs, and inform them that the best mechanism of management is by communities seeking solutions themselves. The GCRMN is sponsored by the Intergovernmental Oceanographic Commission, the United Nations Environment Programme, and the World Conservation Union.

The GCRMN is a partnership of communities, governments, and scientists collaborating in networks to gather data on the status and trends in reef health and to raise awareness among user communities about the problems facing coral reefs. The strategic plan is available from the sponsoring agencies.

The long-term goal is to involve all users, especially local communities, in reducing anthropogenic impacts and ensuring that reefs are managed for sustainable benefits. The short-term goals are to provide communities with the capacity to assess the status of reefs, observe the links between damaging activities and reef status (such as marked declines in fish stocks or loss of coral cover), and make data available to implement effective management of the resources. For example, there is a need to demonstrate that the establishment of fishing reserves, marine protected areas, and local management regimes to outlaw damaging practices can conserve coral reefs and provide sustainable economic returns.

The structure of the GCRMN consists of six regions throughout the world, based on the UNEP Regional Seas Programme. Within each region, there may be one to many nodes that will be effectively independent in budgeting, monitoring, and reporting. The regions are the Middle East; Western Indian Ocean and Eastern African States, with two nodes; South Asia; the East Asian Seas, with five independent country nodes and two others serving groups of countries; the Pacific, with six nodes: and the Caribbean and Tropical Americas, which will contain many nodes to be decided with the CARICOMP network.

Integrated and Interdisciplinary Strategies to Resolve Reef Problems

Just as the problems are multifaceted, so solutions will require a range of disciplines. Integrated coastal management (ICM) is seen as the best method to resolve problems of overexploitation and destruction of coastal resources. ICM involves all stakeholders in integrated management of the coasts and immediate catchment area.

There are sufficient numbers of biological and physical scientists involved in coral reef conservation and management; there are increasing numbers of well-trained resource managers in industrial countries and some (but not enough) being trained in developing countries. Many social scientists are starting to study coral reef user communities and determine how destructive patterns develop to advise on socially acceptable ways of resource management. There are, however, few specialists in laws on ownership and control of coastal areas previously regarded as common property. There are also few specialists able to assess the economic value to communities of sustainable use of coastal resources. Most economic studies on coral reefs have been made through the auspices of the World Bank.

All information must then feed into political processes, but without political will at the decisionmaker level, efforts at local area management will be futile or directly thwarted by competing political interests. There are insufficient political lobbyists urging the need for sustainable resource management. The GCRMN seeks the involvement of all disciplines in the search for solutions.

The critical actions to minimize reef damage are through increasing user awareness and providing education on the causes of problems and on relatively simple remedies. The GCRMN will involve schools and other groups in reef monitoring in parallel with education on how reefs function and how they are damaged by direct human pressures.

The GCRMN is providing communities with basic training in underwater assessment methods and direct socioeconomic surveys, to enable communities to contribute directly toward preparing local, national, regional, and global coral reef status reports. Data on reef status and trends from the GCRMN will be given to management agencies, especially for areas under active management, compared with nearby unmanaged areas.

At all times GCRMN and ICRI will work towards minimizing damaging activities and stress positive, sustainable uses for coral reefs: sustainable fishing, including the live capture of reef fish, harvesting of juvenile and larval fish for raising in cage culture; mariculture of algae, fish, and invertebrates; harvesting of sand and coral rock within the production capacity of reefs; and sustainable tourism. Frequently, tourism is regarded as a problem, whereas it is potentially the most sustainable way to generate income from coral reefs. Most tourist operators do not wish to damage the resources that attracts tourists, but they may do so through a lack of information on cause and effect. There is an urgent need to incorporate tourist operators within reef management teams.

Conclusions

The GCRMN will succeed by:
- Developing independent networks of countries with similar interests and problems to share skills and enthusiasm
- Training all stakeholders in basic and effective methods of assessing reef status and analyzing data
- Ensuring that training occurs at the community level and that collaborative networks are established among communities, governments, and scientists
- Obtaining low levels of sustained funding to allow communities and governments to conduct monitoring and education
- Producing annual reports on the status of coral reefs for communities and decision-makers.

To achieve these, there is a need for low-level, sustainable funding for GCRMN Nodes and coordination and for the ICRI process to focus coral reef remedial action at the level of the user. The cost of initiating an average-sized node is anticipated to be approximately US$100,000, with recurrent expenditures decreasing, until countries are self-financing after about three to five years.

Thus, we have sufficient knowledge about the biology, geology, and physics of coral reefs to implement sustainable management. We understand how many coastal communities use and interact with their resources to recommend sustainable management strategies. There is sufficient experience in coral reef management to apply to all reef areas and to most user communities.

Calls that not enough is known about the biology and geology of coral reefs to manage them are false; claims that the size or shape of marine protected areas cannot be determined or assessed for effectiveness are naive. Overexploitation is the experiment; establishing protected areas is the normal, or "control," situation that existed for thousands of years.

We lack economic, legal, and political advice and expertise on the ground and where decisions on coral reefs are made to integrate knowledge and experience from the other disciplines.

We need many disciplines and the political will to assist communities in managing their own resources sustainably. The GCRMN seeks such assistance at the ground level to help conserve coral reefs for future generations.

Partnerships for the International Coral Reef Initiative

Timothy E. Wirth
U.S. Department of State

I am here to talk about a specific and unique partnership that has made significant strides toward preserving this precious ecosystem—the International Coral Reef Initiative, or ICRI.

ICRI was founded to mobilize governments and a wide range of other stakeholders whose coordinated, vigorous, and effective actions are required to address the threats to coral reef ecosystems. ICRI encourages stable coral reef management practices worldwide, including measures to prevent illegal fishing practices, achieve stable fisheries, and protect the ecological systems that support them.

The ICRI framework for action states: "Achieving the ICRI purpose requires the full participation and commitment of governments, local communities, donors, NGOs, the private sector, resource users and scientists; therefore true partnerships, cooperation and collaboration exemplify the ICRI activities."

I have been involved with ICRI since its inception in 1994, and am very pleased with the numerous positive results—and positive partnerships—that have come out of it.

ICRI's first task was to build a fundamental global partnership in support of coral reefs. International activities under ICRI have included a major diplomatic campaign and a series of local and regional workshops convened in the Pacific, the tropical Americas, the South and East Asian seas, East Africa, and the western Indian Ocean. Through these events and others, partner governments have concentrated on highlighting the threats to research and encouraging a stronger focus on the tropical, coastal, and marine environment.

The regional workshops have generated extensive regional cooperation to help individual countries manage reefs. The workshops also illustrate that partnerships between governments must extend beyond the international diplomatic community. The diplomats must bring the message home to their policymakers that the world community is concerned about reefs. We must also heed the voices being raised in communities around the world that effective management is needed if we are to achieve long-term stable use of coral reef ecosystems.

The ICRI Global Workshop was held in the Philippines in 1995. The setting made it crystal clear that in many regions of the world local communities are a fundamental part of the global partnership to manage coral reefs sustainably. This has been recognized in widely accepted principles of integrated coastal zone management, which are becoming more and more widely adopted around the world. The importance of local community involvement must be reflected in local, national, and regional policies and programs.

In the past few years ICRI has been successful in gaining global consensus on the importance of conservation and stable use of coral reefs. The decisions and resolutions of the major global environmental bodies, including the Commission on Sustainable Development, the UNEP

Governing Council, the Convention on Biological Diversity, and the Intergovernmental Oceanographic Commission reflect this global concern.

As reflected by this conference, the donor institutions are strong partners in the coral reef initiative. Some of the strongest initial impetus for ICRI came from bilateral aid agencies, from the United Kingdom, France, Sweden, Australia, Japan and the United States who are supporting major coastal zone management initiatives around the world. The World Bank and the regional development banks are strongly involved in coral reef and coastal zone programs, and this command must increase as the commitment to stable development is deepened.

Another partnership that is gaining momentum is that of the Global Coral Reef Monitoring Network. This network is designed to link scientists, resource managers, and coral reef users into national and regional networks that collect, assemble, and synthesize information on the state of coral reefs. The network supports our efforts to understand the trends in coral reef health, and to manage them for sustainable use, taking into account the needs of local communities.

Nongovernmental organizations (NGOs) have been partners in ICRI since its inception. Their commitment to raising awareness of the plight of the reefs, and to instigating action to protect them is as long-standing as any of the partners to this effort. Nowhere is this more visible than in the efforts to stop cyanide fishing for the food fish and aquarium trades. NGOs have been critical in raising awareness of the issue—the masterful publicity campaign launched before the Biodiversity Convention Conference of the Parties in Jakarta in 1995 kicked off the most recent global wave of mechanisms on destructive fishing methods.

I can say from experience that NGOs have been outdoing the State Department in diplomatic approaches to high levels of government in the Asian region. They have been developing and implementing alternatives to cashing in on coral reef fish for the food and aquarium trades and investigating aquaculture alternatives. They have been working with industry to identify sources of cyanide and the means to test for it in fish, and they have been setting up testing facilities to help the world monitor and stop this destructive trade. Government and multilateral donor support of such outstanding efforts is essential. The U.S. government, for one, is ready to do what we can to tackle our own responsibilities as a major importer of fish from Korean coral reefs. And I am very pleased that the private sector is also more and more involved in looking for solutions to the cyanide problem.

This brings me to the final partner I want to mention—the private sector. The private sector is starting to become more involved in our overall effort to manage the threats to coral reefs and coastal zones. At the Middle East Seas Regional Workshop two weeks ago, the impact of burgeoning tourism development was identified as one of the major threats to reefs in the region. In each island nation of the Caribbean, planeload after planeload of Americans and Europeans lands each day. Everywhere around the world we can see runoff from offshore investment activities flowing out and choking reefs.

We need to bring the private sector more fully into this coral reef initiative partnership. Among us today are many who have found exciting ways to draw the private sector into looking for constructive solutions. When we share our experiences, we find that private, commercial interests can be willing partners in our search for sustainability. I have found this in my own discussions with the cyanide industry, the tourist industry, the diving industry, and the airlines. Often their willingness to engage is only as far away as our ability to begin a dialogue, to constructively lay out the issues, and to begin the search for common interests. Once they are on board as partners and committed, they will work as hard as the rest of us.

The challenge to involve the private sector faces each of us as partners in the coral reef initiative. We must meet that challenge and build the constructive partnerships will most support concerted action on the reefs.

PANEL ONE

DESTRUCTIVE FISHING PRACTICES

Session Chair: Sofia Bettencourt, World Bank

Abatement of Destructive Fishing Practices in Indonesia: Who Will Pay?

Rili Djohani
The Nature Conservancy

Dynamite and cyanide fishing both have a devastating effect on reefs. However, these issues require specific management strategies because of the different groups and market forces involved. A thorough understanding of the history and nature of destructive fishing practices and of the perceptions of the stakeholders involved is essential to develop effective local and regional management strategies. A combination of enforcement, awareness and training programs, and alternative livelihood programs has proved to be a successful strategy in the abatement of destructive fishing practices in Komodo National Park (Flores). But who is going to pay in the long term? The careful planning and development of ecotourism as a part of a conservation strategy may both contribute to the effective protection of the reefs against destructive fishing practices and generate income to sponsor management (park) strategies.

Background

One of the richest genetic storehouses on earth, Indonesia supports one-eighth of the world's coral reefs. At least 2,500 species of reef fish and 400 species of stony corals inhabit Indonesia's waters. Indonesia's coral reefs are being destroyed at staggering rates. Destructive fishing practices, coupled with uncontrolled rural and coastal development, are severely damaging coral reefs, putting at risk the livelihoods of more than 7,000 villages.

Large portions of reefs are blasted away every day throughout Indonesia, reducing reef flats and upper slopes to rubble. The use of explosives to gather food fish, using bottles containing dynamite or ammonium nitrate, is widespread throughout the archipelago. Although spreads of soft coral may give the appearance of a revitalized reef, this habitat supports very few fish and may even be disruptive in the recolonization of reef-building hard corals.

More recently, the coral reefs are now being threatened by cyanide fishing, which is causing long-term damage to Indonesia's coral reef habitats on a large scale. This poison is used to capture live reef fish for the restaurant and aquarium trades. The cyanide stuns the target fish, such as Napoleon wrasse and groupers, but it leaves a trail of dead, small fish and dying corals in its wake. It may take several decades for a reef to recover. An estimated 29 percent of Indonesia's coral reefs remain in good or excellent condition, leaving over half in damaged or critical condition.

History and Nature of Destructive Fishing Practices

Blast Fishing

Although now illegal, blast fishing has been a widespread technique in Indonesia for over 50 years. The type of explosives used has evolved from dynamite to self-made fertilizer/kerosene bombs wrapped in Sprite soft-drink or beer bottles, which are thrown overboard to catch schooling fish at shallow reef areas. More sophisticated bombs have been encountered in Komodo National Park, in Flores, whereby the fishermen use remote-control mechanisms to explode the bombs away from the boat, reducing the resulting noise. The blast fishermen usually work in pairs or in small groups. Free divers collect the fish individually by hand, or by spear, placing them in sacks before surfacing. Recently, divers have been able to prolong their stays underwater by breathing compressed air pumped by low-pressure compressors (*hookah*) from the boat. Pet-Soede and Erdmann (forthcoming) classified blast-fishing operations in the Spermonde Archipelago (South Sulawesi) in small-, medium-, and large-scale operations. Their data show that there is a strong economic incentive for boat owners to enlarge their blasting operations. The fish is sold at local markets, usually through a system of middlemen (or *punggawa*).

Cyanide Fishing

In the early 1990s, foreign fishing companies began collecting reef food fish for the growing markets in Hong Kong (China)—still the major trading and import market for live reef food fish—Taiwan (China), Singapore, and China. Initially, the companies used their own fishing crews to catch groupers and Napoleon wrasses with cyanide and *hookah*. In a few years, this unsustainable technique was introduced to many fishing communities throughout Indonesia with the help of a network of the local *punggawa*. These middlemen can monopolize this trade in their area via a complete control over fishing communities through a system of credit and debt and the use of their influence to engage government support. The valuable fish are kept in holding pens (*keramba*) until mother ships collect and transport them to overseas Asian markets. The role of foreign fishing companies has been reduced to the trading of the target fish, which considerably lowers their risk of being caught and charged with illegal fishing practices in Indonesia.

Some Stakeholders' Perceptions and Precedents

The major underlying issues for the use of destructive fishing methods are increasing population and competition for fishing grounds. Growing population pressure has a direct impact on the reefs, resulting in overexploitation of fish and invertebrate species. Uncontrolled urbanization and modernization of fishing techniques lead to habitat destruction and rapid depletion of fish stocks. Access to new markets, products, and technology is altering the existence of coastal fishing communities whose livelihood often depends entirely on the sea. It becomes increasingly difficult for the fishermen to catch enough fish for their daily life. They become easy targets for the middlemen who are recruiting fishermen for their business. The *punggawa* provide them food, fishing gear, and boats—building up the debts of the fishermen, who quickly become entirely dependent on the middlemen for their livelihood. At some point, the fishermen do not have a choice but to use the cyanide to catch fish in order to pay their debts on time. Providing alternative livelihood programs that offer economic incentives for changing the behavior of local fishermen should be part of the strategy to abate illegal fishing practices.

Two groups can be distinguished among the dynamite fishermen on the basis of their motivation and engagement in dynamite fishing. The first group consists of those who do not have the means to switch to sustainable fishing practices on their own.

Such a fisherman might say, "I know we are causing damage to the coral reefs but what am I to do? I have no other skills and it is my only income. There will always be fish in the sea."

Members of the police also acknowledge the fact that dynamite fishing is a socioeconomic problem and sympathize with the fishermen, as they are only looking for food. In areas such as Spermonde, the problem is not solved by enforcement alone. On one occasion, the police stepped up enforcement for two days, cracking down on the dynamite fishing. Consequently, there were no fish available at the local markets.

Introduction of other sustainable fishing techniques is essential.

The second category is that of hard-core fishermen who do not fear the law and who take for granted the consequences of being involved in destructive fishing practices. They are usually led by influential and relatively wealthy leaders who organize and train a small group of fishermen in dynamite fishing. These "professional" fishermen will not hesitate to throw their bombs at representatives of the enforcement agencies in the heat of fights at sea. An increased enforcement effort in Komodo National Park has led to the capture and death of a few notorious blast fishermen. Others have since found an alternative livelihood in pelagic fisheries (where they catch Spanish mackerel). The combination of adequate enforcement and local market opportunities led to the decrease of blast fishing in the park.

Cyanide fishing involves an international syndicate with different mobile groups involved in supplying markets overseas. The consensus among the exporters and trading companies of live reef food fish is that it is essential to find alternative fishing techniques that do not destroy the reefs. The aim should be to eliminate the use of cyanide, not the trade itself. However, a question arises: Who is going to pay for the development of new, sustainable harvesting and cultivation techniques that should be more lucrative? The enforcement of laws against cyanide fishing is complicated for the following reasons:

- It is difficult and expensive to detect cyanide in fish, and the impact on the reefs is less visual.
- The transport vessels are registered as cargo vessels; consequently fishing laws do not apply for to these boats.
- The use and availability of cyanide is legal for other industries, such as mining and electroplating, so the poison is readily available.

Fishing companies supply fishermen with air compressors for their diving but often neglect to give them instruction in their use. As a result, death or paralysis from the bends has become widespread. A young fisherman, paralyzed from his lower chest down, was informed of the correlation between the bends and frequent or deep diving. After listening to the information, he said, "I would still go diving again as much as possible, so I can earn more."

It is evident that awareness and training programs will be effective for this target group only if coupled with a more lucrative alternative fishing technique or source of income.

Local Management Strategies

It is essential to differentiate management strategies for dynamite and cyanide fishing, taking into account the local socioeconomic situation in each priority area. Locations near urban centers greatly influence the reluctance of local fishermen to turn to other fishing techniques. In remote areas, much less time is generally needed to gain the trust of fishermen and engage them in alternative livelihood programs. This fact, in turn, will affect the planning and design of the management program. Short-term strategies should be designed to put an immediate halt to destructive fishing practices, and long-term strategies should be designed to devise sustainable solutions.

A combination of enforcement, awareness and training programs, and alternative livelihood programs has proved to be a successful strategy in the abatement of destructive fishing practices in Komodo National Park. Upon request from the Department of Forestry, The Nature Conservancy assists the Komodo National Park Authority with the planning and management of the marine natural resources. The intent is to establish a marine reserve that fully protects the complete natural community structure and habitat of the demersal and sedentary marine ecosystem in all its diversity (Pet and Djohani, 1996). The greatest immediate threat to the park comes primarily from outside fishermen who are engaged in illegal destructive fishing methods. The Nature Conservancy helped form a team consisting of the park's management, police, army, and fisheries. This team now works together to carry out a routine patrolling program. Since its inception in 1995, blast fishing has declined by more than 80 percent. Workshops, presentations, and exhibitions throughout the year help build national and provincial government and local support. Target audiences include planners, legislators, fishermen leaders, schoolteachers, and entrepreneurs. Fishing villages receive posters and comic books that illustrate the impact of dynamite and cyanide use. Economic alternatives for local communities are essential to reducing destructive fishing practices. In close cooperation with outside investors and local entrepreneurs, The Nature Conservancy is helping develop ecotourism, pelagic fisheries, and environmentally sound mariculture. Compatible training programs are set up for communities living in and outside the park to enhance skills and encourage participation in these opportunities.

The challenge is to develop mechanisms that ensure the long-term sponsoring of enforcement, awareness programs, and the development of alternative livelihoods. The private sector, with the support of government, will play an increasingly important role in protecting the coral reefs, generating income for park management, and providing alternative income for local villagers.

Ecotourism: An Important Ally

Ecotourism can play an important role in protecting the marine natural resources in an area. The Nature Conservancy is currently exploring ways to work together with ecotourism developers in the Komodo area, whose businesses help endorse a threefold strategy to ban destructive fishing practices in and around Komodo National Park:

- Increased capacity to monitor the reefs through the presence of ecolodges on islands outside the park and the presence of sea safaris and dive live-aboard vessels cruising in the park
- Increased support to raise the conservation awareness and commitment of the government at all levels
- The generation of alternative sources of income and employment for local communities.

The Nature Conservancy is working with the major ecotourism developer in the buffer zone area with the following goals in mind:

- To influence the planning and design of the a sustainable project that will include the construction of ecolodges on islands and mountains and planning of sea safaris, and, at a later stage, to help monitor the tourism activities such as diving, hiking, sportfishing, and kayaking in the park.
- To ensure the involvement and employment of local communities in ecotourism activities.
- To develop mechanisms for the generation of income for park management from the ecotourism revenues. Local entrepreneurs have already sponsored the installation of mooring buoys at popular dive spots in and around Komodo National Park. Cruise boats and other tour operations will be targeted as well to contribute to park management.

Regional Recommendations

Strategic alliances are required to effectively address the issues of cyanide and dynamite fishing in Indonesia and the Indo-Pacific region. Moreover, it seems virtually impossible to organize and cover the costs of enforcement, awareness, and alternative livelihood programs throughout Indonesia without the involvement of the private sector. The careful planning and development of ecotourism as a part of a conservation strategy may contribute to the effective protection of the reefs against destructive fishing practices and generate income for the sponsor's (that is, the park's) management strategies. Those who are concerned with the region must:

- Visualize and explain the impact of destructive fishing methods to key policy- and decisionmakers at regional and international forums
- Inform and engage the international private sector, in particular those in the field of ecotourism, in local conservation, and in management of marine natural resources
- Develop mechanisms in which tourism revenues will flow back to park management
- Ensure local social benefits derived from international tourism activities, for example, through marketing of local handicrafts and training of local guides.

References

Djohani, R. 1995. "The Combat of Dynamite and Cyanide Fishing in Indonesia: A Strategy to Decrease the Use of Destructive Fishing Methods in and around Komodo National Park." The Nature Conservancy, Jakarta.

Pet, J. S., and R. Djohani.1996. "A Framework for Management of the Marine Resources of Komodo National Park and Surrounding Areas in Eastern Indonesia." The Nature Conservancy, Jakarta.

Pet-Soede, P., and M. V. Erdmann. Forthcoming. "Blast Fishing in Southwest Sulawesi: An Increasing Demand for Fertilizer." The Nature Conservancy, Jakarta.

Is Harvesting Wild Groupers for Growout Sustainable?

R. E. Johannes and N. J. Ogburn
R. E. Johannes Pty. Ltd.

One way of reducing the impact of the live reef food fish trade on grouper stocks is to encourage the expansion of grouper farming, which is carried out in a number of Indo-Pacific countries. There is considerable room for expansion by means of culturing these fish—in abandoned shrimp ponds throughout much of Southeast Asia, and using cage culture in some areas, such as eastern Indonesia.

But despite more than a decade of research in at least 16 different countries commercial success has proved elusive because of the fragility of grouper larvae, the difficulty of obtaining suitable food for them, and cannibalism. Mortality rates have been either uniformly high or frustratingly and unpredictably variable.

Taiwan, China, has reportedly had some recent success in the hatchery raising of estuarine groupers *Epinephelus coioides* and *E. malabaricus* commercially. But the technology, which has been developed by the private sector and carefully guarded, is not available for export. Moreover, the price of hatchery-raised juveniles in Taiwan, China, has been too high for competition to compete in the export market. So grouper farming in other countries continues to rely heavily on wild-caught juveniles.

There are reports of dwindling supplies of wild juveniles in some areas, for example, *Epinephelus akaara* and *E. coioides* in Hong Kong, China, and the adjacent waters of mainland China. There are also a number of general statements made in various reports and papers suggesting that supplies are dwindling in other countries. But no research has documented these declines or established any cause. Is it overfishing of the juveniles, overfishing of the adults that produce the juveniles, habitat degradation and pollution, or a combination of these? Or is it an artifact of the great natural interannual variation in recruitment that is known to occur in a variety of species of groupers?

It is widely believed that reef fish populations are limited not by competition or available habitat, but by recruitment—that is, by the numbers of larvae that manage to complete their oceanic/pelagic life stage, locate a suitable reef, and settle there. If this were strictly true (more recent research by a number of workers casts some doubt on this, however), it would imply that removing juvenile groupers from the wild to farm them would be robbing Peter (wild stocks) to pay Paul (aquaculture). If grouper stocks are limited by habitat availability or predation, however, there is less likelihood that harvesting wild juveniles in moderation would deplete wild stocks.

A variety of poorly documented methods are used to harvest wild grouper juveniles in a number of Asian countries. The Philippines has one of the longest histories in this regard. In a project sponsored by The Nature Conservancy, we examined some of the methods used there in order to the determine the species caught, the possible social and ecological impacts of these fisheries, and long-term trends in availability of grouper juveniles. To obtain anecdotal information in the absence of published data, we sought the opinions of the fishers.

We found evidence of only two species of grouper juveniles, *Epinephelus coioides* and *E. malabaricus*, being caught in large numbers. These are the same two species produced in hatcheries in Taiwan, China.

The capture method that appeared most ecologically and socially sustainable is that of using artificial habitats made of brush, rock, or wood and referred to as *gangos*. Constructing and operating *gangos* is an occupation economically within reach of very poor families. *Gango* owners in northern Cebu estimate the labor and material costs of obtaining and transporting nest-building materials to nest sites at 200 to 400 pesos (about $US6 to 12). They state that costs may be recovered in as little as two harvests (typically between one and two months apart). The materials for the net used to encircle the *gango* and capture the fish cost about 700 pesos (approximately $US22).

Although normally described as reef fishes, juveniles of both *E. coioides* and *E. malabricus* settle in estuarine areas in and near mangroves. They move to coral reefs only after achieving a size of about 1 kilogram. Between 70 and 90 percent of Philippine mangrove areas have been destroyed in recent times. It is possible, especially under these circumstances, that the shelters used by fishers to attract the juvenile groupers in such areas increase the likelihood of their survival.

In any event, it is noteworthy that the majority of grouper fry collectors we interviewed around all four of the main Philippine islands we visited—most of whom had been operating for two decades or more—said that they perceived no long-term decline in abundance of grouper fry or juveniles. At most locations *gango* operators said that although the numbers of *gangos* in their waters had increased markedly since

they started using them, they saw no decline in catch per *gango*.

The exceptions to this were fishers in estuaries near Roxas City, Panay. They reported a marked and prolonged decline in the availability of juvenile groupers, which they said paralleled declines in abundance of most other estuarine species. They saw the cause as environmental degradation, especially sedimentation. Severe sedimentation and shallowing of the estuary, owing to deforestation in the adjacent watersheds, have been documented in these waters, as well as a significant reduction in water circulation and quality because of the uncontrolled proliferation of fish ponds.

The Nature Conservancy is sponsoring the introduction of Philippine *gangos* in the Komodo area of eastern Indonesia. Its purpose is to provide alternative employment for fishers presently using destructive fishing practices, and to encourage the greater farm production of groupers so as to help reduce the pressure of the live reef food fish trade on wild stocks. The oft-cited problem of obtaining suitable food to feed these carnivorous fish is not an issue in this region, since an unexploited fish stock unsuitable for other purposes has been identified.

Our study covered portions of only one country, and only two species of juvenile groupers. If reef fish farming is to achieve its full capacity to take advantage sustainably of the large and fast-growing demand for live reef food fish, then more such efforts should be made to investigate the biology of, and fisheries for, the juvenile reef fish of species that are (or could be) caught for growout in the western Indo-Pacific region. There will be little incentive for the industry—which is composed of innumerable small competing units—to fund such research. The task would therefore seem to fall logically to governments, aid agencies, and large NGOs (nongovernmental organizations).

Destructive Fishing Practices in the Asia-Pacific Region

Nancy MacKinnon
The Nature Conservancy

Destructive fishing practices have seriously damaged many of the world's richest and most diverse coral reefs, providing an urgent warning that immediate and far-reaching action is needed. The Philippines stands out as one of the hardest hit areas, with more than 70 percent of its 13,000 square miles of reef in varying stages of deterioration. In Indonesia this trend is being replicated, with only 29 percent of that country's square miles of reef considered in good condition. Among the region's most destructive fishing, trends are:

- Sodium cyanide. Fishermen use cyanide to stun and capture fish for the live reef food and aquarium fish trades. Although the target fish often survive the cyanide assault, the poison leaves a trail of dead and dying fish in its wake. Living coral reefs are also among the casualties. Because of depleted fish stocks and unrelenting market demand, the live reef fish trade is expanding geographically, moving into the western Pacific, in particular Papua New Guinea, the Solomon Islands, and Micronesia.
- Depletion of spawning sites. Commercial fishing companies use helicopters and advanced technologies to locate and deplete spawning sites. Continued pressure could quickly cause fish stocks to collapse, permanently altering entire ecosystems.
- Pesticides and herbicides. Fishermen mix pesticides (such as Endrin) and herbicides (such as Teodal) with drums of sand, which they dump on reefs, killing all marine life in the vicinity. The mixture remains active for three days, continuing to kill fish that enter the contaminated area.
- Explosives. Blast fishing is so widespread throughout the region that large sections of once-vibrant reef have been reduced to rubble. In Komodo National Park, Indonesia, for example, a Rapid Ecological Assessment found the impact on reefs from explosives was moderate to high at more than half of the surveyed sites.
- Meting. "Meting" is an emerging threat that involves the indiscriminate removal of all edible organisms from reefs. Fishermen destroy corals and other organisms by using metal crowbars to rip away coral cover to dislodge abalone, clams, and other invertebrates. This practice leaves behind nearly 100 percent dead coral rubble.

Causes of Destructive Fishing Practices in the Asia-Pacific Region

Destructive fishing involves a complex array of political, economic, and sociological factors The following outlines some of the primary challenges:

- Consumer demand. Unrelenting demand for live reef fish has fueled the dramatic surge in sodium cyanide fishing. China, including Hong Kong and Taiwan, drives the $1 billion-per-year live food fish industry. The United States, Europe, and Japan lead demand for aquarium fish, which totals a small percentage of the food fish trade.

- Uninformed consumers. Though cyanide fishing has received considerable media coverage, consumers remain largely unaware of the real cost of reef fish. To date, there are few mechanisms for consumers to participate in meaningful reform.

- Lack of local marine tenure. Unfortunately, most local villagers lack the authority to protect their own waters. As Dr. Robert Johannes notes, "Fishing crews from outside the region destroy reefs while local villagers are powerless to intercede—either due to local laws, poor communications, or bribery of village or government officials."

- Local economic forces. Poor island nations often trade away their future by depleting and destroying their own marine resources for immediate needs or short-term gain. Especially when locals are powerless to protect their waters, they may use destructive fishing practices to fish their reefs before someone else does. Moreover, as resources become depleted, fishermen increasingly turn to destructive methods to capture what few fish stocks remain.

- Weak policies and enforcement. Many countries allow large-scale commercial fishing yet lack policies that are effective at ensuring that these companies operate on a sustainable basis. For those countries with laws prohibiting destructive practices, governments may lack the infrastructure or political will to enforce those laws.

Conservation Tools

Destructive fishing must be addressed on both regional and site-specific levels. The following are some of the most promising strategies that The Nature Conservancy and others are pursuing:

Regional

Grouper mariculture production. The Conservancy believes that expansion of environmentally sound grouper mariculture is critical to increasing sustainability of the live food fish industry. In addition to relieving pressure on wild fish stocks, mariculture offers alternative livelihood opportunities to divert fishermen from cyanide fishing and other destructive practices. With a goal of eventually gaining market share over wild-caught grouper, the Conservancy will work with regional mariculture experts, local communities, and local business partners to establish a mariculture demonstration center at Komodo National Park, Indonesia, to serve as a model for replication across the region.

Certification for aquarium fish. The World Wildlife Fund, the National Aquarium, the American Marine Life Dealers Association, the Pet Industry Joint Advisory Council, The Nature Conservancy, and others have formed the Marine Aquarium Fish Council (MAFC). MAFC will act as an independent organization that will set standards and oversee voluntary environmental certification in the aquarium industry.

Cyanide testing. The Conservancy is working with the DuPont Corporation to develop simple, inexpensive, and noninvasive cyanide detection tests that will detect minute levels of cyanide in fish, even several weeks after exposure. We hope to develop a legally defensible test to discourage live fish exporters from buying or exporting cyanide-caught fish. Presently, the Philippines is the only country to test fish prior to export, and the fish must be killed to be tested.

Local marine tenure. Patrolling vast waters is costly and often impractical at the national level. Local villagers are not only the best positioned to protect their waters, but also the ones who have the greatest personal interest in ensuring the long-term health of their reefs. The Conservancy supports the reinstatement of traditional marine tenure where it existed previously and the introduction of co-management systems for marine resource management in areas where it not previously exist.

Science and research. The Conservancy and partners are seeking funding for a three-year investigation of the short- and long-term effects of fishing with sodium cyanide and explosives on coral reef communities.

The Conservancy is also considering research on the effects of cyanide on aquarium fish. Should results demonstrate that cyanide compromises the health of fish through increased mortality or reduced reproductive output, consumers can help drive demand for fish free of cyanide.

Prevention in the western Pacific. Live reef fish importers report that the trade is looking to the western Pacific as the "new frontier." Working with the International Marine Life Alliance (IMA) and other partners, the Conservancy seeks to help prevent cyanide fishing in the western Pacific—before the industry can establish an economic foothold. To date, the Conservancy has provided fisheries policy guidance to threatened areas including Papua New Guinea, Palau, the Marshall Islands, and the Federated States of Micronesia.

In addition the Conservancy intends to collaborate with local and regional NGOs (nongovernmental organizations) to develop a regional education campaign targeting coastal villagers, political leaders, and other decision-makers. The campaign will demonstrate the potential ramifications of cyanide fishing through communication materials such as posters, videos, pamphlets, and comic books.

Local

Local NGO development. Local NGOs can provide the most powerful and long-term voice for conservation. Among many valuable functions, local NGOs can guide policy development, oversee community training and education, and help create sustainable economic alternatives.

In Palau the Conservancy helped establish the Palau Conservation Society (PCS). Today, PCS has become the nation's leading advocate for a balance between development and conservation. The Conservancy will remain a behind-the-scenes partner, providing technical support and participating in joint fund-raising until PCS becomes fully self-sufficient.

Alternative livelihood development. At several sites the Conservancy is developing sustainable enterprises, including ecotourism, catch-and-release sportfishing, and mariculture as alternatives to destructive fishing. These sites will serve as "learning beds" to develop models for effective marine resource management that can be applied throughout the region.

Enforcement. Active patrolling and enforcement are essential to marine resource management In Komodo National Park, for example, the Conservancy helped activate police and Park Authority patrols. Because of increased patrolling, and extensive community education, blast fishing declined by 87 percent in 1996.

Training. International Marine Life Alliance offers a comprehensive program to retrain cyanide fishermen. The Cyanide Fishing Reform Program (CFRP) advocates fine-mesh nets for aquarium fishermen. For live food fish collectors. CFRP promotes hook and line in conjunction with the decompression technique of inserting a needle into a fish's swim bladder. In some cases, CFRP provides training in related businesses to diversify fishermen's economic bases.

Marine protected areas/no-take reserves. Among the most promising strategies marine protected areas and no-take reserves not only protect coral reef habitats, they show promise in enhancing fish stocks in adjacent fishing grounds. These areas should incorporate spawning aggregations for protection.

Destructive Fishing with Dynamite

Solomon Makoloweka
Tanga Coastal Zone Conservation and Development Programme

This paper highlights the problem of describing the process used to identify the issues and causes, key stakeholders, steps taken so far to address the issues, obstacles encountered, and lessons learned.

Destructive fishing practices with dynamite have been recorded in the Tanga Region and indeed along the Tanzania coastline since the mid-1960s. The Fisheries Act of 1970 banned the use of explosives. However, a World Conservation Union (IUCN) and Tanga Regional Authority 1987 joint preliminary survey to determine the status of coral reefs in the region showed that explosive fishing was still a problem and had a major impact on the reefs (IUCN, 1987). The Tanga Coastal Zone Conservation and Development Programme's survey in 1995, which involved fishermen from villages, showed that of the 93 reefs in the region 10 percent were destroyed, about 20 percent were still in good condition, while the remaining 70 percent were in a moderate state with a possibility for recovery if no further human activity is continued—such as, by making them protected areas or by controlling access and types of activities (Horrill and Kalombo 1995).

Setting

The Tanga Region is in the northeastern part of Tanzania in the West Indian Ocean. It has a coastline of 150 kilometers where in the north it borders with Kenya. Over 200,000 people live along this coastline, with most of them depending on fishing for their livelihood. Other important economic activities include farming and trade based on coastal resources. Seaweed farming is gaining momentum, while there is potential for tourism development.

The program is a partnership being implemented by the Tanga Regional Authorities with technical advice from IUCN and financial assistance from Irish Aid. Phase I ran from 1994 to 1997; Phase II began in July 1997 and will continue until July 2000.

Environmental Issues

The program conducted participatory resource assessment in nine coastal villages to establish resource use patterns (for example, who uses what and at what levels). It was found during this survey that coastal communities were well aware of most of the underlying causes of destructive fishing practices. The study showed that up to 80 percent of the adult males in coastal villages were involved in fishing, but more people were catching less now than they were a few years back (Gorman 1995). The exercise was facilitated by government extension workers.

Identification of Stakeholders

The socioeconomic survey was followed by a regional workshop organized by the program. This involved representatives of all key stakeholders—for example, representatives of coastal villages, regional and district government authorities, and commercial users of coastal natural resources. The main objective of the workshop was to agree on priority issues, analyze causes, and develop suggestions for possible solutions (table 1). The following were the issues as identified by workshop participants:

- Declining fish stocks
- Low agricultural production
- Beach erosion
- Poor enforcement
- Scarcity of fuelwood and building materials
- Beach pollution
- Lack of social and economic services.

As a result of the workshop, three pilot villages were selected to try possible solutions to their top two most pressing issues. These villages were Kipumbwi in Pangani district, Kigombe in Muheza district, and Mwambani in Tanga Municipality.

The immediate reaction by the pilot villages was to form special committees to take action to deal with fisheries-related issues. The villagers were given basic training in program planning, problem analysis, formation of objectives, work plans, and monitoring.

Since destructive fishing and poor enforcement by government were identified as some of the major causes of low fish catches, the fish scarcity committee in each village resolved to

---

Table 1. Causes and Possible Solutions for the Issue of Declining Fish Catches

Causes
- Uncontrolled mangrove cutting
- Destruction of coral reefs
- Poor gears
- Increase in number of fishermen
- Trawlers fishing close to coast
- Seine nets—fishing of juveniles

Possible solutions
- Restrict illegal fishing techniques
- Mangrove replanting
- Close areas to fishing
- Provision of appropriate gears
- Develop alternative incomes
- Restrict trawlers fishing offshore

Source: Kalombo 1997.

---

carry out gear inspection, inspection of fish killed by dynamite, and both land and sea patrols in their respective areas of jurisdiction. To make the patrols more effective and legally binding, they formed bylaws to apprehend law offenders. The bylaws were later approved by the districts. The village committees have become the focal points for planning and implementation of agreed actions. Both district and program staff from Fisheries, Natural Resources, and Community Development have facilitated the process by providing technical assistance to the villages.

Coral Reef Survey

To determine the status of the coral reefs the program carried out a participatory coral reef survey along the entire coastline. The survey was carried out by Fisheries personnel and involved fishermen in the villages. The surveys were fairly simple, involving mapping, measuring the proportion of live to dead corals, fish population, and fish and coral diversity. The surveys were conducted using an open boat, outboard engine, a global positioning system (GPS), and snorkels.

Results of the survey included the following:
- Reefs were identified—including 14 that had not been charted before.
- Approximately 10 percent of reefs were found to be destroyed, 20 percent were in good condition; the remaining 70 percent were in moderate condition with a possibility for recovery if no further human activity takes takes place.

The majority of the reefs destroyed or in poor condition are near areas densely populated with humans (Horrill and Kalombo 1995). Fishermen helped in collecting data and reviewing the results. The program later fed back the coral reef survey information to all users. Information included reef status, fish population status, coral diversity, importance of the reef for different fisheries, fishing gears, fish species, and which villages use the reefs. This prompted village committees in pilot villages to take further actions intended to boost fish catches. Two of the pilot villages, Kipumbwi and Kigombe,

Table 2. Effects of Reef Closures

- Fish in closed area will be able to grow larger and so produce more eggs.
- Reef conditions will improve, increasing the number of fish shelters.
- Number of fish in closed areas will increase.
- Fish will migrate to other reefs and be caught.
- Fishing area restrictions will leading to overfishing in open areas.
- Fishers' income will decrease with decreased catches because of overfishing.

Source: Kalombo 1997.

opted to establish management areas so that they could try some of the proposed actions, such as closing of some reefs, village patrols, and gear and fish inspections. This led to a series of meetings to reach agreements with neighboring villages using the same reefs. The meetings were very protracted, but the villages reached a consensus to close some of the reefs.

Before reaching a final decision, however, villagers debated the advantages and disadvantages of reef closures and the benefits of long- and short-term closures (table 2).

Since most of the reefs were already overfished, most villagers agreed that there were more benefits in closing the reefs.

Minutes of all meetings, attendance, and agreements with adjacent villages were recorded and endorsed by village assemblies. The same were forwarded to the District Council, where they were again endorsed and passed over to the Director of Fisheries to await final approval.

Tools for Sustainable Development

Training and learning through training instruction in different skills at all levels had to be provided for regional and district government officers, extension workers, and villagers. First, a training needs assessment was carried out for extension workers. The assessment revealed that lack of technical skills was not a problem, but that lack of communication skills was (Chiwile and Salenge 1994).

The total training program included participatory rapid/rural appraisal and learning (PRA) techniques, communication, facilitation, and animation skills; coastal ecology; coastal culture; and analytical and planning skills. The participants also learned how to serve as trainers in planning and business management. The result has been improved relationships and understanding between villagers and government extension workers.

Training in coastal ecology for government staff, such as magistrates and police at the regional and district level, has tremendously improved law enforcement. Other tools used are PRA and animation, which are techniques to stimulate people to identify and analyze their problems, and search for solutions themselves.

Monitoring and Evaluation

A number of tools are being used for monitoring and evaluation, including a logical framework that sets out objectives, results, indicators, and assumptions; periodic remeasuring of the social economic baseline; and monitoring of the health of coral reefs, mangroves, and seagrass beds. Our approach to monitoring and evaluation is like planning and implementation: it must belong to different stakeholders.

The following are recommendations for future actions:

- Start any new program with a "listening" phase. This should be based on participatory appraisals that involve all stakeholders from the beginning in identifying and prioritizing the issues.
- Provide training in participatory problem analysis, planning, and monitoring to both government workers and villagers. This can result in a high level of commitment by coastal villagers to their planned solutions.
- Strengthen capacity at all levels and promote communication between different sectors, different levels, and different stakeholders.
- Train extension workers and selected villagers to be trainers themselves. This appears to be an effective way of improving certain skills and techniques of a larger number of villagers.

- Involving different sectors of government in training courses and seminars has begun to bear fruit. For example, the district registrar has taken the initiative in determining, with district magistrates and public prosecutors, why the prosecution of certain cases, particularly those involving illegal fishing, is generally prolonged and unsuccessful. This has resulted in tremendous improvement in fines imposed and reduction of prosecution time (Horrill 1997).
- Have regular workshops and feedback meetings with stakeholders. Keep all players informed; this will help keep popular support.
- Simple monitoring techniques play an important part in feedback.
- Monitoring systems need to be developed with the participation of the people who have to use them, and they should be appropriate for the resources available to them and their operations. Monitoring tools and procedures must be simple.
- Future financial demands of programs can be minimized by a community-based approach of training villagers as trainers, and by using appropriate and accessible technology.

References

Chiwile, P., and H. Salange. 1994. "A Report of the Training Needs Assessment for the Extension Workers along the Coastal Zone." Tanga, Tanzania.

Gorman, M. 1995. "Report on Socio-Economic Study/Participatory Rural Appraisal Conducted in March/April 1995." TCZCDP, Tanga, Tanzania.

Horrill, J. C., and H. Kalombo. 1996. "Report on the Results of the Survey of the Coral Reefs of the Tanga Region." TCZCDP, Tanga, Tanzania.

Horrill, J. C. 1997. "Evaluation of Enforcement Trials TCZCDP." Tanga, Tanzania.

IUCN (World Conservation Union). 1987. "The Coastal Resources of Tanga Region, Tanzania."

Kalombo, H. 1997. "Artisanal Fisheries Management in Tanga, TCZCDP." Tanga, Tanzania.

Policy Reform and Community-Based Programs to Combat Cyanide Fishing in the Asia-Pacific Region

Charles Victor Barber
World Resources Institute

Vaughan R. Pratt
International Marinelife Alliance-Philippines

Cyanide Fishing: A Poison Tide on the Reef

Since the 1960s, more than a million kilograms of deadly sodium cyanide has been squirted onto coral reefs in the Philippines to stun and capture ornamental aquarium fish destined for the pet shops and aquariums of Europe and North America. More recently, a growing demand for larger reef food fish has vastly increased the incidence and spread of cyanide fishing. Consumers in Hong Kong, China, and other major Asian cities greatly value certain reef fish when they are plucked live from a tank, cooked, and served minutes later, and pay up to $300 per plate for some species. The combined demand for aquarium and live food fish has spread cyanide fishing throughout Indonesia and into neighboring countries such as Fiji, the Maldives, Papua New Guinea, and Vietnam. In the past year, officials in countries as far-flung as Eritrea, the Marshall Islands, and Tanzania have voiced suspicions that their fast-growing live-fish export industries may also be using cyanide.

Far from Hong Kong's restaurants and the pet stores of Europe and North America, fishermen in Southeast Asia, the Indian Ocean, and the Pacific dive into the sea with *hookah* tubes in their mouths—attached to air compressors on small boats—and makeshift squirt bottles in their hands. These fishermen squirt cyanide into coral formations, thereby stunning their prey for collection. Sometimes a crowbar is nec-

essary to pry apart the coral heads and reach the stunned fish that hide in crevices. The rewards are high, with some cyanide divers making more than university professors in their countries, but so are the risks. Untrained in diving safety, many fishermen fall prey to decompression sickness (the bends.) Contributing to this chain of poison are a variety of intermediaries—vessel and holding-tank facility owners, fish exporters and importers—and civilian, police, and military officials who look the other way for a cut of the profits.

Cyanide kills corals and reef invertebrates along with many nontarget fish. Large percentages of the fish that are captured live die in transit because of their poison-weakened state. Deadly in any marine environment, the spread of cyanide fishing is particularly tragic in the countries of the Indo-Pacific region. As the global center of marine biodiversity for corals, fish, mollusks, and reef invertebrates, the region may justifiably be called the Amazon of the Oceans. Cyanide fishing also threatens the livelihood of poor coastal people in the region, where dependence on fish protein is very high and fisheries provide millions with income.

The Philippines, birthplace of cyanide fishing, is also the only country with a program in place to eradicate the practice. Since the early 1990s the Bureau of Fisheries and Aquatic Resources and the International Marinelife Alliance-Philippines (IMA), a nongovernmental organization (NGO), have jointly developed and implemented the Cyanide Fishing Reform Program (CFRP). Experience with the CFRP over the past five years shows that cyanide fishing can be reduced through a combination of the right policies and laws, beefed-up enforcement efforts, enhanced public awareness, cyanide testing of live fish exports, training of cyanide fishermen in cyanide-free live fish capture techniques, and development of sustainable community-based resource management and livelihood alternatives that transform local fishermen into the front line of marine stewards and protectors.

One key aspect of the CFRP's initial success has been initiation of policy reforms in both source and consumer countries to create anti-cyanide fishing incentives and enforcement mechanisms. A second important element has been development of effective partnerships with fishing communities themselves, focusing on transfer of nondestructive technology and improvement of local livelihoods.

This paper identifies the key actors in the live fish trade and analyzes their roles and interests. It then looks at the process by which research and advocacy that first exposed the cyanide fishing problem in the Philippines during the 1980s has been transformed into a new policy framework and program of action on the ground. The paper then elaborates the policy reforms governments of both exporting and importing countries must make to establish incentives for a cyanide-free live fish trade, and examines the community-based strategies that lie at the heart of the CFRP's efforts to counter this ominous threat to the very heart of the planet's marine biodiversity.

Actors in the Live Reef Fish Trade

The live reef fish trade in Southeast Asia has an estimated annual retail value of at least $1.2 billion, about $1 billion from the live food fish trade (mostly with Hong Kong, China), and nearly $200 million from exports of aquarium fish to Europe and North America. Not all of the fish in the trade are caught with cyanide (Australia's live reef fishery, for example, is cyanide-free), but most of them are. To understand the dynamics of this trade, it is necessary to understand the various actors involved and the incentives that currently shape their behavior.

Cyanide Fishermen

The number of cyanide fishermen operating in Southeast Asia and neighboring countries in unknown. Based on estimates in the Philippines, where there are probably about 4,000, the number of hard-core cyanide fishermen throughout the Indo-Pacific region probably does not exceed 20,000. In short, cyanide fishing is not a ubiquitous problem, like slash-and-burn farming, practiced by millions of poor farmers. Nor is poverty the root cause of cyanide fishing, although many cyanide fishermen are certainly very poor. Rather, cyanide fishermen are a fairly small and discrete group responding to very specific incentives: a new technology, a ready market for the product, lax government enforcement of anticyanide laws, and the lack of viable livelihood alternatives. Experience in the Philippines suggests that when cyanide fishermen are introduced to cyanide-free techniques for live fish capture and ensured a fair price for their catch, they are willing and often eager to give up using the poison and to talk about ways to ensure the long-term sustainability of their local reefs and fisheries. Development of reliable alternative sources of income strengthens these incentives, and strict government enforcement of anticyanide fishing laws further reinforces them.

Live Reef Fish Exporters

The number of companies involved in the live fish export business in Southeast Asia is also unknown, but it appears to be expanding rapidly. In the early 1960s, for example, there were only 3 companies exporting aquarium fish from the Philippines, and export of live food fish did not yet exist. By the 1990s there were some 45 aquarium fish exporters in the country, and 8 companies exporting live food fish. At least 10 companies run holding tanks for live food fish in Bali, Indonesia, a major transshipment point. Conservative estimates of the annual volume of Asian trade in live food fish alone range between 20,000 and 25,000 metric tons, mostly from Indonesia, and the real total may be far greater. Philippine government statistics show that as many as 6 million aquarium fish were exported in 1996, and Indonesia is catching up quickly.

Exporters of cyanide-caught live food and aquarium fish are responding to a strong market demand and the lack of meaningful law enforcement and monitoring by governments. Partnerships with the exporters for more sustainable live fisheries are possible only when source country governments take strong action to eradicate the export of cyanide-caught fish and importing countries demand proof that incoming fish were not caught with cyanide.

Live Reef Fish Importers

Businesses that import live food and aquarium fish are in essentially the same position as exporters: absent government pressure to ensure that the fish they import were not caught with cyanide, they have little incentive to take action on the issue. As one large importer of live food fish argued: "We [the Hong Kong importers] do not participate in any catching of fish or its activities. We just finance the people by equipping them with boats and fishing gear. We just buy fish from them. The production side is left to them."

Live Reef Fish Consumers

Consumers have an important role to play in pressuring the aquarium fish industry to take action on imports of cyanide-caught fish. Indeed, publicity and ensuing consumer pressure in Europe and North America has had some impact on aquarium fish importers and led to efforts like the Marine Aquarium Fish Council in the United States, discussed below. Consumer pressure against cyanide fishing is virtually nonexistent among the Chinese consumers of live food fish, though. As one Hong Kong, China, observer noted, "Being endangered actually seems to spur demand."

Divers and Dive Operators

Scuba diving and snorkeling on tropical reefs is a big and growing business throughout the Indo-Pacific region. Divers and dive operators have a strong interest in maintenance of coral reefs and healthy fish populations, and are often vocal in their support for marine conservation. Effective mechanisms have not yet been developed, however, to fully tap this group for political and financial support in combating cyanide fishing, although some efforts such as the Professional Association of Diving Instructors' Project Aware are working to instill greater general environmental consciousness in divers and dive operators.

Engaging these diverse groups in efforts to combat cyanide fishing requires two basic elements. First, government policies must provide a structure of negative and positive incentives that make cyanide fishing unattractive for the whole range of actors involved in the trade and make sustainable alternatives attractive. Second, partnerships must be developed directly with fishing communities currently using cyanide, to assist them in abandoning the cyanide fishing tradition and adopting techniques, technologies, and economic strategies that improve their livelihoods while protecting their rich marine environment.

Policy Reforms to Combat Cyanide Fishing

Cyanide fishing will not end until governments set in place effective policies to eradicate it and to encourage sustainable live reef fisheries. The use of cyanide to catch fish is illegal in virtually every country of the Indo-Pacific region, but the big profits to be made, combined with lack of enforcement and other supporting actions, mean that with the exception of those in the Philippines, these laws do not much discourage cyanide fishing.

Policy reform, in this context, therefore means more than passing laws. It also involves establishment of effective institutions to monitor the live reef fish trade, enforce the laws, and provide economic incentives for fishermen, traders, and consumers to shift to ecologically sustainable, cyanide-free reef fisheries (see box 1). Experience with the Philippines' Cyanide Fishing Reform Program suggests the following priority areas for policy reforms to combat cyanide fishing in the many countries of the Indo-Pacific region where it is a growing threat.

Policy Reforms in Live Reef Fish Source Countries

Establish Cyanide Detection Test (CDT) Laboratory Facilities at All Major Live Fish Collection and Transshipment Points.

A simple test to determine the presence of cyanide in live fish was developed by IMA and the Bureau of Fisheries and Aquatic Resources (BFAR) and has been in use for over five years in the Philippines. Currently five laboratories test over 6,000 samples annually. An effective CDT testing network is key for a strong effort to reduce cyanide fishing. Without testing, authorities cannot determine whether fish have been caught with cyanide or obtain convincing evidence to prosecute violators. To be successful, CDT labs must also be backed up by a larger network of agencies and monitoring posts, and staff trained in sampling prospective live fish shipments and rapid sample transport. Such a network requires directives on participating in sampling and monitoring from central agencies to their local offices, and training in correct sampling and shipping-to-lab procedures.

Although testing is not a panacea, it is the best technical tool currently available to identify cyanide-tainted fish and provide hard evidence with which to prosecute violators. Countries that want to provide incentives to stop cyanide fishing must be serious about developing their capacities to systematically test live fish intended for export.

Establish a National System of Data Gathering and Monitoring That Provides Useful Data for Regulating the Live Fish Trade.

In order to monitor and regulate the live fish trade, governments need accurate and appropriate data. Many national systems for collecting fisheries and export statistics do not adequately disaggregate data, making it impossible to tell, for example, how many individuals of a particular species were collected in a particular location, exported in a given month or year, or who did the collecting and exporting. There is no way to regulate cyanide use in the live fish trade until such data are regularly collected.

The Philippines now collects live fish data in ways that allow the government to keep a watch over total numbers of particular fish species moving through domestic and international airports and major international seaports, activities of exporters, and other relevant information. IMA collects the data through its CDT and monitoring network, and provides it to all relevant national and provincial government offices.

Establish a Firmer Legal Framework to Detect and Prosecute Cyanide Fishing and Trade in Cyanide-Caught Fish, Ultimately Requiring Mandatory Testing and Certification of All Live Reef Fish Exports.

While fishing with cyanide and other poisons is banned in virtually every country in Southeast Asia and the Pacific, a much firmer legal framework in needed to make these bans effective. Once a CDT laboratory and monitoring network is established, all prospective exporters should be required to submit to random sampling and testing, inspection, and government licensing. All shipments should require a certificate showing the origin, volume, and species composition of the shipment, and certifying that it has been subject to random CDT procedures and is cyanide-free.

A mandatory certification system (as was established by law in the Philippines in late 1997) provides key positive as well as negative incentives for exporters. On the one hand, uncertifiable fish become liabilities. On the other hand, certified fish can obtain an "environmental market premium" in markets where importing governments regulate imports and consumers prefer fish caught without cyanide.

Enforcement procedures and penalties must be fairly applied, and should focus on punishing the larger players in the trade, such as exporters and corrupt officials, and not unduly persecute the cyanide divers themselves. Governments might consider enacting strong forfeiture provisions to prosecute large operators. With this approach, violators would lose not only fish that test positive for cyanide, but also equipment such as boats and holding facilities proved to have been used for cyanide fishing.

Nonetheless, local cyanide divers should be educated that what they are doing, for whatever reasons, is illegal and that repeat offenders will be punished harshly. This will be perceived as just, however, only when local fishermen see the big operators prosecuted first. Targeting the big cyanide fishing interests also reduces incentives for local divers to join in the trade.

Ban or Restrict the Export of Especially Vulnerable Species, Such as the Napoleon Wrasse (Cheilinus undulatus).

Blanket bans on the live reef fish trade are both unwise and unworkable and just drive the trade underground. When the Philippines attempted a ban in parts of Palawan province several years ago, cyanide fishermen continued to use the poison, but killed the fish after capture and sold them on the fresh fish market. Also, bans deprive local communities of one of the most lucrative sources of income to be found in the coastal zone. The cyanide-free capture of live fish at sustainable levels with a fair return to local fishermen should be the objective of live fishery policy.

That said, the pressures on particular species may become so great that governments may want to ban altogether their capture and export. For the Napoleon wrasse, highest-valued of the live food fish species, overexploitation may soon reach critical levels, warranting a complete ban. A ban is unlikely to stop the Napoleon wrasse trade altogether, but it may reduce the total volume.

Regulate the Import, Distribution, and Use of Cyanide.

Cyanide has many legitimate uses in industry, but a considerable amount of the poison is diverted into the live fish collection business. In most countries of the Indo-Pacific region, import, distribution, and use of cyanide are virtually unregulated. To remedy this problem, a draft Sodium Cyanide Act that would strictly regulate the import and use of cyanide was introduced in the Philippine House of Representatives in late 1996. The draft bill requires all cyanide imports to be authorized in advance by the government, and requires the poison's sale to be "strictly controlled." Control elements include requirements for traders and end users to seek authorization from the Department of Environment and Natural Resources (DENR) to purchase, distribute, or use cyanide, and to file weekly reports on the sale or use of the substance. Both traders and buyers would be subject to spot checks by the government. Penalties under the act are stiff, with prison terms for unauthorized possession or importation of cyanide ranging from six to 12 years and fines set at a minimum of $10,000.

While this type of law will undoubtedly be difficult to enforce, it should nonetheless increase the price of cyanide on the black market, thus making nondestructive techniques of live fish capture more economically attractive to fishermen currently using cyanide.

Address Corruption Within Vulnerable Government Units Such as Fisheries, the Navy, Customs, and Police Forces.

The ease with which government officials charged with regulating the live fish trade can be bribed in many places works against all of the other incentives that source country governments might put in place to stop cyanide fishing. But with so much money at stake in the cyanide-based live fish trade, corruption is a recurrent problem. Governments can eliminate corruption only if officials at the highest levels take a firm public stand against it and when corrupt officials are dealt with harshly under the law. Heads of vulnerable agencies, such as fisheries, the navy, and customs, must establish firm policies that those convicted of involvement in cyanide fishing will be summarily fired and permanently barred from civil service or military positions. National police agencies and prosecutors can make it known publicly that they will seek the maximum penalties available under the law to prosecute corrupt officials.

The media can help by exposing instances of corruption related to cyanide fishing in the press. Even in societies where the press is restricted, firm government policy statements against cyanide fishing and related corruption should give the press a freer hand in reporting abuses. Finally, an effective CDT lab and monitoring network, backed up by community-based monitoring, can provide government with a great deal of information about potential corruption problems.

Mount Public Awareness Campaigns in the Media and Schools.

NGOs and government leaders should work systematically to build public awareness about the threat of cyanide fishing and the steps that must be taken to stop it. Press releases, symbolic public events, and the steady provision of information to journalists are all tools that can raise public awareness and strengthen other anti-cyanide fishing incentive measures.

In the schools information on the values of marine resources and biodiversity, the effects of cyanide fishing, and the tools available to stop it should be integrated into curricula from the primary grades onward. Cyanide fishing is a learned behavior that becomes a tradition over time. By teaching the cyanide-free tradition in coastal area schools from an early age, countries can help to ensure that children are fully aware of the alternatives to cyanide fishing and their positive consequences.

Divers are also potential allies in raising awareness and gathering information. In the Philippines in 1994, IMA initiated a voluntary Status of Coral Reefs (SCORE) survey, using a simple questionnaire on reef conditions, which divers were asked to complete and return by mail. By mid-1996, 200 of the 4,000 survey forms distributed by IMA had been completed and returned, providing the first new primary data on the condition of Philippine coral reefs since a survey done in 1983, including reports on suspected cyanide fishing locations.

Policy Reforms in Live Reef Fish-Importing Countries

As in any transnational trade, source countries for live reef fish need the cooperation of importing country governments if their efforts to stem cyanide use at home are to be effective. At present, no importing country requires proof that imported live fish were not caught using cyanide, or penalizes firms that import fish caught with the poison. Key steps for setting up more helpful incentives in importing countries include the following:

Monitor Imports of Live Fish and Provide Data to Exporting Countries.

Importing country governments should establish data collection and storage systems to keep track of the number by species of live fish imported, and the country of origin. They should then share that data with relevant government agencies in source countries. In this way, monitoring agencies in source countries can compare their own export statistics with import statistics and thus determine the validity of those export statistics—provided exporting countries begin to collect detailed export data, as the Philippines is already doing.

Phase in a Legal Requirement That All Live Reef Fish Imports Be Certified as Cyanide-Free.

When live fish–exporting countries require cyanide-free certification for all exports, as in the Philippines, importing countries should reciprocate by requiring all live fish importers to provide certification from the source country government that the fish they are importing have been certified as cyanide-free. Since Indonesia and other exporting countries do not currently have testing and certification systems in place, it is probably unrealistic for importing countries to immediately impose a ban on imports of noncertified live fish. But importing country governments, and importers, can move in this direction by gradually phasing in a prohibition on noncertified live fish imports, simultaneously working with exporting countries to develop testing and certification procedures, laws, and technical capacities. Importing governments will also need to establish cooperation with groups such as IMA and the Marine Aquarium Fish Council (discussed below), which can provide independent third-party monitoring of the certification systems that national governments set up.

Provide Donor Assistance to Live Fish-Exporting Countries to Help Them Combat Cyanide Fishing.

Live fish–importing countries that are providers of development assistance (such as the United States, Canada, Japan, and the countries of the European Union) should offer financial and technical assistance to exporting countries, to assist them in developing cyanide-fishing reform programs and certification procedures. The Asian Development Bank has set a good example in this regard, providing some $2.7 million for the Philippines' CFRP as part of a new Fisheries Sector Loan slated for implementation

in early 1998. The U.S. Agency for International Development is also providing support for the Philippines' CFRP, and is currently developing anticyanide fishing activities as part of its Coastal Resources Management Project in Indonesia, in collaboration with IMA.

Strengthen Consumer Awareness about the Impacts of Cyanide Fishing.

As in other areas of environmental certification, it is crucial to build consumer awareness. Where consumers themselves increasingly demand assurances that the fish they are buy-

---

Box 1. Establishing Partnerships with Live Fish Exporters and Importers

Along with establishing partnerships with fishing communities, effective policies to combat cyanide fishing must also cultivate support from other private sector actors in both source and importing countries. Some of the most important steps in this regard include the following:

Ensure that testing of fish for cyanide is done rapidly, fairly, and efficiently. As already noted, establishment of cyanide detection testing (CDT) capacities and requirements is an essential incentive for discouraging cyanide fishing. But speed is essential if cyanide testing is to gain the support of legitimate exporters, who do not want their business unduly delayed by red tape. To that end, laboratories need to follow the Philippines' model and function seven days a week, returning test results to the exporter (with a cyanide-free certificate if the tests are negative) within 24 to 36 hours.

Equally important, the agency managing CDT labs must be trusted to be fair, efficient, and incorruptible by the fish collectors and exporters.

Provide and publicize official cyanide-free certification. As demand for cyanide-free live fish grows in overseas markets, fish that exporters can claim as reliably cyanide-free can command a higher price. This was proved in the 1980s when aquarium fish from the Philippines, tainted with that country's cyanide-fishing reputation, began to command a lower price than the same species from Indonesia—thought to be cyanide-free at the time. Preliminary evidence from the grouper fishery in Coron, Philippines, indicates that a similar market premium is beginning to operate in live food fish markets.

Governments therefore need to formalize and publicize their certification process, both at home and abroad. For the aquarium fish trade, this could be done

at the industry's conventions and in its trade magazines. Food-fish importers, mostly in Hong Kong (China) and southern China, are less organized and less concerned about the environmental impacts of their trade, but this situation is likely to improve over time, as it did in the aquarium trade during the 1980s. Already, the Hong Kong Fisheries Department, World Wildlife Fund-Hong Kong, and other groups are working to raise consumer awareness.

Create partnerships with the private sector in live fish importing countries. The best current example of such a partnership is the newly formed Marine Aquarium Fish Council (MAFC) in the United States, which is the single largest market for Indo-Pacific aquarium fish. In 1996, a number of U.S. conservation organizations and aquarium trade groups met to develop the MAFC as a body that would serve as an industry-independent governing council to establish standards and oversee environmental certification of aquarium fish imports and sales in the United States.

Composed of aquarium fish importers, scientists, and environmental NGOs, the MAFC will establish standards for certifying aquarium fish with reference to collection methods, suitable and nonrecommended species, size limits, holding and transportation methods, and other standards of practice. Costs would be borne by a percentage of the sales price, although grant funding would have to cover startup costs to develop and test applicable certification procedures. Actual certification would be carried out by certification institutions accredited by the MAFC and adhering to the MAFC standards, not by the MAFC itself. The MAFC would require that collectors, traders, and retailers adhere to all standards continuously and would identify appropriate enforcement mechanisms, including the monitoring of the chain of custody from reef to retailer. The council would work closely with the American MarineLife Dealers Association.

ing have not been caught with cyanide, the pressures on live fish exporters and the governments that regulate them to take action will grow rapidly.

It is important to note that testing of live fish imports on their arrival in importing countries is not an effective strategy and is likely to be counterproductive. Cyanide metabolizes out of fish relatively rapidly, and tests conducted at import destinations are likely to be negative for cyanide, regardless of whether the fish was caught with cyanide or not.

Community-Based Strategies

Without fishermen in the equation, there is simply no solution to the cyanide-fishing problem. There is no policy, law, or technology that can replace the need to work directly with cyanide fishermen. Training, community organization, income enhancement, and establishment of community-based coastal management systems in communities currently using cyanide—or vulnerable to its introduction as a live fish trade is established in their area—constitute the core partnership necessary to end cyanide fishing.

Train Fishermen in Cyanide-Free Fishing Technologies.

When fishermen are presented with effective cyanide-free technologies for capturing live food and aquarium fish—and given greater awareness about the legal, health, and ecological risks of cyanide fishing—many choose to convert to cyanide-free techniques.

In the Philippines, IMA has trained over 2,000 cyanide fishermen in cyanide-free live fish capture techniques. A typical one-week local training program targets 20 to 30 fishermen who are currently using cyanide to catch either live food or aquarium fish and have developed an interest, whether through IMA awareness activities or their own experiences, in learning cyanide-free techniques. Initially, three-day on-land "classroom" sessions provide lectures and discussions concerning the arguments in favor of cyanide-free fishing, cyanide-free technologies, postharvest management of catches, coop-

erative marketing and other strategies for adding fisheries production value, and safe diving techniques.

These sessions are specialized to address specific types of live fish capture. Fishermen who primarily collect aquarium species are trained in the use of fine-mesh barrier nets. Fishermen for whom food fish are the target species are trained in hook-and-line techniques for capturing groupers and simple techniques for decompressing the air bladders of captured fish to ensure their postharvest survival and health. Because particular grouper species favor distinctive bait sizes and shapes, bait preparation is a key part of the hook-and-line training as well.

Following the "classroom" sessions, the fishermen and trainers carry out four days of in-water training in either net or hook-and-line techniques. The intensive one-week training is followed by a three-week follow-up period of monitoring by the trainers to ensure that trainees have mastered fishing techniques and proper postharvest care. Other activities, such as organizing local fishing associations and cooperatives and developing value-added livelihood activities—discussed below—take more time and involve periodic follow-up participation by the trainers over months or years.

Using this basic model, IMA in 1997 expanded training programs to many new areas of the Philippines and now operates such programs in five major cyanide-using regions. IMA has also initiated the first Indonesian training program—for 60 fishermen—in North Sulawesi province, working with a local partner organization.

Enhance Local Income from the Live Fish Trade and Other Sources.

Fishermen's incentives to forsake cyanide fishing increase—and partnerships between fishing communities and outsiders such as IMA grow stronger—when local income from sustainable use of marine and other local resources rises. Beyond training in cyanide-free fishing techniques, IMA therefore works with fishing communities to promote a variety of livelihood enhancement activities.

When fishermen can get more money for cyanide-free live fish, they are extremely enthusiastic about converting to cyanide-free techniques. As in most poor fishing communities in Southeast Asia, cyanide fishermen receive only a small percentage of the value of their catch, with the lion's share of profits accruing to middlemen. By helping fishermen obtain postharvest equipment and know-how and assisting them to develop their own marketing cooperatives and outlets, the local share of the profits can be increased.

In the area of North Sulawesi, Indonesia, where IMA initiated a training program in July 1997, for example, the local partner organization is the provincial cooperative of retired military veterans. By providing the fishermen with diving compressors (previously, the only one in the village was owned by a live fish broker with a local monopoly on the trade) and offering higher prices for fish through the cooperative, the program will break the power of the middleman and help the fishermen obtain higher prices for the cyanide-free aquarium fish they capture. The cooperative itself sees a good business opportunity, of course, but perhaps as important, the cooperative's director is also a dive-tour operator concerned about the effects of cyanide on the reefs that have made the province a premier dive destination.

Few fishing communities, however, subsist wholly on the live fish trade. More typically, they pursue a "portfolio" economic strategy combining live fish, fresh and dried fish, agriculture, wage labor, and other activities. An effective livelihood enhancement strategy needs to target all of these activities and introduce new ones where an opportunity exists. Introduction of simple technologies can often add significant value to products that communities are already harvesting and selling. In Philippine fishing communities where the capture and sale of tiny dried fish (*dilis*) is a common activity, teaching simple techniques to spice the fish can raise their value by 40 percent. Where raw oysters are collected, teaching oyster sauce production methods adds considerable value to that product. In some communities, IMA training programs promote nonfishery activities, such as soap making, tailoring, and handicrafts produc-

tion. In short, the IMA training and livelihood enhancement strategy seeks to assist a larger socioeconomic transformation of poor fishing communities toward a better standard of living based on sustainable resource use and capturing a larger share of the local profits for local benefit.

Strengthen Community-Based Management of Local Fisheries and Reefs.

Partnerships with fishing communities must go beyond training and income enhancement, important as these elements are. Sustainable coastal management requires the participation and support of the local communities that directly earn their living from the sea, in cooperation with government agencies—an arrangement often called "co-management." Cyanide fishing, blast fishing, coral mining, mangrove destruction, and many other sources of coastal degradation can be slowed only when the communities on the front line become central players in protection efforts and beneficiaries of sustainable management. This requires policy shifts by most governments, which have traditionally treated coastal zones and fisheries as the exclusive preserve of state power and policy.

In some areas of eastern Indonesia and the western Pacific, long-standing customary systems of marine tenure and management provide a sound institutional basis for community-based efforts. Where customary systems exist, governments should recognize and support them and provide technical and financial inputs to assist traditional communities in adapting to rapid economic and technological changes.

Most coastal communities in Southeast Asia, however, do not possess functioning customary systems for managing and conserving coastal resources. Many are composed of a heterogeneous mix of immigrants and natives who lost such systems long ago. This loss does not mean that viable community management systems cannot be nurtured. The Philippines, where customary coastal management systems have vanished, has the most extensive and active community-based coastal resources management (CBCRM) initiatives in Southeast Asia.

Box 2. Toward a Cyanide-Free Fishing Tradition on Canipo Island, Philippines

Canipo Island is located in the Calamianes group of islands in the north of Palawan province. The area has been a traditional fishing ground for live grouper collection, especially the high-priced spotted coral trout, *Plectropomus leopardus*. For years, hundreds of fishermen used sodium cyanide to collect groupers. In 1993, however, a local businessman engaged in live grouper collection and dismayed at the impacts of cyanide on the reefs, started a cooperative called Kawil Amianam—Filipino for hook-and-line collecting. The group used the traditional hook and line but also developed a method for decompressing air bladders of the captured fish using a plastic straw, which is necessary for the fish to survive when they are rapidly brought from 20 to 25 meters to the surface.

More than 400 fishermen in the area soon joined Kawil because of pressure from the Cyanide Fishing Reform Program, which began operations in the area and opened a cyanide detection test (CDT) liaison office in 1994. Furthermore, Kawil's decompression method exploded the long-standing myth: you can't catch live groupers with a hook and line. In 1994, the Kawil fishermen began having samples of their catch tested by the CDT lab in Manila, with assistance from the CDT liaison office (the fish sampled were air transported to Manila for testing). The results, in the form of a certification that the tested fish were cyanide-free, were returned to the Kawil members within 36 hours, so as not to unduly interfere with shipping of the catch.

In 1995, IMA started working with Kawil to train more fishermen in the area and to assist in modifying the bladder-decompression techique and tools, substituting less stressful large-guage hypodermic needles for sharpened plastic straws. The Kawil hook-and-line and decompression technique is also being transferred to other areas of the country via training programs. Sampling and testing of Kawil's catch has continued for the past two years, and the test results indicate that virtually all members of the group are continuing to use the hook-and-line method and have not reverted to cyanide use.

Major reasons for the preliminary success of the cyanide reform effort in the Canipo area seem to be:

- Dedicated and persuasive leadership of the fisherman's organization
- Fishermen's receiving a higher price for cyanide-free groupers
- Presence of CDT sampling and monitoring personnel in the area
- Self-policing of its members carried out by Kawil.

A successful CBCRM program requires government commitment in policy and law, collaboration with like-minded donors and NGOs, and a "learning process" of drawing on the ideas and innovations of local communities to establish, refine, institutionalize, and measure the accomplishments of CBCRM initiatives.

Build the Capacity of Local Communities to Serve as Front-Line Agents in Anticyanide Monitoring and Enforcement.

Building on training, community organization, and livelihood enhancement initiatives, an effective cyanide-fishing reform program needs to enlist local communities as partners in the specific tasks of monitoring and enforcement (see box 2). Local fishermen are on the water far more regularly and know their areas better than government fisheries officers. With minimal training, which NGOs are often best equipped to provide, these groups can serve as an early warning network, letting officials know when cyanide fishing operators appear in an area. In the Philippines, members of local fishermen's organizations and cooperatives have been deputized as fish wardens to patrol and monitor their fishing grounds.

Although local community groups cannot be expected to directly confront well-organized—and often well-armed—cyanide-fishing vessels, they can perform important norm-setting and self-policing activities within the community. After all, a "community" does not decide to renounce cyanide fishing. More often, one group of individuals within a community may make that decision, while others continue using cyanide. Peer pressure is thus important in spreading the cyanide-free tradition throughout the community.

Conclusion

Cyanide fishing is not the only threat to the coral reefs and other coastal ecosystems of the Indo-Pacific region. Other threats include rapid conversion of coastal habitats such as mangroves for aquaculture, charcoal, and building materials; overfishing because of government-subsidized fleet overcapacity; dynamite fishing; haphazard coastal tourism development; runoff from industrial pollution, mining, urban wastes, and fertilizers and pesticides; and sedimentation arising from deforestation. But the training and community organization strategies essential to stopping cyanide fishing also provide an important catalyst for communities to address a broader range of threats to their local reef environment. And four unique characteristics of cyanide fishing provide hope that it can be stopped or at least significantly reduced faster than some of the other threats to coral reefs:

Cyanide fishing is generally focused on isolated reefs far from the effects of coastal habitat conversion and sedimentation. As a result, the problem is relatively localized and a discrete target for control efforts.

Discovered in the late 1950s, cyanide is a relatively recent fishing technique and has only come into widespread use in the past three decades in the Philippines, much more recently in other countries. Outside of the Philippines, therefore, the practice is not yet deeply embedded in local cultures and economies.

Cyanide fishing targets a very specific high-end market—live food and aquarium fish, with some food species selling for as much as $180 per kilogram and some aquarium species fetching $350 per individual. The consumers and their suppliers are therefore an identifiable and fairly limited group.

As detailed above, there is a clear and not too complicated set of actions to address the problem if governments set the right incentives in place, and partnerships are developed among fishing communities, exporters and importers of live fish, scientists, and NGOs.

The difficulties in stopping cyanide fishing should not be underestimated. It is important to note, though, that people have long captured and sold live fish without using cyanide, and they still do in many places, such as the Caribbean and Hawaii, where live aquarium fish have been collected with fine-mesh nets for decades. Nothing is intrinsically wrong with a cyanide-free live fish trade as long as it is practiced at sustainable levels and protects the coral reef ecosystem that provides fish habitat. But cyanide fishing is fast becoming a deadly tradition in the Philippines, handed down from father to son. It will soon be just as firmly established in Indonesia and other countries throughout the Indo-Pacific region. Our challenge is to eradicate the growing cyanide tradition and replace it with a cyanide-free fishing tradition.

Note

This paper summarizes data and conclusions found in *Sullied Seas: Strategies for Combating Cyanide Fishing in Southeast Asia and Beyond* by Charles V. Barber and Vaughan R. Pratt, published by World Resources Institute and International Marinelife Alliance-Philippines, 1997.

Ocean Harvesting of Ornamental Marine Life: A Mechanism for Reef Preservation

John C. Walch
The Aquatic WildLife Co.

In 1973 Robert P. L. Straughan wrote in *The Marine Collector's Guide:* "Whereas today the average aquarium uses white sterile corals, it is entirely possible that the aquarium of tomorrow will contain nothing but living corals and fish."

Straughan's prediction has indeed become reality. What once required donning mask and fins to experience is now being replicated in homes and offices around the world. Today's living reef aquariums mirror all the splendor and beauty of a healthy, natural coral reef. Maintenance of an enclosed marine ecosystem is an excellent way of learning and sharing the secrets of life on a coral reef. I have noticed that children in contact with marine life have a heightened concern for the marine environment. While not everyone has the means to travel to see coral reefs first hand, exposure to properly established reef aquariums in the classroom or in private homes may increase the sensitivity of future generations for the need to protect the world's reefs. Today's inland expeditions to life on the coral reef can also serve as a mechanism for reef preservation.

While it may appear somewhat contradictory, harvesting ornamental marine life from coral reefs could also serve as a tool for coral reef conservation. With proper management, guidance, and the continued improvements in the marine aquarium hobby, this could indeed be true.

Historically, the marine aquarium trade has had a less than clean environmental reputation.

Collection of ornamental marine fish and invertebrates has in the past been considered a factor that has a negative impact the on coral reefs. Overfishing, destructive harvesting methods, the removal of large coral colonies to serve as bleached decorations in aquariums, and high mortality rates at both the distribution and consumer levels are all issues stated by the environmental lobby as reasons to ban the trade of ornamental marine life. While some of these issues may have had a degree of legitimacy in the past, most, if not all, are no longer matters of concern.

As the collectors, exporters, wholesalers, retailers, and consumers gain experience and knowledge, changes and improvements are continually being made. Overfishing to the point of extinction may well be a legitimate point of concern regarding certain large-scale commercial fishing activities related to the food fish industry. Or, in the case of the sea horses, possible extinction in an attempt to satisfy the traditional Chinese medicine market may be a legitimate issue. However, the concern of overfishing carries little credibility when applied to the present methods of collecting ornamental marine fish. The demand for ornamental marine fish is increasing at a steady rate; however, it will never reach the magnitude associated with food fish.

The negative impact on population densities from responsible collection of ornamental marine life has always been much less severe and more localized than the effects of pollution, sedimentation, and tourism. Even if this is true, however, it does not necessarily make the practice acceptable. It is in the best interest of everyone—including the aquarium trade—to preserve the reefs. The simple recognition that ornamental marine life is a valuable consumer product provides an incentive for its conservation. The problem arises when the collection methods used are destructive to the surroundings or threatening to a sustainable population density of a given species.

The solution is complex and involves a number of diverse interest groups and a series of related actions. To achieve the collective goal of coral reef preservation, the individual goals of each party must be considered and seriously pursued. Using the aquarium trade as a model, we must first identify the parties, their personal needs, and individual and collective goals.

We can start at the source of the product—the village fisherman—rather than with the end consumer. His personal goal is a simple one: he needs to care financially for his family. However, the income he derives from the aquarium trade can be greatly affected by local and international laws and the availability of product. Without beneficial guidance regarding the changing desires of the trade and the influence of a stewardship program, his personal and immediate needs may indeed overshadow any long-range planning or conservation approach. By educating fishermen about the technological advancements over the years in responsible harvesting techniques, the proper storage and handling of their product, and the potential of mariculture, local income and coral reef health can collectively benefit.

Guidance and stewardship programs may be easier to administer in countries where fishing rights to a reef are controlled by the adjoining village, as opposed to areas where the implicit rule is "Take it before someone else does." In the countries that allow open fishing on all reefs, there is a need to establish some type of "ownership" program, either through additional educational programs or through governmental controls, such as a permitting process.

A good example in the Indo-Pacific region is the popular aquarium species of anemone fish. Under an "open reef policy" the fisherman collects not only the juvenile anemone fish but also the anemone—along with the adult pair of fish. When asked why this was done, fishermen always answered, "If I do not take them, someone else will." However, when there is area-wide coordination, education, or a regulatory permit policy, adult anemone fish will be left and only juveniles will be collected. This will allow collectors to return to the anemone on a regular basis to harvest the new juveniles. Such programs can prevent a tragedy of the coral reef commons.

Sustainable harvesting practices work only if all the fishermen support them. This is the challenge facing the parties involved in the educational process and local governance. While the motives may vary, the end goal of fishers and conservationists may be the same—to ensure that there is a continued supply of anemone fish in population densities that will allow harvest without threatening their existence. Maintenance of these population densities will not only require replacing destructive harvesting methods with sustainable ones, but may also require education to minimize negative terrestrial activities that are also affecting life on the reef.

Consumers have already demonstrated their desire to purchase animals that are collected without the use of explosives and cyanide poisoning. The growing awareness of fish health has increased the number of animals being purchased from countries that do not use these destructive methods, and the popularity of aquacultured marine life. The consumer has also learned that sustainably harvested and maricultured ornamental marine life are, in the long run, worth the additional expense because the animals thus obtained are more likely to live.

The Aquatic WildLife Company is located far from a natural coral reef in the foothills of the Appalachian Mountains in Cleveland, Tennessee. Yet we are very concerned and cognizant of what is happening to the world's tropical coral reefs. Hard coral propagation techniques developed and perfected within our 24,000-gallon land-based mariculture facility have already been transferred to villagers in the Solomon Islands so that they can help us meet our growing demand using ecologically responsible methods. We also closely follow the ever-changing marine aquarium hobby and in many cases we set the trends. Both Dana Riddle (manager of our Marine Research Project and author of *The Captive Reef*) and I spend much of our time promoting consumer education through articles published in trade journals and personal speaking engagements at regional and international aquarium meetings. Our popular ecoReef™ aquarium system was designed to sustain a natural and healthy balance between the living marine organisms, and we incorporate features that were once considered controversial but are now considered essential. Our research on how to maintain the brilliant colors of *Acropora* species corals in captivity, nutritional requirements of both fish and invertebrates, flow rates,

and the lighting requirements for photosynthetic animals have all been beneficial to the survivability of animals by aquarists.

The Aquatic WildLife Company is dedicated to protecting the aquatic environment and will continue to develop propagation techniques, improve the methods used during the handling and shipping of marine life, advance the hobby when and wherever possible, and be willing to share the knowledge gained with any interested parties. We assert that a critical and effective mechanism in protecting and preserving the natural resources of the world's coral reefs may well be to develop a stronger alliance with the aquarium trade, expand education about sustainable harvesting techniques, and continue to promote the benefits of maricultured ornamental marine life.

Macroalgal Culture as a Sustainable Coastal Livelihood in Coral Reef Areas

José A. Zertuche-González
Universidad Autónoma de Baja California
Instituto de Investigaciones Oceanológicas

Mitigation of destructive reef practices requires not only educational and regulatory programs but also the provision of alternative livelihoods for people living in coral reef areas. Commercial activities performed around coral reef areas should be environmentally compatible with the corals but should also be socially compatible with the traditional activities of coastal inhabitants.

In this paper, the culture of seaweed on reef flats is proposed as an ecologically and commercially viable alternative that could divert destructive fishing activities to an environmentally friendly endeavor.

Seaweed culture in reef flat areas has been practiced since 1971 in the Philippines. To date, there are no reports of a reef area being destroyed by the impact of seaweed culture. For over 25 years, reef flats have continuously produced tons of seaweed, while coral, other invertebrates, wild algae, sea grasses, and fish live and flourish there.

The seaweeds commonly cultured in tropical regions are sold as a source of carrageenan (*Euchema* and *Kappaphycus*) and agar (*Gracilaria*). These seaweeds, however, are also consumed directly or in soups and beverages as part of the local diet.

Besides an economic benefit, seaweed culture in these regions has offered additional environmental and social benefits. Seaweed cultures can absorb the excess of nutrients produced by terrestrial farming and local villages or from tourist development, thereby preventing the growth of opportunistic plants that often kill corals. The development of cultures provides an additional source of organic matter for herbivores (fish and invertebrates) that in turn provide additional opportunities for fishermen.

Seaweed farming is an activity in which women can work, thus obtaining additional income for the family. As a sustainable livelihood, seaweed farming prevents migration to urban areas and helps development in the province.

Some environmental problems have been related with seaweed culturing, but usually they can be easily prevented. The use of mangrove stakes to hold culture ropes is a new threat for mangroves. This practice has been reduced by informing farmers of the importance of mangroves in maintaining good water quality (necessary for seaweed culture) and by encouraging them not to remove full plants, but instead to cut only branches, which are capable of regenerating. The removal of eelgrass (initially indicated as preparation of a site for seaweed culture) is no longer recommended, since, empirically, it has been observed that seaweed grows better on eelgrass than on sand, apparently because of nutrient availability. Other problems, related to waste generated from farm materials and from domestic material from people living in these areas, are usually controlled because of the simple fact that farmers are concerned with keeping water quality high to permit better plant growth.

Seaweed farming has been extended to other countries of East Asia and Africa. Modest attempts are now being performed in the Caribbean. Concern has risen because of the introduction of nonindigenous strains to these areas. Regarding the introduction of *Eucheuma* and *Kappaphycus* to these countries, there are no reports of negative effects. The introduction of these species in Cuba has been carefully studied, and so far, no negative effects have been observed. An increase in the diversity in areas where the algae have been introduced, because of to the additional food and added niche for local species of fish and invertebrates, is one of the positive effects observed.

Although seaweed farming in reef flats has gone on for over 25 years, very few studies have been performed concerning its social and ecological impacts. Farming methods practiced today are basically the same ones proposed by Dr. Maxwell Doty three decades ago. Therefore, much remains to be done in order to improve the benefits (or avoid problems) generated by seaweed farming. For instance, to improve this livelihood for seaweed farmers, technological advances are necessary to increase production of seaweed per unit of time and area at a lower cost. Aspects such as farm management, to reduce the impact of herbivores and pest weeds, or the increase in quality obtained by genetics and strain selection, are topics where research is required in order to increase yield and quality. Equally important is the assessment of seaweed farming on social and political issues. It is important to determine how successful seaweed farming has been in increasing the living standard of people who practice it. What influence does it have on family and community integration? It is important to know the compatibility of seaweed culture with other commercial activities in time and space (such as the use of land and waterfront). Assuming the culture of seaweed is feasible in these areas, an understanding of the social and political aspects is essential in order to decide the feasibility of seaweed farming in a particular area and country.

A combined effort of academia and industry allowed Dr. Doty to initiate seaweed culture on reef flats. It is estimated that around 40,000 people in the Philippines alone are thriving because of this activity, and coral reefs are still there. We can only speculate about the impact of these people on the coral reef in the absence of seaweed farming, but most likely there would be far less coral than there is now.

There are many other regions in the world where seaweed farming could provide a way to preserve coral reefs. In some countries, particularly those in the Caribbean, there exist academic and private efforts, often uncoordinated and with very limited financial support, attempting to develop seaweed farming. Academia, industry, and developing agencies need to undertake joint efforts to see that these opportunities become a reality.

Discussion

Audience question: I would like to ask if the panelists could comment on the anthropological perspective of trying to switch traditional capture fisherman to something like aquaculture or agriculture. I had done some research in the past which shows that sometimes there's a rejection of a move of something that's seen as traditionally much more like farming or fishing that is more acceptable. And I was wondering if the panelists have had any experience with that?

Solomon Makoloweka: In this regard, actually, with the coastal people in the area where we are working, there are fishermen and agriculturists. Although 90 percent of the people are fisherman, according to a survey which was carried out, but still those same people do practice farming, but they have these attendant problems: by improving, or trying to eliminate some of the obstacles in farming, some of the people can be redirected to exploit fully the resource.

Bob Johannes: The situation where you have people that are simultaneously both farmers and fishermen is very widespread in the area that we're talking about, which makes it a little easier. Also, sometimes when you make a transition, a culture is forced to make a transition from one type of living to another, it's also simultaneously being transported—like the transmigration program in Indonesia—and this makes it doubly difficult. I have seen situations where mariculture didn't seem to go down very well in a tra-

ditional, purely fishing society—In Palau, for example, the Palauan fishermen are used to freedom and their own schedule, and they don't take kindly to having to routinely check on ponds, so that didn't go down very well. So I think the problem you are raising is one that you can expect to be serious in some areas and not a problem in others, and you just have to adapt accordingly.

Bill Kiene, Smithsonian Institution: Much of the focus of the discussion has been on alternatives for local, poor fishermen, as well as developing their culture incentives to supply the market for these fish. Bob [Johannes], you had a picture of a large wrasse there [during your presentation]. The potential value of those live fish in places like Hong Kong is tremendous; there was a report of over $10,000 dollars paid for one of those fish. If you develop industries—for example, a gold mine—a company does this, it's not necessarily going to stop a local person to dig his back yard for gold if it's there. Is there any effort to educate people around the world that are consuming these fish, that it is not necessary to have a status-symbol meal to survive?

Vaughan Pratt: There has been a lot of work going on in the past couple of years in Hong Kong trying to educate the consumer. Unfortunately, eating cyanide-caught fish is not a public health problem. If people were dying, then they would think twice about it. The problem we're dealing with—the people eating the fish are the same people we're fighting with to not use ivory and other endangered species as well. And the campaign hasn't worked to educate them about saving a furry animal, much less getting them concerned about a coral reef, so we have a difficulty in that. So it boils down to—if we can't influence the consumer, then maybe we can influence the importers, and that's what we're working on now—to get them involved in the more sustainable capture of these fish. Then it all boils down to what we've all talked about today—if we teach a cyanide fishermen to farm or to any other alternative but we don't get him off of this [cyanide], when he decides not to farm anymore he only has this to go back to. So, it's back to the whole chicken and the egg—we really need to get them off the [cyanide] bottle into another form of fishing, or make what they're catching now done better without using cyanide, and then try other alternatives. But working on the consumer in Hong Kong—it's been done, it's being done, and I really don't think they're going to be the big key to the solution.

Jack Sobel, Center for Marine Conservation: The panel has defined destructive fishing in a fairly narrow way, treating things such as dynamite fishing—and the really egregious examples that are very obvious and blatant. And that may be appropriate for many of the countries in which the panelists have focused their efforts. However, in areas like the wider Caribbean where activities such as cyanide and dynamite fishing and other superegregious methods are not very widespread and not causing widespread harm, you still have extraordinary problems with simply overfishing the resource and removing critical components of the ecosystem. I'm wondering if we need to look more broadly at the question of what is destructive to reefs, and addressing not only these most egregious examples—because if that is all we address—in many places we are still going to be left with collapsing ecosystems that are a result of what would not be classified based on these definitions as destructive methods.

José Zertuche: Well, we no doubt are overfishing—I am referring to any species, not only fish—is one of the main problems. One does not need cyanide to remove fish from a coral reef. I guess that all of these observations that have been repeated again and again are good, because that tells us that there are many problems that require many solutions. Some people just mentioned the issue regarding consumers, and it is clear—pardon the comparison—but it is similar to the drug war. If we do not work on people who consume drugs, it will be very difficult to address drug trafficking. Of course, overfishing is just one way to harm coral reefs. Regulations are needed at all levels—the same type of education—all the way to sanctions applied to local fishermen, you should have a counterpart for the consumer, too.

Bob Johannes: These days a great many people who are concerned with the fisheries conservation in the coral reef context look upon marine reserves offering the most hope. We have a discussion panel on marine research in this conference, so we are covering the issue to some extent.

Nancy MacKinnon: Regarding marine reserves, fishing and spawning aggregations, I think a lot of people would say it is a huge problem, and more research is needed to understand where those aggregations occur, so they can be incorporated into marine protected areas.

Walter Adey, Smithsonian Institution: While direct reef destruction is probably a primary problem at the moment, coastal eutrophication and siltation is not far behind. Worldwide, coastal eutrophication and siltation results from farming. I would be very concerned with an emphasis of shifting to farming rather than mariculture as a way of solving direct destruction of the reef. I think that is simply putting off the problem for a few years.

Solomon Makoloweka: I talked about improved agriculture—that would take care even of the hazards of improper agriculture of the coasts, so this would be a very improved technique of farming—that should take care of the anomalies which would otherwise be hazardous.

Herman Cesar, World Bank: I would like to ask a question about "political will" to Rili [Djohani] and to Vaughan [Pratt]. It seems that one of the striking differences at the moment between the Philippines and Indonesia is that in the Philippines, there has been a gradual change in political will, where a lot of destructive practices are now being much better enforced than they used to be—whereas in Indonesia, that does not seem to be the case yet. I would like to ask the panelists what they see as the way to go about on the one hand community-based management—such as the private sector partnerships, teaching, and training—these micro-improvements—and the political will question on the other hand. It seems that Indonesia, at the moment, is still fighting such an uphill battle, whereas the Philippines are now going, from legislative and enforcement points of view, so much easier that now it is more of a nice downhill track. I would like your comments.

Rili Djohani: It is a difficult question, I think. I agree it is very difficult to get political will from various government agencies involved in the conservation management of marine resources in Indonesia. Again, community-based management may work in remote areas where there is not a lot of influence from urban centers, but you will always run into the problem when there is a conflict between the use of a resource between local communities and, say, a fishing company. For example, foreign fishing companies with a permit from the central government. It is very difficult to empower a local agreement saying a community has the exclusive right to use this resource versus more lucrative agreements with the private sector which have been agreed upon in another part of Indonesia. So I don't really think that in the short term community-based management will work in Indonesia. That's why I repeat again that alliances with the private sector, which will actually bring in the necessary capital and power to the local area,

will better enforce protection of reefs rather than proceed with the idea of local communities in the short term. But again in the long run, I think we should work on how we can establish exclusive user rights for local communities in Indonesia, but it will take a long time in figuring out the legal basis to get the right or the political clout in Indonesian to work on those sort of issues. In the meantime, I think you have to work with the private sector in particular to protect the reefs—either in remote areas, or an area's nearby urban centers. Again ecotourism might be a very good vehicle to start with, or sustainable agriculture enterprises in buffer zones of national parks.

Bob Johannes: The question was why the difference between Indonesia and the Philippines in the rate of improvement of political awareness? I think it was Churchill who said that democracy was the worst system of government, except for all the rest [laughter]—I think the big difference between Indonesia and the Philippines is that the Philippines is a democracy and it is very clear in the newspapers that anyone who wants to speak out against anyone, including the president, can do so with almost impunity. Whereas in Indonesia, in order to make political change you have to have pressure on politicians from the public—you don't get it in Indonesia, because people are afraid of being critical. It is a big difference and I think it's part of this problem. The problem that pertains to both countries, however, is the enormous corruption at virtually every level from almost the highest, and perhaps the highest, right down to the local policeman. In that sense, both countries have a big, big problem.

Vaughan Pratt: Let's remember that the political will in the Philippines came at a great cost, because it took a revolution for it to happen. It took six to seven years for a new government to institute democratic policies. But in 1991, at the end of President Aquino's term, they implemented a local government code which devolved all national powers to local governments, which gave mayors and all the governors more power—power over forestry, power over their coastline. And that turned more territorial use right management over to coastal communities. And in doing that, coupled with education programs, the community has become more aware of being in charge of what's theirs. And that has spurred more local law enforcement groups, where people go out and patrol their areas to protect what they have. And that's the difference. And the other thing is that President Ramos is a diver, and the fact that he dives as much has he can, he knows what we're talking about, and his honesty has filtered down to the local communities where corruption is much less than it used to be. So there are all these factors all together, and if Indonesia can replicate that in any means, then hopefully we'll have some hope of saving the reef.

Alexander Stone, Reef Keeper International: I want to refocus attention to Jack Sobel's point about the fact that if we are going to talk about reef destructive fishing practices we need to, at least on a second-tier level, also focus on activities over and beyond the use of dynamite and cyanide. In the wider Caribbean and in many U.S. coral reef areas as well, there are practices which—it is not just question of being responsible for over-fishing—it's a question of being responsible for degradation and destruction of the habitat. That includes roller trawls, the use of fish traps (in Hawaii), the use of certain nets and the way they are used, and certain shrimp trawling methods also. So, I just want to make the point and put it on the record that the use of other fishing gear is not just a problem with reefs because of over-fishing, there's a habitat destruction component to the use of that gear. And if we here in the World Bank and our other constituencies are going to target reef destruction fishing practices as an action item, we need to expand our context beyond what we have been talking about.

Sofia Bettencourt: I can answer that. From our opinion, and I think some of the panelists have made reference to this, the threats have to be targeted on a site-specific basis and on a regional basis. So what we have is a pragmatic approach of targeting the most important threats first, and these most important threats will vary from site to site and from region to region. I fully agree

with you that we need to consider the whole range of destructive fishing practices, gears and other means that can destroy the habitat of coral reefs, but these will have to be targeted on a per-region basis. The issue of cyanide, and to a lesser degree the issue of explosives, has taken so much prominence because it is a regional threat—it cuts across countries. Therefore, it requires a regional strategy. The issue of habitat destruction by fishing gears seems to be more site specific, as is explosives, and therefore may require more site-specific strategies that maybe an international resolution cannot tackle. But I agree that it should be brought to the table. Tomorrow we will have time for our breakout discussion, and I encourage members from the public to come to this meeting and bring with them solutions that may be targeted toward these site-specific threats.

Robin Marinos: I have been to three meetings this week and they all have to do with coral reefs, overfishing, and so forth. And I find everybody's talking and I don't know who can have an effect on this—we're at the World Bank meeting here. Evidently the World Bank has a lot of influence—and I would ask what kind of immediate action can the World Bank or other organizations connected to the World Bank have, especially upon governments like the Indonesian government? I have evidence that it is openly involved in overfishing, what I consider illegal fishing, and actually the live turtle trade—the slaughter of green sea turtles. At the moment there are about 15,000 to 20,000 being slaughtered openly—you can go there any day of the week and watch them, and they are catching them with cyanide, bombs, whatever. What can these organizations do immediately to provide the right kind of pressure that the governments finally turn out and stop being involved? In Indonesia the case is clear. We're all talking, and no one's doing. We have to start doing things—whether its monetary pressure or whatever. That's why I'm here. I'd like to have answers to these comments.

Sofia Bettencourt: Perhaps I can respond, since I am the World Bank staff member on the panel.

We are looking at several levels. In Indonesia specifically we are now assisting the government of Indonesia in developing a coral reef rehabilitation and management program. This will be a 13-year program which the World Bank will help support. It will have other donors involved, such as the Asian Development Bank, the Australians, and the Japanese. It's a concentrated effort that will initially target policies, strategies, and a very large awareness campaign, and it will start with pilot sites that will then expand to a second phase. But we are going to be working on enforcement and legal issues, and on strategy and awareness as exactly the time to tackle political will and trying to target the larger public. In addition to that we have done a very large study. My colleague, Herman Cesar, has completed a very large study on the economic value of coral reefs, and he has been able to offer to politicians (the study has been translated into Indonesian and has been presented in several fora around the world) trying to determine the economic cost of reef destruction. These figures are now in the hands of politicians. They are being cited by ministers in Indonesia. It takes time, but I think we are working towards this period at a more global level, we have been active in conveying fora such as these, so we can get various stakeholders to speak together. We have also recently launched a "Marine Market Transformation Initiative" trying to work with the private sector and other partners to develop incentives at the market level to curb, among others, destruction on the reef.

Audience question: I think it is a very good suggestion among so many—the alternative livelihood to be provided to the coastal community—especially those who are depending on fishing. Some suggestions have also been made, but I think that the whole question of coral reef systems and their sustainability is not to be considered only on the basis of one system alone. A suggestion has been made for agriculture development in the coastal areas and alternative source of ecotourism, which is, of course, a source of economy in many, many countries. The problem is adjusting to alternatives sources or alternative livelihoods. I think we have to take into consideration the environmental implications of any activity. There is a case study of El Nidio [inaudible], for example, deforestation in coastal areas causes sedimentation and loss of fisheries on coral reefs. And if we have to develop agriculture as a livelihood in the area where coastal reefs are to be protected, we have to feel the consequences of these actions. For example, the discharge of pesticides or the sedimentation due to rainfall, and all this sort of thing. If we allow ecotourism beyond a certain minimum level, we are likely to cause a stress to the coral communities also. So my thinking is that in suggesting all these alternatives, we have to look into the implications of these actions on the reef system as a whole.

Sofia Bettencourt: We are fully aware that indeed there are impacts—the secondary impacts of introducing alternative income generation. And I think that the strategy has been one to look at being pragmatic—and seeing if we have a large threat at the moment. We may not be able to tackle all the threats at once, and we may be able to develop an alternative income generation that in the short term reduces the impact on the reefs. But then at the same time, try to get a mitigation process. For example, assessing the carrying capacity of the area before introducing that sort of income generation. I think what we are debating now is being as pragmatic as possible in trying to curb the very urgent threats and then trying to tackle the other ones. But I think you have a very, very good point—before introducing these alternative income generating solutions, one should be doing a study of carrying capacity to find out what their impacts in the long term may be.

Rili Djohani: I think often it's also not a matter of introducing new, alternative livelihoods, but just looking at an area which is trying to liaise with ongoing developments, and whether we like it or not, those developments will proceed. What we are now trying to do is be very strategic about these alliances and see how we can make it as sustainable as possible, and how can we articulate benefits for conservation if it's near a national park and so on. So I wouldn't say it's always an introduction of new, alternative livelihoods, but very often we try to link with ongoing developments. It is also building on the history of an area—what kind of practices are used, can these be expanded or not? It's not really the introduction of an entirely new alternative livelihood in most of the areas we work in.

Ariel Cuschnir, Unigroup International: I am a marine biologist. I would like to raise the issue of nondestructive fisheries. Taking into consideration two topics, one is the increasing world demand for marine and coastal coral reef organisms, either for the food or aquarium industries. On the other hand how fragile marine coral reef ecosystems can be. For example, Dr. Johannes mentioned before groupers—we know from the scientific literature that groupers that reach 12 centimeters in size, the recruitment on a reef by that fish will take between one and three years. So taking into consideration the two factors of both demand and the fragility of the coral reef environment my question is: Shouldn't we raise the issue of how sustainable our current fishing techniques are?

Bob Johannes: I think the issue is being raised constantly in the literature on coral reef fisheries—how much fisheries it can sustain. There are more and more bits and pieces of information put together to try to arrive at some kind of rule of thumb, but it is not a very easy question to answer. You can come up with a general answer, but when it comes down to specifying how much this particular reef can yield, that's much harder. In other words, I don't have a really satisfactory answer to your question, nor do I know of a recommendation for research or anything else that would provide a good answer anytime soon.

Ariel Cuschnir: I think it is a very important point, but the main message that I get out of these comments and questions is that any solution that we provide, we need to see the consequences. Either it is something that is compatible with our solutions or not, and what else can be effective. No doubt, any of these solutions will have to have some sort of research background that support them, and many of them will demand some research to follow it. And none of the resources will be a solution forever. All of them will have their limitations, and what I think is that when we provide these solutions, we have to include a very careful follow-up with serious research that can tell us up to when and how these solutions can be good. For instance, talking about seaweed culturing, we can consider many favored things. There is some evidence that it [seaweed culturing] will increase biodiversity, maybe will increase the number of invertebrates and fishes that will live there, it will help to clean excess of nutrients and on and on, so an advocate of seaweed culturing can tell us many of these things. But on the other hand, there is also some constraint. There is some consideration or worries about the introduction of commercial strains, just to give an example. So those things—if we are going to provide seaweed culturing as a solution—that is something that has to be looked at very carefully. There are some good examples of it, for instance introduction now of Ecuma [inaudible] in Venezuela and Cuba. It was done through the government; and promoted by the government; in one case it even received support from Mexico, and has been doing very careful research into the impacts that these will have on coral reefs.

Bob Johannes: If I could take a different tack on your question, I think we have now recognized in fisheries in general, that there's too much natural variation from one year to the next in recruitment and stock growth and so forth, that we are never, never going to be able to manage fisheries in any optimal way—the way we used to think we could. Optimum sustainable yield, optimum economic yield, whatever. And that we're going to have to settle for something cruder—and that is "precautionary management." I think the precautionary approach as used in coral reef areas—the most obvious example is the marine reserve—and when in doubt close a big chunk of reef and that way you guarantee that you're not going to have calamitous stock collapse, at least. You're not going to have optimum harvest rates either, but that's out of the question—you might as well forget about that. But I think you have to go one step further, and this I don't think many people have realized yet. It simply not possible to do the research that is necessary in order to get the kind of information the textbooks tell you is necessary to manage fisheries throughout the tropics. There are vast areas of reefs, mangroves, soft bottom communities, for which we have no information. My belief is that we must think about what 10 years ago would have been unthinkable. And that is what I call "dataless management." That is closing areas of reef where we don't have any direct data. Now dataless management does not mean information-less management. You have two sources of information: you have the research that is done in similar areas elsewhere that can be extrapolated with some confidence, and you also have local knowledge of fisheries from other people who depend on these resources. So I think we have to stop talking about vast amounts of additional research—we can't afford them, they're not costeffective, we don't have the people power anyway, so get on with it by more and more precautionary, and dataless, (sometimes precautionary) management.

Walter Adey, Smithsonian Institution: What Bob Johannes says is absolutely correct, but for people in the room that might not recognize— decades of research tell us that most reefs—while they may have a very high GPP, or gross primary productivity, they have a near zero net primary productivity. The normal, obvious way to change this is to raise nutrients. You can't do that with a reef. The basic overall point is that the production, overall, that can be taken out of a reef is seriously limited. Now everything else he said goes from there, but I think everybody should remember that, and all the scientists in the room I'm sure know that already.

Summary: Sofia Bettencourt: If I could summarize some of the results that we discussed here: We discussed destructive practices comprising poison and explosives, and we started touching on the removal of the habitat, which I think should be a topic for tomorrow's discussion as well. Among the causes that we identified are increasing population, markets that have a high demand for these products, an increase in fishing technologies, weak enforcement, competition for scarce resources, a social structure that lends itself to these practices, such as a middleman structure existing in Indonesia and in other parts of Southeast Asia. Availability of explosives and cyanide and destructive inputs to these practices, tradition, and lack of political will. We've identified a range of possible solutions. These will be discussed in further detail tomorrow. One solution that has been proposed is to basically have a very strong combination of processes, such as enforcement, awareness, training, and alternative income generation— and that one such intervention is simply not enough. We also talked that it may be interesting and important to separate between shorter-term measures—things that need to be done to immediately remove the threats to the reefs, and longer-term policies that need to be in place in order for the programs to be sustainable. We talked about the need to involve communities in identifying their problems, and also in reviewing the results of the monitoring, so that their awareness can be increased as to the real status of the reef. And you would be surprised how effective that can be. We have been in a village, for example, where a person went down diving, and took a video of the reef, and showed it back to the village, and at the same time showed them the video of a healthy reef—and the reaction of the villagers was outstanding. We discussed the need to provide ownership to the communities either through user rights or through alternative income generation that they can feel are theirs. We talked about various forms of alternative income generation that may be sustainable, such as user-pay schemes, involvement of the private sector in ecotourism. We talked about fish nests as a possibility for habitat enhancement in spawning grounds of groupers. We talked about ornamental fish culture, and we talked about the need to introduce site-specific solutions rather than generalized ones. Finally, we talked about the need to involve the intermediaries and the consumers in the overall strategy.

PANEL TWO

ILLEGAL AND SUSTAINABLE TRADE IN REEF PRODUCTS VERSUS CERTIFIED TRADE AND SUSTAINABLE BIOPROSPECTING

Session Chair: Michael Rubino, International Finance Corporation

Convention on International Trade in Endangered Species of Wild Fauna and Flora

James Armstrong and Jared Crawford
Convention on International Trade in Endangered Species of Wild Fauna and Flora

The international trade in reef products is a substantial industry that is challenging to monitor and regulate, especially in the case of corals.[1] The total international trade in reef species may only be guessed at, since little or no recording of such trade is done by importing and exporting countries, and this will continue to be the case until reef species are listed in the appendixes of CITES (the Convention on International Trade in Endangered Species of Wild Fauna and Flora).[2] While international trade in some reef species of conservation concern from large traders such as the Philippines and Indonesia has declined slightly in the recent past, trade from small island states has remained steady or has increased. Numerous heavily traded species such as sea cucumber and sea urchin are not currently listed in the appendixes of CITES.

CITES provides proven mechanisms for regulation of international trade and achieving sustainability in the trade of over 2,000 reef species and many more marine species. Each party to the convention is required to designate one or more "management authorities" to be responsible for administering the convention and one or more "scientific authorities" to advise on scientific and technical issues, including assessments of the threat that may be posed to species by international trade. Parties must establish legislation that prohibits international trade in specimens in violation of the convention, penalizes such trade, and allows for confiscation of specimens illegally traded or possessed. The convention classifies threatened species in three categories:

- Appendix I: Species threatened with extinction that are or could be affected by trade. All seven species of sea turtle are included in Appendix I.
- Appendix II: Species not necessarily in danger of extinction but which could become so if trade were not strictly regulated. Ten species of clams and a similar number of conch species are included in this appendix, as well as some 2,000 species of coral.
- Appendix III: Species that are protected by the states that list them and for which those states seek the cooperation of the other parties in ensuring that illegal trade does not take place.

Explicit guidelines, or biological criteria, are used to determine whether a species is threatened with extinction prior to considering any proposal to list a taxon in the appendixes of CITES.

System of Permits

Any international trade, meaning any export, re-export, import, or introduction from the sea of animals or plants, or any part or derivative of a species included in the appendixes of the convention, requires the issuance of a permit or certificate by a management authority. The procedures for issuance and use of the permits or certificates vary according to the appendix in which the species concerned is listed. The convention provides minimum controls for conservation purposes for trade in certain species of wildlife, but the parties are free to reinforce the protection provided. Stronger measures may even include the forbidding of all trade in species of wildlife. Despite perceptions to the contrary, the permit procedures in CITES are not complex.

The Standing Committee of the Conference of the Parties to CITES provides policy advice to the Secretariat of the Convention. Technical guidance is provided to the parties by four permanent committees: the Plants Committee, the Animals Committee, the Nomenclature Committee, and the Identification Manual Committee.

Nondetriment Findings

The Conference of the Parties to CITES recognizes that commercial trade in marine and reef taxa may be beneficial to the conservation of species and ecosystems when carried out at levels that are not detrimental to the survival of the species in question. The nondetriment finding is at the core of CITES, and it is a requirement specified in Articles III and IV of the convention. In classifying species and determining whether the populations are robust enough to be traded internationally, the scientific authority determines, through scientific procedure, whether international trade will jeopardize the survival of the species.

The sturgeon is one such case where international trade was determined to be a significant factor in the drastic decline in population. The combined impact of overfishing and pollution on sturgeons, valued mainly for caviar, led to the proposal at the most recent meeting of the Conference of the Parties to list all 23 species of the fish in Appendix II except for those which were already listed in Appendix I. In many areas where caviar had traditionally been harvested in a sustainable manner, sturgeons were now being killed in large numbers to extract caviar and supply meat and fins. The current appendix listings are intended to assist range states in regulating the trade in caviar and to limit it to sustainable levels. Additionally, the parties are called on to conduct scientific research on the sustainability of sturgeon fisheries, curtail illegal

fishing, promote regional agreements between states, and establish mechanisms to enforce the Appendix II listings. International and nongovernmental organizations, specialized agencies of the United Nations, and industry have been asked to provide financial assistance for projects on sturgeon species.

The success of CITES may also be measured by the number of species listed in Appendix II that have never been moved to Appendix I. Numerous species, including fur seals and narwhales, have been maintained in Appendix II with continued commercial trade permitted at levels that are not detrimental to them.

CITES promotes projects to determine the population status of species and to assess the effects of international trade. Recognizing the importance of the fisheries trade and the need for effective regulation, several projects involving marine species have been conducted; one such is the recently completed survey of corals in the Philippines, which investigated options for sustainable use.

Enforcement

Enforcement of the convention is the responsibility of the parties and their respective management authorities, customs, and police services. Enforcement assistance is also an important focal activity of the CITES secretariat, which regularly publishes reports on infractions or the types of fraud or smuggling employed. Where serious infractions exist, the standing committee may take appropriate measures to remind states of their obligations. The extent of illegal trade in CITES-listed species is by nature difficult to evaluate. One of the secretariat's priority activities is to combat illegal trade, in cooperation with the national authorities designated by the parties to the convention, Interpol, and the World Customs Organization.

Capacity Building

Recognizing that proper implementation of the convention in many countries requires increased capacity and information exchange, programs are in place to provide technical assistance and promote bilateral training of CITES parties. Capacity-building efforts also include the development of projects with the parties and liaison with donor agencies. Detailed reviews have been carried out to determine the status of national legislation for CITES implementation, and the CITES secretariat puts a great emphasis on training the staff of management and scientific authorities as well as customs agencies worldwide. International trade in marine species of conservation concern presents additional challenges, as agencies and laws regulating fisheries are often distinct from those that address environmental issues. Special attention has been given to addressing the capacity-building needs of small-island developing states as well as efforts to influence the nonparties from this group to join the convention.

CITES provides sound mechanisms for regulation of a sustainable trade in reef species through a worldwide network of management and scientific authorities and established legislative requirements. As noted by the Centre for International Environmental Law (CIEL), CITES does not compete with other regimes relating to marine fisheries. Rather, it is a safeguard that protects species of conservation concern when other measures have failed, and it provides an important tool for helping to achieve sustainable fisheries. Through strategic partnerships with organizations such as the World Bank, CITES can assist range states in developing the capacity required to trade these resources in a sustainable manner.

Specifically, collaborative action will seek to achieve:

- Amelioration of conflicts between national fisheries and environmental legislation
- Application of lessons learned through previous trade studies and assessments
- Enhanced and effective national legislation

- Improved grass-roots and community-based management of coral reef resources
- Improved monitoring, recording, and reporting of trade
- Maximized conservation benefit through judicious management of bioprospecting
- Sustainable conservation of reef species through use of CITES trade mechanisms
- Understanding the status of key species and the impacts trade has on these keystone taxa.

Marine Taxa

Marine taxa listed in CITES include:
- 2,000 taxa of hard and soft coral
- 130 whale taxa
- 32 taxa of clams
- 19 seal taxa
- 18 taxa of turtles
- 8 albatross and frigate bird taxa
- 6 taxa of sirenians
- 5 fish taxa
- 3 penguin taxa
- 3 gull taxa
- 1 crocodile taxon.

Notes

1. When the Philippine ban on coral trading was lifted in 1992, some 7.5 million specimens of coral from 63 taxa were exported from that country in less than nine months! (IUCN)

2. CITES, also known as the Washington Convention, was adopted in 1973 and came into force on July 1, 1975. It is an intergovernmental treaty, with 142 parties, that provides the necessary framework for regulating trade in threatened species of wildlife. The overriding goal of the convention is to ensure that international trade in specimens of wildlife does not affect the survival of species, and to demonstrate that the effective and sound management of resources may be beneficial to the conservation of species and ecosystems and to the development of local communities.

Reef-Destructive Practice versus Opportunities for Sustainable Mariculture: Coral Reefs and Pharmacologic Potential

David J. Newman
U.S. National Cancer Institute

The coral reef, be it shallow or deep, is an incredible and as yet almost untapped source of what a natural-products chemist would call "secondary metabolites." By this, one means chemical entities that are not essential for maintenance of life (growth and reproduction) in an isolated setting, but are usually produced when an organism is under stress. Such stresses in a marine environment are usually associated with the absolute requirement to maintain a foothold on some living space. Although mobile animals in the marine environment can roam far and wide to obtain nutrients, almost all invertebrate animals that one sees when inspecting coral reefs are effectively immobile and thus require that nutrients be presented to them via a flowing water column (for example, they are filter feeders). In order to attain this desired state, they must actively compete for the (relatively) very small amount of real estate that there is in, on, or about a coral reef.

I like to use the analogy that the "happy" coral reef, meaning one that is not being actively disrupted by outside forces (be they fishing with dynamite or raised temperatures or excess nutrients from sewage), is a very tight-knit community and can be considered to be the marine equivalent of a rain forest insofar as its vast variety of different species (or biodiversity) is concerned. Although one reads and hears a vast amount about the loss of species from deforestation of rain forests, I would be willing to argue that the loss of biodiversity is potentially much greater whenever an established coral reef is destroyed.

Since the advent of scuba, which was brought to fruition roughly 45 years ago by the man in whose memory we are gathered here today, Jacques Cousteau, scientists of all disciplines have been able to gather information as to the makeup of reef communities. With each new piece of information, it has become more and more obvious that a viable reef community is just that, an interactive commune of all manner of species and that the individual species do not exist in isolation, each having a part to play in the maintenance of the commune.

Some simple examples will suffice to make my point. When the surface temperature of the Caribbean was elevated a few years ago (as may well happen in the Eastern Pacific and other areas this coming year because of El Niño), the algal symbionts in the corals were expelled. As a result, one of the major sources of nutrient in corals (the products from the photosynthetic processes of the zooxanthellae) disappeared. The second is from areas in the Philippines (in parts of Negros and Cebu) where fishing, instead of using nets or lines, is practiced using dynamite or hand grenades. Although a large number of fish are collected this way, the explosives not only stun or kill the fish, they also destroy the reef. As a result, the reef fishes no longer have the nutrients produced by the reef invertebrate and algal communities to feed on and so either die or leave, thus removing what is probably the major source of protein for the local inhabitants, leading to long-term economic harm for the immediate benefit of a few. On the Coromandel coast of India, even today, coral reefs are used as a ready source of raw material for the local manufacture of cement. Removal of the coral has led to the demise of the reef fish population and the loss of a ready and cheap source of protein for the subsistence economies of the immediate area. This is the same result as in the Philippines but from what appeared initially to be a much more benign cause, the production of building materials.

Pharmacologic Potential of Coral Reefs

As a result of the extreme pressure for space and nutrient in a reef, there is in effect chemical warfare going on continuously between the inhabitants of the ecosystem. Anyone who has seen the demarcation line of dead cells that is drawn between two sponges of different genera when they touch, or has wondered why a highly colored nudibranch without any obvious protective armor has not become a tasty breakfast for a cruising fish or other predator, can see the effects of specific secondary metabolites.

These phenomena were fairly well known to marine biologists and a few chemists who liked to skin-dive prior to the advent of reliable scuba, and the chemical literature of the 1940s and early 1950s gave an indication of the potential of the marine environment, a prime example being the reports by Bergmann and Feeney (1951) of the isolation and purification from Caribbean sponges of the chemical compounds that ultimately led to the antiviral drugs Ara-A and AZT and to the anticancer agent Ara-C.

Over the last 25 to 30 years, the immense potential of the marine environment as a source of lead chemical structures has begun to emerge. Initially, these explorations could best be described as "grind and find" operations where invertebrate organisms were simply taken, effectively at random, from reefs, ground up, and used to provide extracts, and then the chemicals that they contained were isolated and identified, simply as a chemical exercise (the marine equivalent of phytochemical investigations of plant

sources). Approximately 20 years ago, more systematic investigations began, in which materials were tested for their effects in various pharmacologically oriented screens (anti-infectives, cytotoxicity, simple immunology, inflammatory processes, for example) and the catchphrase became, and has remained, "bioactivity-driven isolations." What this means is that now the extracts are tested against a wide variety of pharmacologically relevant screens, and only if an "activity of interest" is seen is the material further worked on—initially by chemists and then by other scientists.

Economics is the major reason for this change in isolation philosophy, and for an economic reason that is not always appreciated outside of the scientific or technological community. Since the infrastructure required to investigate any natural product in a rapid screen is very costly (24-hour stable electrical power, access to robotic systems, high-speed computation, access to state-of-the-art chemical instrumentation), only very well funded researchers in major universities or in well-financed biotech/pharmaceutical companies generally can afford to expend the funds necessary to pursue such leads, so any lead that is pursued should have the potential for further development. At the moment, only countries with secure, well-funded economies can afford to undertake such studies on their own, and even then, only a very few actually have the necessary infrastructure to further develop any lead. It must be emphasized that in general, the structure that is found in nature is normally only a lead, not a drug, and vast sums have to be spent to further develop the material before its "chemical descendant" can be considered as a clinical candidate.

Although the above could be thought of as excuses for not pursuing such agents, in fact, Mother Nature has proved time and again that she is a much better chemist than any mere mortal. In a recent analysis, Cragg and others (1997) demonstrated that over 60 percent of all antitumor agents and anti-infective agents introduced worldwide between 1983 and 1994 had a natural product structure in their background. Although pharmaceutical houses had generally moved away from studies of natural products in the last few years in favor of products from combinatorial chemistry, there are now moves toward reinvestigating selected natural sources for their potential as leads to new structures. However, these forays back into the field of natural products by some pharmaceutical researchers are being conducted with care and generally only if quality and sources of supply can be guaranteed.

In practice, what this means in the marine environment is that companies have to be assured that the materials that they test must be available in the event that more material is required for further studies. What does this statement imply for the source country? It means that any collections made must be stored frozen, fully identified taxonomically, that the location must be known accurately (such as, through the use of GPS—global positioning system—coordinates). High-quality underwater photographs must be taken, and then high-quality voucher specimens must be deposited in a recognized repository. Only if these requirements can be met is an organization normally willing to spend time and money in working on a given material.

Potential Areas for Help

How can the more developed countries realistically aid in these endeavors? In the case of the United States, the National Cancer Institute (NCI) has really moved to the forefront in the collection and processing of marine samples in order that they may be investigated for their potential as leads to pharmacologically relevant compounds. Dr. Patrick Colin, of the Coral Reef Research Foundation, presents information (pages 74–76) on the NCI collection program from the perspective of the collector. The NCI collects via a specific collection contractor who is bound by the NCI letter of collection that specifies, in advance, that any organization working with these materials must involve the source countries in the event that a compound isolated from the raw material proceeds on toward clinical trial, and this must occur whether the material is the pure natural product or has even been made synthetically after the natural product has

been identified. Furthermore, any contractor collecting for the NCI must obtain prior permission from the central government of any source country and abide by the restrictions it imposes with respect to collection areas and time. In fact, the NCI requires that the export permit from the source country be sent with the samples when they are air-freighted to the United States.

Costs

Overall, it costs the NCI approximately $700 per sample to collect, identify, process, and store the material that a coral reef provides. To then screen one sample in the antitumor screen—one time—costs the NCI approximately $250, and the rule of thumb is that it takes about 5,000 samples to be tested before one of them will make it to the next stage in the process toward a drug entity. In general, the chance of any one sample making it to market is well over 1 in 50,000, but the more different types of screen that a single extract can be put through, the higher the probability that it will be a hit in one of them. With the permission of the source countries, we are now letting many organizations look at the samples collected, under conditions requiring that the source countries be involved in the later development of any materials that come from the screening. Because of differences in patent law between the United States and other countries, we cannot assign patent rights in advance of a discovery, nor can we state that an individual is, or is not, an inventor in advance of any discovery, nor are we permitted as an agency of the U.S. government to require specific royalty payments in any agreement written in advance of a patentable discovery.

What can the World Bank and other funding organizations do? As mentioned above, one of the major requirements for collection and screening of samples (not only those from the marine environment) in the source country is a stable scientific infrastructure. Provision of scholarships, and perhaps more important, the provision of an adequate source of scientific instrumentation and supplies for work to be performed in the source countries, will materially aid in the realization of the value of a country's natural resources. One of the most frustrating things that can occur for source country scientists is to be brought over to the United States (or another industrial country) for training, and then on return to their home countries, realize that they cannot apply their skills because of the lack of items that are taken for granted in the developed world. There are large numbers of extremely talented individuals who cannot achieve their goals because of a lack of infrastructure and scientific supplies in the source countries.

In the short term the World Bank could help by subsidizing training for source country scientists in methods of scientific collection and taxonomy, which do not require too much specialized equipment initially, and to provide access to the information banks of the developed world (oceanographic data is available on the Web, for example, using GIS technologies). Perhaps the major reason why this was successful was that they were (and are) able to present to any potential collaborator, a catalog of species and their habitats prior to any screening. This type of endeavor, such as a cataloging of the fauna of a given area, fulfills many purposes, not the least of which is being able to present to potential collaborators an idea of what diversity exists in a given area. Such information really becomes important when any form of mariculture of an invertebrate is considered. With information as to current fluxes, types of growth patterns, and so on already under way, the chances of success are much higher than they would be if starting from scratch.

As an example of such studies, one may point to the work of the NCI with the New Zealand government on the in-sea aquaculture of a deepwater *Lissodendoryx* species that produces the antitumor candidate Halichondrin B. In this, a sponge that normally grows at a 100-plus meters has been successfully grown at 10 meters and still produces the metabolite of interest. This would not have been practical in the absence of the oceanographic expertise that was available within New Zealand.

Finally, a comment should also be made on the apparent monetary value of a collection. Although it costs the NCI over $700 to collect a marine sample, the intrinsic value of any given sample is only a few dollars. If, however, some biological assay can be run in the country that demonstrates activity, then the value rises by at least an order of magnitude, if not more, as that country has now proved its ability to provide biologically active materials. Thus, yet another area for help would be in the provision of funding and training for the use of simple biological assays, thereby giving a significant "value-added" component to a country's reef resources.

References

Bergmann, W., and R. Feeney. 1951. "Contribution to the Study of Marine Products. XXXII. The Nucelosides of Sponges." *Journal of Organic Chemistry* 16: 981–87.

Cragg, G. M., D. J. Newman, and K. M. Snader. 1997. "Natural Products in Drug Discovery and Development." *Journal of Natural Products* 60: 52–60.

Coral Reefs: Conservation by Valuation and the Utilization of Pharmaceutical Potential

Walter H. Adey
Smithsonian Institution

Coral reefs, as a marine biome, provide the largest diversity per unit of global area on earth. One estimate (Reaka-Kudla 1996) proposes that coral reefs have about 1 million species, with only about 10 percent described. It has been estimated that rain forests, the most diverse terrestrial biome, contain over 2 million species, but in an area 20 times larger than that of coral reefs. With ships and scuba, most of the diversity of coral reefs is more or less easily accessible, while much of the rain forest terrain is difficult to penetrate and is accessible only by rivers. The great diversity in rain forests is mainly in the monophyletic groups of chlorophytic higher plants and arthropod insects, while the diversity of coral reefs is distributed across more than 38 phyla and innumerable taxonomic subgroups. Coral reefs offer a phyletic diversity that is nearly an order of magnitude greater than that of rain forests, again greatly increasing the potential for obtaining unique compounds of pharmaceutical interest.

The Need to Conserve Coral Reefs

The commercial value of coral reefs for tourism, the hobby industry, and as a source of seafood is enormous. Unfortunately, coral reefs are exceptionally sensitive to human exploitation, as well as local and global pollution. They can also be harmed by global climate changes caused by our activities. Worldwide, coral reefs are showing signs of deterioration and in some cases overt destruction. Unfortunately for coral reef conservation, unlike rain forests, where the destruction for logging and farming can be seen from satellites and is obvious to anyone on-site, the early stage of coral reef degradation is rather subtle.

The human species is presently destroying the coral reefs of the world. Already 10 percent are irretrievably lost to coastal siltation and human eutrophication that allows algal growths to smother and kill the reef-building communities (Crosby and others 1995). Another 25 percent are deteriorated and endangered. Dynamite, electric shock, chemicals such as arsenic and rotenone, fish traps, and overfishing in general are destroying and depleting the fish and shellfish predator species that are important in maintaining the health and continuation of coral reef communities. Human perturbation may be the cause of worldwide episodes of coral bleaching, in which corals lose their symbiotic algae. Also, human activities may be responsible for the worldwide outbreaks of coral diseases such as black band disease, which is caused by a cyanobacterium. The nations of the world are shocked by this deterioration and have declared a worldwide coral reef initiative (Crosby and others 1995) to analyze the damage, propose solutions, and initiate appropriate conservation programs. The Coral Reef Alliance, together with more than 40 other organizations, has designated 1997 as the International Year of the Reef. To lose forever the majority of coral reefs of the earth would be an ecocide, unforgivable by future generations. It would also provide the significant potential for the loss of numerous pharmaceutical compounds even before they are discovered.

Natural Products Obtained from Coral Reefs

In recent years, there has been substantial progress toward developing new pharmaceuticals from marine organisms (numerous publications summed up by Fenical 1996, and Hay and Fenical 1996). The filter-feeding, or grazing, macropredators (such as sponges, bryozoans, sea squirts, and sea slugs) that yield the best results have a combination of the following traits: sessile, stationary or slow moving, soft-bodied and without structural defenses, brightly colored, light-refracting or with contrasting markings, and possessing endosymbiotic microorganisms that can produce additional toxins. Most important, they are avoided as prey by most predators. Also, motile and sessile predators produce toxins to catch their prey. Some of the most powerful toxins ever tested are found in marine macropredators, such as jellyfish, sea snakes, gastropod cone shells, and puffer fish (Halstead 1988, Meier and White 1995). Toxins work by disrupting cellular functions and may provide the molecules we need to cure human diseases.

In the clear waters of coral reefs are found the world's greatest assemblages of such promising candidates for possessing secondary metabolites with useful bioactivities. Already, promising new drugs have been found in sponges and other ocean invertebrates and larger algae, some that are in preclinical development and others beginning clinical trials (Carte 1996).

The Potential for Meso- and Micropredators

Just as there are numerous larger invertebrates that are predators, or have chemical defenses to other predators, there are many more small and microscopic species, colonial bacteria, protists (single-celled organisms that develop no tissues and have advanced membrane-bound nuclei), and small and micrometazoans, (tiny, multicellular invertebrates) that are themselves predaceous or are eaten by larger predators and have developed chemical defenses. Such defenses are espe-

cially prevalent in slow-moving and sessile forms. In addition these micropredators have evolved highly effective chemical offenses to allow them to incapacitate and ingest their prey. Protists have effective delivery systems called extrusomes where the chemicals are stored and concentrated. Some of these micropredators also have microorganisms living inside them, such as algae, many of which possess powerful defense chemicals. These micropredators live with their cells exposed directly to other microorganisms and may have chemicals with antibiotic properties.

When standard agar culture methods are used to isolate bacteria from the sea, less than 5 percent of the species, as shown to be present by DNA methods, are successfully cultured. Similarly, standard methods for collecting meso- and micropredators in aquatic environments yield only a small percentage of those that are present. Commercial interest in natural products chemistries, prior to the often long road to laboratory synthesis, is often thwarted by the rarity of the species with compounds of interest. As we will also describe briefly below, our broad success with large numbers of species in coral reef microcosms and mesocosms suggests the potential to locate, monitor, and then, most important, culture in quantity those species having compounds of interest.

Culture Systems for Pharmaceutical Development

For 20 years the Marine Systems Laboratory has been a world leader in the development of laboratory aquatic ecosystems (Adey 1983, Adey and Loveland 1991, Adey 1995). Numerous coral reefs have been included in the over 100 ecosystem years of laboratory experience in this field.

Here we will briefly describe a 400-liter Caribbean coral reef ecosystem that has been subject to biodiversity research for the past year. This experimental unit, established 11 years ago and closed to significant biotic introductions for the past six years, has been maintained under a tight engineering and operational regimen that would be expected to demonstrate a strong parallel with the wild ecosystem. It is noteworthy that the system calcification rate (the single best indicator of long-term reef function) has consistently remained at about 5 kg/m^2/yr, or 25 percent above published pantropic means for reef flats and upper fore reefs (Crossland and others 1991).

This calcification rate is particularly important for maintaining diversity. It is calcification and the continued building, at macroscopic and microscopic scale, of structure and spatial heterogeneity that in large measure provides wild reefs with the highest specific biotic diversity on earth. In addition, the gross primary production level, as measured by oxygen produced in photosynthesis, is approximately 10 g O$_2$/m^2/day. This lies well within the range of wild reefs (Crossland and others 1991) and thus provides the moderately high levels of energy input, up through a complex food web, that most theoretical diversity models in the current literature require to maximize biodiversity. Finally, this unit has received its wave/current energy input only through bellows pumps that greatly enhance larval survival, while water quality control is managed by algal turf scrubbing, a process that avoids filtration.

Although analysis of the organisms in this microcosm will continue for several months, of the phyla that commonly occur in coral reefs worldwide, and for which adequate analytical capability was available in this study, 27 out of 29 possible phyla were demonstrated. Over 500 species in 343 genera and 231 families have been documented to date in this microcosm; roughly two-thirds of these can be termed macroorganisms and one-third microorganisms. Virtually all of these taxa reproductively maintain populations. Continued new additions to the list suggest that a final count would be over 700 species. In considering this amount of biodiversity, it is noteworthy that microbes (most bacteria and viruses), fungi (primarily phycomycetes), parasitic taxa, and mostly nonmarine taxa have not yet been treated. Also, for several minor phyla, as noted, we have yet to initiate a search with techniques appropriate to their location. Thus, the numbers stated are minimal.

Pharmaceutical Value

Many families of organisms in this microcosm are likely to have species with chemical compounds of potential pharmaceutical value, several of which have been identified. The fact that these species are widely spread over many higher-level taxa only enhances the possibilities for obtaining numerous unique chemistries. Especially noteworthy, in this context, is that the majority of the populations in this system were derived from a single site in the tropical west Atlantic. Equally promising, these results were achieved without major dedicated funding, suggesting that the considerable genetic/natural product chemistry potential of coral reefs throughout the tropics can be localized in laboratories and tested and cultured to production levels at quite moderate cost, without any degradation of wild systems. Such microcosm systems have been demonstrated at warehouse scale for the aquarium trade and could easily be adapted to pharmaceutical identification and production. Thus, wild reefs would not need to be subjected to bioprospecting. "Genetic prospecting," by highly trained crews, requiring only small quantities of reef material to achieve introduction of many hundreds of species into reef microcosms, would be adequate. The development of a large-scale culture industry using the genetic resources of coral reefs would provide a conservation drive to this most endangered of earth's biomes that is unlikely to be achieved by any other means.

References

Adey, W. H., 1983. "The Microcosm: a New Tool for Reef Research." *Coral Reefs* 1: 193–201.

———. 1995. "Controlled Ecologies." Entry in *Encyclopedia of the Environmental Sciences*. San Diego, Cal; London: Academic Press.

Adey, W. H., and K. Loveland. 1991. *Dynamic Aquaria: Building Living Ecosystems*. San Diego, Cal; London: Academic Press.

Carte, B. K. 1996. "Biomedical Potential of Marine Natural Products." *BioScience* 46 (4): 271–86.

Crosby, M. P., S. F. Drake, C. M. Eakin, N. B. Fanning, A. Paterson, P. R. Taylor, and J. Wilson. 1995. "The United States Coral Reef Initiative: An Overview of the First Steps." *Coral Reefs* 14:1–3.

Crossland, C., B. Hatcher, and S. Smith. 1991. "Role of Coral Reefs in Global Ocean Production." *Coral Reefs* 10:55–64.

Fenical, W. 1996. "Marine Biodiversity and the Medicine Cabinet: The Status of New Drugs from Marine Organisms." *Oceanography* 9(1): 23–27.

Halstead, B. W. 1988. *Poisonous and Venomous Marine Animals of the World.* Princeton, N.J.: Darwin Press.

Hay, M. E., and W. Fenical. 1996. "Chemical Ecology and Marine Biodiversity: Insights and Products." *Oceanography* 9(1):10–20.

Meier, J., and J. White, eds. 1995. *Handbook of Clinical Toxicology of Animal Venoms and Poisons.* New York: CRC Press.

Reaka-Kudla, M. L. 1996. "The Global Biodiversity of Coral Reefs: A Comparison with Rain Forests." In M. L. Reaka-Kudla, D. E. Wilson, and E. O. Wilson, eds., *Biodiversity II: Understanding and Protecting Our Natural Resources.* Washington, D.C.: Joseph Henry/National Academy Press.

Marine Pharmaceuticals from the Reef: A View from the Field

Patrick L. Colin
Coral Reef Research Foundation

The shallow-water areas of the world tropics, which include coral reef` sea grass beds, mangroves, and other habitats, contain a high species diversity of organisms living in close proximity to one another. Many of the organisms have evolved complex chemical compounds for defense, predation, aggression, and other unidentified functions. These are the sorts of chemical compounds that can be developed into drugs to treat a wide variety of afflictions.

For the past six years I have headed a program collecting samples of many invertebrates and marine plants for screening by the U.S. National Cancer Institute (NCI). Our responsibilities under this contract are to do the initial collections, photograph and document the samples, and, if necessary, be able to relocate and recollect samples for further development work. This is very exciting work because we are the ones who acquire the raw material to begin the process of finding new pharmaceuticals from the sea.

We, not the NCI directly, usually open contact and initially deal with the government agencies of the sample source countries and serve as the conduit for distributing testing results to the various countries.

There is a huge gulf of misunderstanding regarding this type of activities. Suspicions abound, unfortunately sometimes with justifiable reason. The negative aspects tend to get all the press. Cases where metric tons of one species are collected off reefs to provide a few milligrams of some compound are presented as the norm, tarring all with the same brush of ravaged reefs left in the wake of irresponsible collectors.

There are a number of aspects of the NCI approach to discovering and exploiting new marine biochemicals that favor, I believe, a sustainable use of the shallow tropical environment. Initially, the samples collected for and extracted by the NCI are relatively small, usually about 1 to 1.5 kilograms, although a lesser amount can be taken if the organism produces a high yield of extract. Samples are frozen and shipped in that condition from collecting areas to the NCI laboratories in Frederick, Maryland, maximizing the yield of extract from each sample as compared with other means of storage before extraction. The 1-kilogram wet weight of a sample ideally produces about 2 to 20 grams of aqueous and organic extract. These two extracts, which might contain dozens of different compounds, allow sufficient material to undertake the initial screening tests and provide, if needed, for follow-up testing. Also some isolation, purification, and elucidation of chemical structure of promising compounds takes place. The quantity of extract obtained from the original samples is usually sufficiently great that it is usually unnecessary to do time-consuming and expensive recollections every time an initially promising sample is identified. However, the original sample does not normally provide enough compound to undertake extensive testing or commercial development of a drug. There simply isn't enough compound contained in 1 kilogram of initial sample to allow that.

The collection of a 1-kilogram sample is usually environmentally benign. We do not collect hard (stony) corals or threatened, endangered, or protected species. Prime target groups are sponges (Porifera), ascidians (Urochordata), bryozoans (Entoprocts), nudibranchs (Mollusca), soft corals (alcyonacea), and algae. In practice, it is almost impossible, after the fact, to identify where on the reef samples have been collected. This sort of collecting is not a "clear-cutting" operation; rather it is a delicate, very selective cropping of a limited number of organisms out of everything occurring over a broad area. On an average collecting trip with two to four dedicated collectors in the water for a few hours each day, 10 to 15 samples per day is normal, with an exceptional area producing 25 to 40 samples.

The smaller the sample weight needed for screening, the greater the number of species within an area that can be sampled. The 1-kilogram level is a reasonable compromise, with enough species in a diverse area to keep a small team of collectors busy for several weeks. Once an asymptote on species to collect has been reached for a given area, it is either time to move or to change the quantity required for a sample. We also use a process of what I like to call "progressive discrimination" in working a sample area. First the easily collected species are taken. Then progressively more difficult samples are worked on. I believe this strategy results in the maximum number of likely samples for screening, maximizing the chances for a "hit." One might argue that this only helps deplete the rare organisms on the reef, but this assumption flies in the face of biological fact. Nearly all benthic organisms in shallow water are patchily distributed, and what may be uncommon or rare in one area may be abundant in another nearby, apparently identical, area for reasons unknown to us.

The NCI in its international collections program views the countries where collections are made as collaborators who are entitled to be fully informed as to the results of the testing program and fully involved to the maximum technical level that is appropriate. The latter effectively translates into having host country scientists or students involved both as a learning experience and as direct contributors to the technical work. Most natural products are too difficult to synthesize and the NCI (and licensees) are committed to obtaining natural products from the source countries where technically possible. An example of this commitment is the mariculture of the sponge *Lissodendoryx* species in New Zealand for the compound Halichondrin B. In the cases where additional material is needed to continue development work on the very small percentage (around the 1 to 2 percent level) of samples that ever reach this advanced stage, the host country is fully informed and permission is obtained prior to collection of additional material.

The NCI is involved in drug discovery, not drug development and sales; in essence it operates as an honest broker between the pharmaceutical company and the source countries. Its contract collector, such as our organization, also cannot benefit economically from any discoveries. This means the NCI and its collectors have no incentive to deal with the host countries in less than a totally honest manner. In reality, it is in the NCI's and its collectors' self-interest to work closely with and protect the host countries' interests. The more access we have to sample a country's biota, the higher the chance of finding useful compounds, something that makes us all look good and helps fulfill the promise of medicinals from the sea. This is a worthy goal as long as the interests of the host country are protected by all parties.

Given these pluses for the NCI program, it is surprising how hard we have to work to find and persuade countries to allow us to collect their organisms for screening. There appear to be several reasons for this. First, there is the huge amount of confusion and outright suspicion mentioned earlier. This revolves around issues of intellectual property rights, royalties, licenses, and such. However, we believe that with an informed understanding of the issues most countries will see that allowing bioprospecting under an agreement similar to the one utilized by the NCI is a good policy; countries that don't allow such activities run the risk of being left behind by those who do. Second, some countries have their own national programs and do not welcome or need overseas researchers. That is understandable in some cases, but of little advantage for countries that do not have such programs. Third, some countries are, unfortunately, not interested unless there are economic benefits up front, something that organizations like the NCI do not provide.

Biological resources that are never screened will not provide benefits to anyone. If the decision is made to allow collections, it is important for countries to require written agreements with researchers or collectors that clearly specify who the country is dealing with, what will be done with the samples collected, require that the country be fully informed of developments from materials from their country, and ensure that the country will have the ability to negotiate fair compensation for any discoveries made from their country. The NCI collection programs meet all these requirements and have written collection agreements that cover these issues. Without such knowledge and agreements, everything is left to the goodwill of corporate executives and lawyers.

The final point I would like to make is that marine natural product collections provide a fantastic opportunity to increase knowledge of species-level diversity and taxonomy of the often-difficult groups of marine organisms, particularly invertebrates, that are of most interest to marine chemists. The earlier marine natural product chemistry literature is replete with poorly identified organisms being the source of novel organics. Often there are few adequate voucher specimens or photographs of the organism, and only rarely is there a reference that can be cited which includes an accurate description and photographs of the organism. Our group has taken the approach of trying to maximize the biological information, particularly taxonomic, obtained from marine invertebrate collections for screening by the NCI. This is done through high-quality voucher specimens and photographs taken on-site. It is no accident that a large number of new taxa are being described from our collections, usually by the taxonomists who are paid from the NCI contract to make the final identifications. While these new taxa are usually described in specialist literature, our group is also dedicated to making this information available to a more general scientific audience through publication of general field guides. *Tropical Pacific Invertebrates* is our first such effort and will be followed by a series of volumes specific to phyla being prepared by our specialist taxonomists over the next several years.

The discovery of a remarkable medicinal compound from a coral reef area, sufficiently valuable to provide the impetus for conservation of reefs, has not yet occurred. It is this dream, however, along with the prospect of discovering new biological information, that keeps us excited about this type of work.

The Marine Aquarium Fish Trade

Daniel Pelicier
Professional Aquarium Fish Collector and Exporter

Private marine aquariums have begun to be popular only recently. Few hobbyists, however, have been successful in keeping the organisms in their aquariums alive for any length of time, mainly because of the rapid deterioration of water quality. This situation has improved dramatically within the last decade, when more sophisticated pumping and filtering systems have become available. At the same time, the rapid expansion of air transportation by jet planes has made it possible to transport live marine organisms over large distances from countries with reefs to the main markets, which are in the United States, Europe, and Japan. This triggered an explosive increase in demand, and many developing countries with coral reefs, such as the Philippines, Sri Lanka, and Indonesia, saw a great potential for earning hard currency. The bulk of the organisms traded today in the marine aquarium trade consists of fish, (the Philippines alone exported some 6.3 million aquarium fish in 1996), but also invertebrates such as shrimp, anemones, and tube worms are in great demand. Also, lots of so-called live rock is exported. This is usually dead coral, which contains a multitude of boring and encrusting organisms such as calcareous algae, tube worms, hydroids, and anemones. Live rock is used as decoration and as substrate. Although the dream of many aquarists is to have a miniature living coral reef, keeping corals alive in an aquarium has proved exceedingly difficult. Corals require special light conditions and extremely pure, oligotrophic (nutrient-poor) water to grow. It has been said that only when you starve your aquarium do the corals start to grow. Only recently, with advanced techniques and filtering systems, has it become possible for the dedicated hobbyist to keep corals alive.

Stakeholders

Of course, the explosive demand for marine aquarium organisms has led to a proliferation of suppliers. Originally, all aquarium fish were caught by hand with no other equipment than a mask, a snorkel, sometimes flippers, and a little scoop net. This is difficult, however, as reef fish hide in crevices in the coral. Consequently, all kinds of methods have been devised to chase the fish out of their hiding places. At first crowbars were used to break the coral, but at present chemicals, mainly cyanide, are squirted into the coral. The fish come out stunned and are scooped up and placed in tanks with clean running water, after which many are resuscitated. After this treatment they will usually live long enough to be shipped out and sold, but eventually cyanide-caught fish die because their internal organs have been damaged. After the collector has left, the cyanide cloud drifts along the reef, killing everything in its wake. In the Philippines alone, an estimated 65 tons of cyanide are sprayed on the reefs each year to catch aquarium and food fish. Not surprisingly, there is a lot of opposition to the aquarium trade because in many places it destroys the reefs and the fish populations. But collecting for the aquarium trade is an important source of income in many developing countries. The marine aquarium trade has become big business, and it has been estimated that its aggregate annual retail sales value amounts to about $300 million. It would be unrealistic to try to ban the aquarium trade completely, and therefore the big question is: Would it be possible to sustainably use these reef resources in a nondestructive manner? I have been an aquarium fish collector and exporter in Mauritius for 30 years and am convinced that the answer is affirmative. Although I do not have exclusive fishing rights anywhere, I have been the only one to exploit a number of reefs, which I consequently consider as my own fishing grounds. They have provided me with a steady supply of aquarium fish over the years while their habitat has remained unchanged. To achieve this I do the following:

- I catch everything carefully by hand, using only a hand net.
- I work deep, below the depth of most finely branching corals, and therefore run less of a risk to damage the reef.
- I work mainly among coral rubble and boulders, also because there my net does not get caught so easily and the fish can't hide so well.
- I carefully put my fish in containers underwater rather than keeping them in nets or plastic bags, to avoid stress. I decompress my fish, bringing them up in stages. The decompression tables for the various fish are the result of my 30 years of experience. Sometimes this requires leaving the fish behind at a certain depth when I go home, to be picked up later, something I can do only in a secure environment where my buoys are not stolen. Some fish I decompress by inserting a hypodermic needle into their swim bladders underwater.
- I know the biology of most of my target species, such as the cleaner shrimp *Lysmata amboinensis* or the endemic Mascarene clown fish *Amphiprion chrysogaster*. The shrimp population shows natural cycles of abundance and decline, and I mainly catch them just before their population would

crash anyway. The clown fish keep a "reserve" of juveniles below the rim of tentacles of their host anemone, whose growth is impeded by the presence of the adults. When I remove only one of the adults, one of the juveniles quickly grows up and replaces the one I have removed, also assuming the sex of the one missing from the pair. Thus, I minimize the risk to reproduction. In the lagoon, I have cloned sea anemones to provide an "anemone plantation," which is rapidly being colonized by clown fish, which I can exploit.

- I do not catch any fish that cannot be kept alive in the aquarium and advise my clients on which species can live together with each other and with invertebrates such as coral.
- I carefully observe the population of my target species to make sure I do not deplete any distinct population and catch pairs of certain species to be kept together in the aquarium.
- I package and ship my fish myself in specially sealed plastic bags filled with seawater and oxygen. My loss between catch and arrival of the fish overseas is less than 10 percent, while a loss of some 70 percent is not uncommon in many other areas. Because I deal directly with my clients, they know they will receive quality fish and are therefore prepared to pay premium prices. Many exporters elsewhere just buy from freelance collectors and therefore have no idea how the fish are caught.

Conclusion

Aquarium fish collecting can become a sustainable source of income, but to do it right requires dedication and training. When carefully done, aquarium fish collecting constitutes for many species only a minor factor in the determination of their population size in comparison with other factors such as natural predation, availability of hiding places, pollution, and storm events. There is a lot more to the trade than scooping fish out of the sea, putting them in a plastic bag, and sending them off. The fact that a fish has not been caught with cyanide does not necessarily mean it has been harvested sustainably or is not damaged.

Recommendations

- Probably the best way to change behavior and eliminate mala fide traders and bad collectors would be through economic pressure. Bad collectors and exporters should go out of business because they are known to and boycotted by a unified organization of importers.
- The aquarium fish importers, hobbyists, and conservation organizations should get organized and set standards, oversee certification of imports, and help the exporting country with training and certification of exporters. In the United States, there is a good start with the establishment in 1996 of the Marine Aquarium Fish Council and the American Marine Life Dealers Association. In Europe, many countries lack a similar organization. The United Kingdom has a trade association, the Ornamental Fish Industry, which has taken some action.
- There should be a strict cyanide testing and export licensing system in the exporting countries, like the one started by the International Marinelife Alliance in the Philippines.
- Licensing of all aquarium fish collectors. At present only the exporter requires a license. An importers' association could send inspectors to the developing countries to check on collecting and shipping practices.
- An area-based management system whereby a particular operator is assigned a specific reef area. In this way the operator has a long-term interest in keeping "his" reef intact and productive.
- The compilation of a list of marine organisms that cannot be caught, because capture would endanger the species or the species cannot be kept alive or can only be kept as a juvenile.

Role of the World Bank

The World Bank could:
- Incorporate sustainable aquarium fish collecting in the projects it finances for reef management as an alternative source of income to destructive reef exploitation. Training in sustainable collecting methods and handling of aquarium fish, certification of collectors and exporters, testing for cyanide, and institution building to oversee the trade should be integral parts of such programs.
- In its policy dialogue with governments of coral reef countries, stress the importance of coral reefs and assist these countries with the implementation of enforcement of the regulations against destructive practices such as cyanide and dynamite fishing. Destruction of natural resources should not be a reason for a country to turn to the Bank for development assistance.
- Finance—through loans or the Global Environment Facility (GEF)—the establishment and management of a Global Representative System of Marine Protected Areas.

The Marine Aquarium Fish Council: Certification and Market Incentives for Ecologically Sustainable Practices

Jamie Resor
WWF-USWorld Wildlife Fund (WWF)-United States

Coral reefs are a critical habitat for the diverse marine life that is vitally important to the environmental and economic health of tropical nations with substantial coastal areas. If managed properly, they can provide important resources for local sustenance as well as commercial trade in food fish and aquarium organisms. Display of reef organisms in public and private aquariums is one of the best means to enhance public awareness of reef biodiversity and the need to conserve reef ecosystems. However, coral reefs face numerous threats, including pollution, agricultural runoff, industrial excavation, and destructive fishing practices. Consumers in the United States, Europe, and East Asian countries may often unknowingly contribute to one of these threats through their support of the trade in marine aquarium fish and invertebrates that is partially supplied with marine organisms collected from coral reefs using harmful practices.

Such collection practices, which include the use of sodium cyanide and other harmful chemicals, cause destruction or irreversible damage to coral reefs. The adverse effects of these practices have been well documented in the Philippines and Indonesia. In addition, there has not been enough research done to determine what is sustainable in terms of collection practices for any species.

Many individuals and organizations[1] familiar with the aquarium trade—including conservation organizations, government agencies, public aquariums, hobbyists, scientists, and the aquarium trade itself—have publicized the problems and have designed programs to address parts of it (as examples, the training of fishers to convert cyanide users to nets instead, and improved animal husbandry); however, the problem has yet to be addressed comprehensively from reef to consumer, and there has been no market incentive to encourage proper collection. The central question that arises is: What can be done to create the necessary market incentive to encourage the utilization of best management practices for the harvest of fish and other marine organisms for the aquarium trade?

Proposed Solution

To address this question, a cross section of organizations representing the aquarium trade, conservation organizations, public aquariums, hobbyists, and scientists proposes to establish a Marine Aquarium Fish Council (MAFC) that would act as an independent governing council to establish standards, oversee environmental certification, and promote conservation education. Actual certification would not be done by the MAFC but rather would be undertaken by MAFC-accredited certification institutions that would apply the standards developed by the MAFC. The goal of the MAFC will be to ensure that collection, handling, and sale of marine organisms from coral reefs uses best management practices and is ecologically sustainable, socially beneficial, and economically viable. It is currently envisioned that the MAFC will begin with a nine-member board. Board members will represent environmental organizations; aquarium fish exporters, importers, and retailers; and public aquariums. In addition, the MAFC will have an advisory board to permit broader participation and guidance on a wide range of issues.

The Concern and Role of the WWF

The WWF's goal is coral reef conservation. Thus, we have tried to facilitate the collaboration of a diverse set of organizations to develop guidelines and criteria for how environmental certification could be used as a tool for the industry and conservationists to accomplish five things:

- Acknowledge by means of an independent certification process those industry participants who are already using best practices for the collection and handling of marine fish and also help maintain important livelihoods for thousands of fishers in coastal areas.
- Reduce substantially the use of destructive fishing practices by use of market forces to encourage consumers to request environmental certification.
- Develop a logo that would be credible in the eyes of the consumer. Such credibility is possible only if it is substantiated by a certification process that is sufficiently independent of industry.
- Reduce the chance that cumbersome regulations or outright bans might be implemented by government agencies as a political solution that would not necessarily achieve the desired conservation results.
- Promote a healthy trade in aquarium fish (and other marine organisms) as a means to enhance conservation of coral reefs and also serve as an important venue for awareness building among aquarium hobbyists and the general public.

Current Situation

Over the next few months, the MAFC plans to undertake pilot certifications of five or six reef col-

lection-to-consumer operations and one or two captive propagation facilities to field-test proposed guidelines and protocols. As part of these pilot certifications, the MAFC is proposing to hold a workshop in late 1997 or early 1998 to vet the proposed protocol in more detail among a wide range of stakeholders. Given that the majority of aquarium fish collection in the world is undertaken in the Pacific, the current proposal is to hold the workshop in the Philippines or Hawaii.

Over the next few months, several issues require close examination and resolution. These include:

- How much will certification cost and how will the costs be covered? How can certification be equally feasible for small collectors, larger collectors and wholesalers, and captive propagation firms?
- What is realistic for reef monitoring? What are best practices for cost-effective reef monitoring programs?
- How can the MAFC best collaborate with existing certification and permitting programs in different parts of the world?
- Can the MAFC develop a logo and a consumer preference that will help industry achieve a price premium for certified fish?
- What can be learned from the MAFC initiative (and vice versa) that is relevant to potential certification for the live food fish trade and food fish in general?

Recommendations for Assistance

Reef managers and scientists: Identification and design of cost-effective monitoring programs that could be applicable in reef areas under a variety of circumstances.

Nongovernmental organizations and academic institutions: Identification or strengthening of existing monitoring capacity (for collection and handling practices) that local institutions have or are willing to develop in order to keep certification costs down, particularly where there are no formal efforts under way.

The World Bank and policymakers: Continued support of the concept of independent certification as a tool for conservation. Continued involvement of the World Bank through Market

Transformation Initiatives (forest and marine) and its expected participation in the MAFC as a member of the MAFC advisory group. Facilitation of more exchanges and dialog to share best practices for sustainable fishing and ways to use independent certification as a tool for reef conservation. Availability of technical assistance funds and small- to medium-scale investment capital for collector associations and exporters in client countries who are interested in participating in independent certification.

Note

1. A partial list of collaborating organizations includes: American Marine Life Dealers Association (AMDA), Ocean Voice International-Canada Aquarium for Wildlife Conservation, WCS Ornamental Fish Industry (OFI) Ltd.-UK American Zoo and Aquarium Association (AZA) Pet Industry Joint Advisory Council (PIJAC), Flora and Fauna International (FFI)-UK, The Nature Conservancy (TNC), National Aquarium in Baltimore (NAIB), World Wildlife Fund (WWF), and New England Aquarium.

Discussion

Stephen Colwell, Coral Reef Alliance: One of the things that always plagues me, and when I discuss with people from other countries comes up, is if all of the facts laid out about bio-prospecting are true, which is to say there is no up-front payment—a 20-30 year payoff— you're talking about pharmacophore development rather than drug development, so that the connection of royalties is low and there are only a certain number of pharmaceutical companies that are cooperating. Are we really setting forward an incentive for conservation? Not doubting at all that there is a value there for humanity, and for the potential drugs that may come out, but for those source countries, how convincing an argument is that when, again, they're looking at putting food on the table tonight. Or even tourism, where the payoff they can see is an immediate future?

Pat Colin: In essence there is very little incentive for conservation coming out of this kind of work initially. I wish there was more but there isn't.

David Newman: I would second what Pat says in practice. We're using conservationist methods to collect, but as Pat carefully put it, something that isn't screened, you don't know what's there. Perhaps the statistic I gave earlier, which may have skated by— if you look at the drugs that are currently in the armamentarium of the physician, there were 60 percent of them in the three major killing areas of disease—that come from a natural source. And rather, in our screening we are finding that the marine environment is producing some of the most exquisite toxins—and all anti-cancer drugs are by definition toxins—that you have ever seen. We're dealing with materials where the classic "angel on the head of a pin" doesn't even come close. I've seen materials in the lab that at 10–12 molar (and bear in mind that Avogadro's number is 10–23, which means you've got a very small amount) kill cells stone, cold dead. They will not be drugs, but they will be leads to drugs. And I'm afraid that, as emphasized, this is not a conservation aspect that one can point to. Ultimately it will be. But at this moment the question that Mr. Colwell asked is quite valid. This does not put something on the table. But let me give you an example in the terrestrial sphere. Inbio, in Costa Rica, started with a different premise. And that was if they know what [the] flora and fauna are, and they know they can go back and get it, they can sell that information to pharmaceutical houses (for example, to Merck at $1.1 million). In the marine environment, we're still at the stage of not knowing how many things are there, where they are, or what they can do. So we're a very long way at looking at it as a conservation aspect, but as a resource aspect it's immense.

Carl Gustaf Lundin, World Bank: I am with the Blue team of the Environment Department of the World Bank. We produced a book called

Marine Biotechnology in Developing Countries a couple of years ago. And we tried to go through a broad range, including some of the topics we talked about here, and how one can go about looking at marine resources in different ways; that's available in the bookstore. We also arranged a conference in the Asia-Pacific Region, in Thailand, called Marine Biotechnology and the Asia-Pacific region. So we have tried to, at least, get the ball rolling a little bit on these topics, although I must admit in terms of our portfolio, it has been very weak until now, and is definitely not something that we can take much credit for. In any event, I wanted to perhaps switch to Daniel Pelicier and ask him a question. Something that sometimes troubles me is the fact that we actually have to wait quite a long time before we extract fish or other marine organisms until they would replenish. If we take a country like Mauritius, which has some extensive reefs, how many people could live the way you do? What are the types of numbers we're looking at? Are we looking at an order of magnitude of 10 different groups that could do this? Or are we looking at a group of a hundred, or would we be looking at a group of 1,000?

Daniel Pelicier: The area I prospect myself, working alone, is less than 10 kilometers of the coast. So you know the size of my island [inaudible]—this is not even 5 percent of the coast. My interest in working there is to take care of my fish—I don't want them to be transported immediately after capture. The more you stress a fish the less it will live in an aquarium. My method of catching is really as simple as that—just take care of the fish properly and really don't stress it, and I will not have any problem. If I go and work elsewhere, I have to transport them and I've had no success doing that. But a place for people to work, if they want to install themselves—away from my area [laughter]—they can start in their area and do the same. All around the island is fishable.

Audience question: My question is addressed to Mr. James Armstrong on the issue of trade and environment. We all know that the World Trade Organization is the main body that regulates

international trade across countries, and the WTO is pretty much pro-trade. I don't know to what extent environment is sinking into the WTO organization? To what extent does your convention deal with WTO in terms of the legalities of global trade in endangered species and other marine products? My second question is that WTO, in its former incarnation as GATT, ruled in favor of Mexico in the famous tuna-dolphin case against the U.S. I'm sure cases are going to come up in the future, and I want to know if your convention is planning to deal with such situations, or how GATT or WTO will deal with such situations in the future?

James Armstrong: The CITES convention is formally linked now with the WTO's. We have actually a formal observer status on the Trade and Environment Committee of the WTO, which is a committee that's formed with representative parties to the WTO meeting to discuss issues like the shrimp-dolphin issue which is before them at the moment. I must say, however, that historically CITES has been considered outside of the main trade commodity activities of the WTO—being seen historically as a convention that has dealt mainly with megafauna—African fauna such as elephants, ivory trade, et cetera. It's in recent years where CITES has actually moved to look at significantly traded commodities like fish, fishery species, and timber—that the WTO has approached CITES to see that we could get together and resolve any of the problems or incompatibilities that there might be. I must say that one of the great incompatibilities that exist in this trade and environment debate which is raging currently, and is focused in Geneva with the agencies like WTO, and issues like the shrimp-dolphin case which is before it at the moment, is the complete polarity of language that we use in our various professions. The trade community talks in ways—using the same terms that we might use in CITES, but mean completely different things. For example, in CITES a quota of an Appendix 1 species (sometimes we allow trade in Appendix 1 species under strict quotas) for CITES, a quota therefore, is a trade-facilitating mechanism. To the trade community a quota is a negative restriction on trade. It is challenging for the two agencies to communicate when we use the same language but it means completely different things. And so the agenda for our convention and WTO is to work closely together so we can at least understand each other and move on over those problems. In last 25 years, and CITES will be 25 years old next month [November, 1997], there has never been an action considered incompatible with the WTO, or the old GATT arrangements. It doesn't mean that there couldn't be in the future—and certainly some of the issues recently at the last Conference of Parties meeting in Harari, particularly the elephant decisions there, may well raise some concerns by party states to the convention, and we could see ourselves having some interesting discussions with the WTO over that.

Alexander Stone, Reef Keeper International: Mr. Armstrong, you mentioned in your comments that CITES now is committed to an action plan, which has as one of its planks, the promotion, facilitation, and encouragement of national legislation, where it is perceived to be needed. Obviously, the context we're talking about is national legislation in the producing country. My question has to do with whether CITES feels that it has a mandate or a responsibility to try and do the same thing with regards to the consumer countries. I am very concerned, for example, that in the United States we have effectively shut down coral collection in all U.S. marine areas, but we're probably one of the top two or three coral importers in the world. I think it's an extremely hypocritical situation at best. And even though the USA is a big industrialized country and has a quadrillion NGOs in it, maybe we ought to be able to clean up our own act. Still, that is not to say that in these types of situations CITES assistance wouldn't be a big help. So my question is whether CITES feels it has a mandate or a jurisdiction to address the situation in consumer countries? Again, as somebody said: if people didn't buy drugs, there wouldn't be any drug dealers.

James Armstrong: There are two elements to this question which need to be discussed. One is national legislation in both the importing and exporting countries—consumer and developing countries. But there's also this issue of perhaps a stricter domestic measure that you're referring to in the case of potentially the U.S. making a decision not to allow the import of species that are on, say, Appendix 2 of CITES, and for which the convention says the trade is allowable, and in fact facilitated. If the exporting country has done its nondetriment finding and through that nondetriment finding is stating as a sovereign nation allowed to trade, and that trade is sustainable or not detrimental to the survival of that taxon that's been traded. And we can talk very briefly about stricter domestic measures in a moment. But just to give you the background to the program of work that the convention is involved in, in its legislative project, unlike any other convention that I'm aware of, and I'm not aware of any convention having undertaken a study of national legislation requirements to implement its convention. But some five years ago, concerned as we were in this old convention, that many parties did not have the necessary national legislation to even implement the basic requirements of the convention they were a signatory to, the parties to the convention undertook a study—an assessment of the status of the national legislation in all of the parties that were signatories to the convention. As of this year we have done 125 assessments out of the 142 parties, and we're concluding that study now over the next two years—in time for the eleventh meeting of the Conference of Parties—that will be held in Indonesia in November, 1999. By that time we should have had all of the countries considered. What we looked at was what were the basic requirements to be included in the national legislation to enable implementation? We found, in fact, that there were only four basic requirements...that a scientific authority has to make. The second thing is that it has to have the power of seizure of illegally collected material. It has to have the ability to prosecute those seizures, and I have forgotten the fourth one actually, but it relates also to this prosecution power. Remarkably, we have found that most or many countries—particularly in regions like Africa and Asia—fell into what we call category 2 and 3—the third category being that none of those four elements were included in their legislation. Many parties sit in that state at the moment, unfortunately. Very few sit in the first category of having adequate legislation to facilitate the convention. And so this is really one of the issues I have been speaking to this week with the World Bank—that we should be getting together as a convention with groups, funding agencies like the World Bank, so that we can actually see how we can enhance these programs with national legislation and build capacity in these countries that require it. So that's happening both at the consumer country level, and we're doing it across the board, we're not just looking at the exporting countries—and you'd be surprised at some of the countries who are very developed and have enacted inadequate legislation. A number of countries in the E. C., for example, are in category 3, which is pretty deplorable. And incredibly, we actually have a power within our convention to bring about the prevention of trade—we have sanction powers. In fact, the parties are so concerned now about some of these countries who—despite the efforts of the parties to upgrade their legislation—have resisted undertaking that, and these parties will be subject to sanctions in which all trade with that country will be prevented. How that sits with the WTO of course, will be interesting. The second point, then, is despite whatever might be allowed under the convention, the convention also allows full parties to take stricter domestic measures. And so in the case of the U.S., it might choose not to allow the import of coral, because it believes—despite what the sovereign nations exporting those coral might be saying—that is not in the interest of the species concerned. We can go into a wonderful debate about how you can determine a nondetriment finding on coral that's harvested destructively. Can such a thing exist? Is it completely incompatible? There are countries, currently, in our convention that impose stricter domestic measures; Australia has stricter domestic measures—it has a stricter domestic measure policy in relation to certain imports that it will not allow, despite those exports being allowed under the convention. The E.C. commonly restricts the imports of species. In fact, this can be seen in the convention as a worry and a concern, because if trade is truly sustainable—if the exports are truly sustainable from a developing country—then to have an importing country put a stricter measure in place precludes any benefit flowing back into conservation programs in those countries. And so these are tricky issues at an international level that are being discussed in our convention at the moment.

Jan Post, World Bank: I had an earlier question that basically, Pat Colin has already answered. And this was almost the same as what Stephen Colwell had asked—what is bioprospecting going to do for the preservation of reefs? If I understand you correctly, you say that we find some promising compound, we unravel the chemical structure in the laboratory, we synthesize it so that we're not in the long term dependent upon some kind of restriction and other things in developing countries. Walter Adey says if we can't unravel the biological or chemical structure, we can make a mesocosm and we start cultivating an organism. There's a third example to my knowledge, which is in the Bahamas, where they actually have a plantation of gorgonians which would probably require too much of a mesocosm to be ecologically sustainable and economically viable. There I can see these organisms can actually contribute to conservation because those people will not want their waters to the polluted and it provides $600,000 dollars worth of royalties to the country of the Bahamas, and it provides a sustainable income to the fisherman. Is this a correct picture? And if so, what are the possibilities? Do you see much scope for this last example to expand to other areas of the world?

David Newman: Yes, in fact I didn't mention the [*Pseudopterogorgia*] plantation in the Bahamas, which Bill Fenical at the Scripps Institution of Oceanography set up with the Bahamian government. That actually is a rather entertaining one, because the material it produces is the active component of Max Factor's Resilience—antiwrinkle cream. And it is in fact an anti-inflamatory that is not a human-use pharmaceutical. If you want to call it a human-use cosmetical, you can. And Bill set up an excellent operation in the Bahamas. That was a compound that came to fruition in something like two years from its discovery. The agents we're talking about are very much longer-term than that, but you have a very valid point. There are two other areas where conservation systems are being used quite well. In the case of Halichondrin B, where I mentioned we collected 1 metric ton. Because of time, I didn't add part of the $300,000 dollars we put into New Zealand—and New Zealand matched it—went into in-sea aquaculture of that organism, and it is now happily producing Halichondrin B and other constituents (which we're looking at) at 10 meters [depth] in Wellington harbor, rather than 100 meters off of the Kaikoura shelf. There's yet a third: Bryo-statin, which was my lead-off example. I mentioned that there are only three colonies that we know of in the world that produce this material. The U.S. government has put over one million dollars into a very successful in-sea and on-land aquaculture of the particular producing organism *Bugula neritina* in conjunction with a small biotech company in California—and they have successfully produced this material and are continuing to produce it both in-sea and on land. I will take issue with Walter, you can culture many examples of marine fauna, but unless you start with a producing culture—that is, a material that produces the agent of interest, your chances of actually making what there is on the reef are pretty slim. In fact, I would say that they are almost vanishingly small. A good example of this is when Dr. Colin, at my request, did a survey of a material known as *Dorypleres splendens*. It also is known as *Jaspis* spp.—depending on the taxonomist— because we were very interested in a material known by two names: Jaspamide and Jasplakinolide. We looked at 37 different examples of this, culled from a variety of sources from the Pacific, four of them produced the material of interest. The other 33 are genetically, morpologically, photographically, and any other way you would like to look at identical. If you set up a mesocosm, with one of those 33, you do not get Jaspamide/Jasplakinolide. If you set it up with one of the other four you may get

Jaspamide/Jasplakinolide. So yes, there are examples of conservation that have been quite successful, but it's the long-term discovery that basically means—if you're looking for a pharmaceutical—you first have to discover it, then you have to show it is of use, then you have to look to see how you can work with it. In the case of Bill Fenical's work with *Pseudopterogorgia*, it was much faster because it was not a human-use pharmaceutical. Though it did, in fact, get FDA approval, but there was no necessity. You could go from discovery to use in something under three years.

Barbara Ornitz, Shellman and Ornitz: I do a lot of talking to schools and all sorts of groups of people about coral reefs and why they're important. One of the issues that really "rings" with people is this pharmaceutical use. Almost everyone has someone in their family, friends, or relatives who have got a problem with cancer or some other disease. So my question is, if we're talking about sustainable bioprospecting, what do you know, panel, about education that's being used? What tools are we using to reach the consumer public to cause the public to say: "Let's exercise the caution, let's take care of these reefs, because they may solve a problem that I have or someone in my family has—we need to preserve them for future generations?"

Walter Adey: What I would suggest, without answering David's question, because I think the answer is in the question itself—Yes, absolutely correct, there are varieties, and some of them have the compounds and some of them don't. I don't think that takes away the value of mesocosm production one little bit. But what I would suggest as an answer to how bioprospecting helps conservation today, what I would point out, for example, is that not so long ago the FCC sold off frequencies— television frequencies, radio frequencies—for very large sums of money. These are even more abstract than the organisms on the reef. To me, coral reefs are genetic resources; they don't need to be any more than genetic resources. To look at them as physical production facilities makes no sense—from looking at their ecology. But looking at them as genetic resources, that's an entirely different matter. What is wrong with an intergovernment approach that joins with industry and says: "Industry, do you ever want to get these compounds—which we all know are going to be so valuable in the future? Then you will join with us and parcel out these genetic resources."

Providing these considerable sums of money right up front, and down the road, and providing conservation at the same time. To directly answer your question, you're absolutely right. The American public, the public around the world would be saying: "We worry more about health than anything." We have a literal health boom in this country right now. It should not be hard to sell that to our government—that coral reef genetic resources should be treated like airwaves. Why not?

David Newman: In answer to the young lady's question, there's actually a large amount of literature. There are a significant number of videos—one was put out on a program called "How Do They Do That?" We were profiled in that—that was over the taxol story which, as a woman, you would definitely appreciate as the first anti-ovarian drug with any real working activity against resistant ovarian cancer. The answer is that we do try. The problem is that scientists are usually very, very stiff—cut-and-dried—and we don't answer the question, "What is the next cure?" We go off into realms of science. We're usually, probably our own worst enemy. So if there are people out there who are willing to translate our science into something that the general public will say "Please send money", we'll be more than happy to take the money. Thank you.

Summary: Michael Rubino: I've been asked to give a quick summary, and some suggested themes for tomorrow's discussion for this panel. Today, we've gotten a brief update on regulatory approaches to these issues, and the importance of complementary national programs. We've also heard about the elements of a certification program, or a marked-driven approach—in this case for the aquarium reef trade. Issues of costs, monitoring, collaboration arrangements, and third party certification. We've also heard about and discussed the relationship between bioprospecting and conservation. As we see more and more marine or reef bioprospecting types of activity, the implementation issues include things like sharing of benefits, and how do we go from rare organisms compounds to large-scale production, and still advance the conservation agenda?

Suggested themes for tomorrow—just two of them and they're really related: What types of key pilot projects, demonstration projects, or commercial projects would you suggest need to be launched to garner lessons learned, to work out the practical details, in effect, to show how it's done in each one of these three areas: regulatory, market-driven (or certification), and research and development? And then, because we're here under the auspices of the World Bank Group, those of us who work within the Bank are quite interested in how can the World Bank Group—through its partnerships with NGOs, and other stakeholders, through its loans to governments, through its investments in the private sector—how can we work with you to advance this agenda, through these pilot projects, demonstration projects, and commercial projects? So, many thanks to the conference organizers, thank you to the panelists and discussants, thank you for all of your questions, and we look forward to your discussion tomorrow.

PANEL THREE

MARINE PROTECTED AREAS

Session Chair: Jan Post, World Bank

The Relationship of Tourism-Related Revenue Generation to Coral Reef Conservation

Donald E. Hawkins
The George Washington University

In order to appreciate the potential contribution of tourism to conservation, the economic significance of the tourism industry as a whole must be understood. Travel and tourism is the world's fastest growing economic activity. Travel and tourism now drives over 10 percent of global GDP, consumer spending, and capital investment in 1997, and is projected to do the same in 2007, according to the World Travel and Tourism Council and the WEFA Group, as described in table 1.

Unfortunately, accurately determining ecotourism's (or coral reef-related travel) segment of the world travel and tourism market is problematic because of various methodological problems, not the least of which is the varying definitions of nature-based tourism and ecotourism that abound in the international travel industry.

Table 1. Economic impact of travel and tourism on the global economy, 1997 (estimated) and 2007 (projected) *(percent of world)*

Measure	1997	2007
GDP contribution	US$ 3.3 trillion (10.7)	US$ 6.3 trillion (10.9)
Consumer spending	US$ 2.1 trillion (10.9)	US$ 4.0 trillion (11.2)
Capital investment	US$ 801 billion (11.8)	US$ 1.6 trillion (11.8)

Source: World Travel and Tourism Council, London, 1997.

The distinction between nature-based tourism and ecotourism can be somewhat ambiguous and certainly confusing to those with limited exposure to this segment of the tourism industry. Generally, ecotourism is considered a subset within the nature-based tourism market and is characterized by a dedication to small-scale development and strict conservation objectives. Nature-based tourism is defined less rigidly and encompasses more types of development and activities, but also maintains a commitment to sustainability through the mitigation of negative ecological and social impacts.

For the purposes of discussing a link between tourism and conservation, the critical distinction to be made is not between nature-based tourism and ecotourism, but between sustainable tourism and mass tourism. Important benefits to conservation can be achieved by using sustainable tourism to:

- Provide a source of financing for parks and conservation
- Serve as an economic justification for park protection
- Offer local people economically sound and sustainable alternatives to natural resource depletion or destruction
- Promote conservation and build support with commercial constituencies
- Create an impetus for private conservation efforts (Brandon 1996, p. 1).

Sustainable tourism development in coastal areas will only provide these types of conservation benefits if certain conditions are met: First, the natural attractions of the region must be competitive with those of other international destinations; second, protected area authorities must exist that are capable of implementing conservation policies and managing tourism impacts; and third, long-term financial support for protected area management must be ensured. Obviously, this third condition for success—guaranteeing long-term financing for coral reef conservation—is the focus of this panel. Let us first review revenue sources related to the tourism sector.

Revenue-Generating Mechanisms

Governments have traditionally targeted the tourism sector as a source of revenue. Only recently, however, has tourism been used by some countries to generate revenues dedicated to conserving the natural areas that are the foundation

---

Table 2. Mechanisms to capture tourism revenues

User fees are charged to people who use an area or facility. Examples include admission to parks or monuments, fees charged to divers, special fees for accommodations, trophy and hunting fees, or even special fees for rescue services (in the case of mountaineering).

Concession fees are charged to individuals or groups licensed to provide services to visitors at selected sites. Common types of services include food, lodging, transportation, guide services, and retail stores.

Sales and royalties are a percentage of earnings from activities or products of a site tourists visit. Examples are sales and royalties from books, photographs or postcards, films, or pharmaceutical products made at or from products at the site.

Taxation of goods and services used by tourists are a common way to generate revenue. Hotel, food, and airport taxes are among the most common.

Donations can be solicited from tourists for special projects or routine maintenance. Examples include restoration of historic buildings, archeological excavation, improved species protection or habitat purchase, or community development activities such as schools or clinics.

Source: Adapted from Brandon 1996, p. 8.

---

of their tourism industries. While the revenue-capturing mechanisms summarized below are generally self-explanatory, each has advantages and disadvantages that are worth discussing.

User fees are a popular instrument for capturing revenue and particularly relevant in the discussion of tourism in parks and protected areas because they are deemed equitable (only those who use a site pay the fee) and the link between tourist use and conservation can be clearly demonstrated. A contentiously debated issue relating to user fees is the appropriate level of the fee to be charged. Numerous studies of parks and protected areas worldwide have demonstrated that, in the vast majority of cases, fees are too low to cover the costs associated with tourist use of natural resources. User fees have increased (often with a two-tiered system in place to keep fees low for nationals and higher for international visitors), but government and industry concerns regarding the negative impact of fee levels on tourist arrivals continue to limit the economic contributions of user fees to conservation despite evidence that most tourists are willing to pay substantially higher fees than those currently in place.

Hotel and airport taxes are another widely used method of collecting revenue from tourism. One problem with these types of levies in terms of conservation financing is that they are applied in a broad manner—to business visitors, domestic travelers, and students, as well as nature-based tourists—making the visible link between the tax and conservation extremely weak. Creating a tangible connection between a tax and conservation is critical, as nature-based tourists are more willing to pay higher fees or taxes when they believe their money will make a direct contribution to conservation of the areas they are visiting. Another problem associated specifically with hotel taxes, particularly with respect to nature-based or ecotourism development, is that small-scale accommodation initiatives, such as community-based lodges and home stay programs, often have problems complying with the collection and reporting regulations of such taxes. This can discourage local entrepreneurial initiatives that are critical to distributing the benefits of

Figure 1. Relationship of revenue-generating options to reef conservation

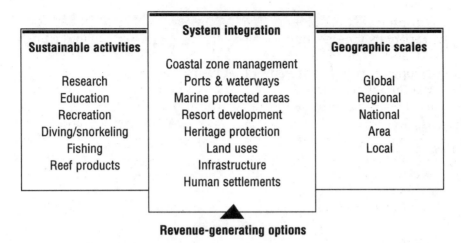

Revenue-generating options

tourism within communities (Brandon 1996, pp. 9–11).

Finally, concessions and royalties have the potential to raise significant amounts of money at well-known and highly visited sites because of the enormous demand for goods and services. The economic potential of these instruments has not been realized in most cases because governments rarely auction off the licensing of concessions at their true market values. Ultimately, the real problem with concessions and royalties, as with all the revenue-capturing mechanisms discussed above, is that they are only tools by which governments can generate funds from tourism. Translating tourism revenues into actual conservation funding is another matter entirely and represents a number of extremely difficult challenges.

So how can the seemingly intractable dilemma of ensuring long-term conservation financing be addressed? There are no easy answers. We need to relate the revenue-generating options discussed briefly above with a more comprehensive understanding of the complex and overlapping marine, coastal, and terrestrial systems

which affect reef conservation in a variety of geographic scales, as presented in figure 1.

Any strategy to increase revenues for reef conservation will have to take into account specific measures to assure that reef-related activities (particularly scuba diving and snorkeling) will be conducted in a sustainable manner, as encouraged by the Coral Reef Alliance. Most important, there is a need for a systems integration approach that relates marine, coastal, and land uses to coral reef impacts. With decentralization coupled with privatization of governmental functions, it appears to me that the emergence of a sustainable tourism movement worldwide will be an important mechanism for private sector direct funding or collateral support for providing the revenues and best practices needed for coral reef conservation.

Reference

Brandon,   Katrina.   1996.   "Ecotourism   and Conservation: A Review of Key Issues," *Environment Department Paper 033*, World Bank, Washington, D.C.

Permanent No-Take Zones: A Minimum Standard for Effective Marine Protected Areas

Callum M. Roberts
University of York

Fishing is a major force of change in marine ecosystems. It leads to loss of diversity and habitat damage and has been recognized as one of the major threats to the biological integrity of marine habitats worldwide (Ginsburg 1994, Dayton and others 1995, NRC 1995, Roberts 1995a, Safina 1995). Fishing is reaching farther and farther across the expanse of the seas. This growing influence leaves few refuges of wild and untouched habitat. The eagles, bears, and buffalo of coral reefs are vanishing as surely as they have from much of North America.

Fishing: A Growing Threat to Marine Biodiversity

Take the Caribbean, for example. My own research over the last three years has documented the loss of some of the largest, most spectacular fish species from huge areas of their former ranges: species like the tiger grouper, yellowfin grouper, and midnight parrot fish. Reefs are being stripped of large vertebrate species in the way the Americas lost their megafauna when people first colonized 11,000 years ago. Like the Pleistocene overkill, this loss is not being accomplished through systematic and bloody slaughter. Nor is it a consequence of the greedy expansion of industrialized fishing. Rather it is a creeping loss accumulating through the gradual spread and intensification of traditional fishing methods, pushing populations of the most vulnerable species across the narrow divide between sustainable harvest and local extinction.

Importance of No-Take Marine Reserves

It is a remarkable fact that the majority of marine protected areas offer no protection whatever from fishing. For example, only 0.14 percent of the combined area of California's 104 marine protected areas have been closed to all fishing (McArdle 1997). This is tantamount to declaring open season on all the wildlife within our terrestrial protected areas. If such hunting were allowed, could we really justify calling them protected? For just this reason, most marine protected areas don't yet deserve the name, even if existing regulations were fully implemented. They still lack one of the most vital forms of protection we can offer.

No-take marine reserves provide an extremely effective means of addressing the fishing problem, particularly for coral reef habitats. A large and rapidly growing body of literature confirms that if you protect reef fish stocks, then fish live longer and grow larger (PDT 1990, Roberts and Polunin 1991, Dugan and Davis 1993, Rowley 1994, Bohnsack 1996). Research also shows that over time reserves come to support populations of species with life history characteristics that render them highly vulnerable to overfishing in the unselective fisheries characteristic of coral reefs: long life, slow growth, late reproduction, low population density, and ease of capture (Polunin and Roberts 1993, Roberts 1995b, Russ and Alcala 1996). Even in relatively lightly fished areas, differences in catchability and life history mean that the most vulnerable species will still be severely overexploited (Roberts 1997). I have become convinced that no-take marine reserves offer the only real hope of preventing local and even global extinction of large numbers of species that are intensely harvested by unselective mean.

Preventing fishing has the added advantage of preventing habitat damage by fishing gear. Reef conservationists' concerns are rightly focused on the most destructive means, such as dynamite, cyanide, and drive net fishing (Rubec 1986, McAllister 1998). But almost any gear can cause damage, and where fishing effort is high reserves can offer important respite from their cumulative impacts. We are only just beginning to appreciate the threat posed to many invertebrate species by fishing gear damage (Dayton and others 1995). For species that release eggs and sperm directly into open water, reproductive success may depend critically on population density. Density can be easily reduced by fishing gear below levels necessary for successful fertilization of eggs.

The problem of overfishing is so widespread that the existence of at least one no-take zone should be considered an essential minimum standard for marine protected areas. There is a paradox here. While the effectiveness of a protected area will be greatly enhanced by the incorporation of such an area, proposing no-take status has been repeatedly demonstrated to be one of the greatest impediments to creating a protected area. For an eloquent example you need look no further than the Florida Keys National Marine Sanctuary (Bohnsack 1997). Inclusion in the preferred management plan of no-take reserves covering 6 percent of the Keys provoked intense controversy. Minority interest groups eventually pared them down to a mere half percent, enough remaining to establish a principle but not enough to safeguard biodiversity in the Keys. The dilemma for those seeking to establish protected areas is whether to press for no-take status at the time of establishment or to drop it in the hope of achieving it later. The best course will depend on local circumstances, but I think that no-take status should feature somewhere in all initial proposals.

Improving Compliance with No-Take Status

No-take regulations are easier to enforce, in principle, than complex systems of rules governing what can and cannot be fished. Bitter experience shows that getting regulations to stick requires more than just legislation; it needs long-term education and policing. This costs money, and to be effective, protected areas must swiftly become self-financing to stand a chance of success. In the Caribbean, there are now numerous examples of successful reserves where financing has been based on user fees levied on tourists (Hooten and Hatziolos 1995).

Once established, the benefits of a no-take area for tourism begin immediately with the removal of fishers and build up rapidly as stocks of large and exciting fish grow. From a fisher's perspective a no-take zone is a mixed blessing. It carries an immediate cost in the form of lost fishing grounds with only the prospect of better times ahead. The economic benefits that no-take areas can provide to fisheries are expected to be substantial and accrue through export of eggs and larvae from protected stocks to fishing grounds and emigration of adults from reserves (Bohnsack 1996). However, these benefits will take time. Models suggest fishers are likely to incur losses over a minimum term of three to five years, until stocks build up sufficiently for benefits to feed through into fish landings (Sladek Nowlis and Roberts 1997). In many coral reef areas the contrast between the rapidly growing prosperity of the tourist industry and the increased hardship suffered by fishers may cause such severe social conflict as to undermine a protected area before it has time to become effective. Such has been the case in St. Lucia, where a change in government led to reevaluation and near collapse of an ambitious and timely management initiative: the Soufriere Marine Management Area (George 1996). Forty percent of this area consists of no-take reserves, and the short-term cost to subsistence fishers, although little in monetary terms, has proved hard for them to bear. For a subsistence fisher the initial cost of creating no-take areas may make all the difference between just getting by and not getting by at all.

The Caribbean model for self-financing protected areas channels all the money from tourist user fees directly into running costs. Perhaps a better model would be to charge more and channel some revenue into a fund to provide development assistance to fishermen losing out in the short term through no-take area creation. In this way fishers would have a greater stake in the success of tourism, would suffer less while fish stocks build up, and would have a greater incentive to abide by no-take regulations. Surveys suggest that tourists would be willing to pay substantially more toward parks than the modest fees they currently pay (Allan Smith and Tom van't Hof, personal communications). The problems in St. Lucia appear to have been solved for the time being through an offer of government compensation to fishers. Development funds channeled from users via the protected area might provide a more enduring solution.

Networking No-Take Reserves

For coral reef areas, almost no marine reserve is too small to benefit from no-take status. In St. Lucia we have found a reserve measuring a bare 150 by 175 meters, which has supported a remarkable buildup in fish stocks compared with adjacent unprotected reefs (Roberts and Hawkins 1997). Of course, marine species have very open populations, with local replenishment often depending on reproduction elsewhere. Consequently, populations in small reserves cannot be self-sustaining. To offer any hope of maintaining viable populations of the large species threatened by overfishing, reserves must interact with others in networks spanning regions. Recent work I have done exploring connectivity patterns in the Caribbean suggests that interaction distances among reefs are relatively short, of the order of 100 to 200 kilometers, although some reefs interact over much longer distances (Roberts, forthcoming). If larvae behave in ways that increase local retention, and recent work suggests that many do (Boehlert

1996), then interaction distances will be even shorter. The existence of short interaction distances has several implications. The first is that to interact effectively, reserves must be established in dense networks, much denser than the present sparse and scattered distribution characteristic for most of the world's oceans. The depressing fact is that the miserable half a percent of the seas currently declared protected is utterly insufficient to safeguard marine biodiversity (particularly as hardly any of this area is no-take).

Two other implications of short interaction distances among reefs offer more encouragement for conservation. International cooperation in marine resource management is essential to the creation of effective networks. Until now such networking has scarcely been attempted, perhaps because people have been put off by the apparent difficulty of deciding who should be partner states in management coalitions. Surface current patterns impose direction and distance constraints on connectivity of living marine resources, and mapping current flows allows management partners to be readily identified.

A further obstacle to creating management networks has been a perception that the more states you add, the less likely you are to reach agreement on substantive issues. Short interaction distances imply that the numbers of partner states necessary for any given nation will actually be rather small and lie well within practical bounds. Even for a region as politically diverse as the Caribbean I found the average number of partner states (upstream and downstream) to range between just four and seven. What I am advocating is a shift away from thinking in terms of vast regional management coalitions to a system of smaller groupings of nations concerned more intimately with ensuring mutual success in natural resource protection. Such groupings will overlap one another but could be embedded within broader international coalitions that agree on guiding principles for management. However, their more limited membership would be better suited to tackling the details of local agreements.

A final consequence of short interaction distances among reefs is that establishing reserves need not be seen as altruistic act only creating distant beneficiaries far downstream. Instead, it means that reserves should provide local benefits too. Since most efforts to establish no-take reserves stand or fall on the perception of local benefits, this is welcome news.

Acknowledgments

My work in St. Lucia has been in collaboration with the Department of Fisheries and the Soufriere Marine Management Area. My sincere thanks to the many people within both organizations who have assisted and facilitated these studies. Thanks also to Scuba St. Lucia for their generous support of fieldwork. The United States Agency for International Development, the United Kingdom's Darwin Initiative, and the Natural Environment Research Council have funded research in St. Lucia. The ideas within this paper have benefited from discussions with many people. Particular thanks are due to Michael Allard, Bill Ballantine, Jim Bohnsack, Sarah George, Julie Hawkins, Tom van't Hof, Josh Sladek Nowlis, Sue Wells, Kai Wulf, and Horace Walters.

References

Boehlert, G.W. 1996. "Larval Dispersal and Survival in Tropical Reef Fishes." In N. V. C. Polunin and C. M. Roberts, eds., *Reef Fisheries.* London: Chapman & Hall.

Bohnsack, J. A. 1996. "Maintenance and Recovery of Reef Fishery Productivity." In N. V. C. Polunin and C. M. Roberts, eds. *Reef Fisheries.* London: Chapman & Hall.

Bohnsack, J. A. 1997. "Consensus Development and the Use of Marine Reserves in the Florida Keys National Marine Sanctuary." *Proceedings of the Eighth International Coral Reef Symposium,* Panama, 1996.

Dayton, P. K., S. F. Thrush, M. T. Agardy, and R.J. Hofman. 1995. "Environmental Effects of Marine Fishing. *Aquatic Conservation: Marine and Freshwater Ecosystems.* 5: 2–28.

Dugan, J. E., and G. E. Davis. 1993. "Applications of Marine Refugia to Coastal Fisheries Management." *Canadian Journal of Fisheries and Aquatic Sciences.* 50: 2029–42.

George, S. 1996. "A Review of the Creation, Implementation and Initial Operation of the Soufriere Marine Management Area." Department of Fisheries, St. Lucia.

Ginsburg, R. N., ed. 1994. "Proceedings of the Colloquium on Global Aspects of Coral Reefs: Health, Hazards and History, 1993." Rosenstiel School of Marine and Atmospheric Science, University of Miami, Florida.

Hooten, A. J., and M. E. Hatziolos. 1995. *Sustainable Financing Mechanisms for Coral Reef Conservation.* Proceedings of a workshop. Environmentally Sustainable Development Proceedings Series No. 9. Washington, D.C.: World Bank.

McAllister, D. E. 1988. "Environmental, Economic and Social Costs of Coral Reef Destruction in the Philippines." *Galaxea* 7: 161–78.

McArdle, D. A., ed. 1997. *California Marine Protected Areas.* La Jolla, Calif.: University of California.

NRC (National Research Council). 1995. "Understanding Marine Biodiversity: A Research Agenda for the Nation." Committee on Biological Diversity in Marine Systems, National Academy Press, Washington, D.C.

PDT (Plan Development Team). 1990. "The Potential of Marine Fishery Reserves for Reef Fish Management in the U.S. Southern Atlantic." NOAA Technical Memorandum NMFS-SEFC-261.

Polunin, N. V. C., and C. M. Roberts. 1993. "Greater Biomass and Value of Target Coral Reef Fishes in Two Small Caribbean Marine Reserves." *Marine Ecology Progress Series* 100: 167–76.

Roberts, C. M. 1995a. "Effects of Fishing on the Ecosystem Structure of Coral Reefs." *Conservation Biology* 9: 65–91.

———. 1995b. "Rapid Build-up of Fish Biomass in a Caribbean Marine Reserve." *Conservation Biology* 9: 815–26.

Roberts, C. M. 1997. "Ecological Advice for the Global Fisheries Crisis." *Trends in Ecology and Evolution* 12: 35–8.

Roberts, C. M. Forthcoming. "Connectivity and Management of Caribbean Coral Reefs." *Science.*

Roberts, C. M., and J. P. Hawkins. 1997. "How Small Can a Marine Reserve Be and Still Be Effective?" *Coral Reefs* 16: 150.

Roberts, C. M., and N. V. C. Polunin. 1991. "Are Marine Reserves Effective in Management of Reef Fisheries?" *Reviews in Fish Biology and Fisheries* 1: 65–91.

Rowley, R. J. 1994. "Case Studies and Reviews: Marine Reserves in Fisheries Management." *Aquatic Conservation: Marine and Freshwater Ecosystems* 4: 233–54.

Rubec, P. J. 1986. "The Effects of Sodium Cyanide on Coral Reefs and Marine Fishes in the Philippines." In J. L. MacLean, L. B. Dizon, and L. V. Hosillos, eds., *The First Asian Fisheries Forum.* Manila: Asian Fisheries Society.

Russ, G. R., and A. C. Alcala. 1996. "Marine Reserves: Rates and Patterns of Recovery and Decline of Large Predatory Fish." *Ecological Applications* 6: 947–61.

Safina, C. 1995. "The World's Imperiled Fish." *Scientific American* 273: 46–53.

Sladek Nowlis, J., and C. M. Roberts. 1997. "Theoretical Approaches to Marine Reserve Design." *Proceedings of the Eighth International Coral Reef Symposium*, Panama, 1996.

Tropical Marine Reserves Should Encompass Spawning Aggregation Sites

R. E. Johannes
R. E. Johannes Pty. Ltd.

Many coral reef food fishes aggregate in large numbers at specific locations, seasons, and moon phases in order to spawn. Such fishes include groupers, snappers, emperors, jacks, mullets, bonefish, rabbitfish, and others. A variety of such species will often spawn at common sites.

These aggregations are prime targets for fishers, who often take large catches from them. In consequence, a number of them have been wiped out, along with the fisheries they supported. This is best documented for groupers but is by no means limited to them. In the western Atlantic, grouper aggregations with a history of heavy fishing pressure have disappeared in Puerto Rico, St. Thomas, Florida, and the Dominican Republic, along with the fisheries they supported. In addition, marked declines in aggregations size have been noted in Belize, Bermuda, and elsewhere in the region.

Although statistics on grouper stocks in the Pacific are scant, groupers have been virtually eliminated by overfishing in at least five locations within Palau, the Cook Islands, the Society Islands, the Tuamotus, and on the Great Barrier Reef. At three of these locations fishing over spawning aggregations has been specifically implicated. It may also have been a contributing factor in the other two.

It is very likely that a great many other aggregations of groupers and other species have been eliminated without written record because of the slowness with which marine biologists, especially in the Indo-Pacific, have recognized and acted upon the need to locate, characterize, and protect them. The problem is almost certainly accelerating, not only because the fishing pressure of growing populations, but also because of the ease with which fishermen can relocate aggregations today with global positioning systems, and the targeting of spawning aggregations by the billion-dollar-and-fast-expanding live reef food fish trade centered in China.

The most widely discussed marine conservation measure in shallow tropical waters is the marine reserve. Proponents often assert that the most important function of marine reserves is to protect spawning stock biomass and ensure recruitment to fished areas by means of larval dispersal. Clearly, for that reason, the boundaries of such reserves should, wherever practical, encompass spawning aggregation sites. Moreover, the presence of an important spawning aggregation site would in some cases be justification in itself for the establishment of a marine reserve. Such, for example, is the main reason for the Palauan government's declaring Ngerumekaol a marine reserve.

There is little evidence in the literature, however, indicating that spawning aggregation sites were given any consideration when the boundaries of most marine reserves were drawn. Badly needed, therefore, are:

- Efforts to locate and characterize spawning aggregation sites.
- Spawning aggregations and associated sites

101

are very poorly documented except for portions of the western Atlantic and certain Pacific Islands. The Great Barrier Reef is an example of an important reef area where very little has been recorded concerning the timing and location of such aggregations, let alone efforts made to protect them.

- Fishers often know far more about the location and timing of spawning aggregations than researchers. Indeed more than 20 different researchers have acknowledged in their publications that it was fishers who enabled them to locate the spawning aggregations that they subsequently studied. For this reason the assistance of fishers should be sought when searching for and characterizing these sites.

Protection of Important Spawning Aggregation Sites

Those who plan to establish or redefine a marine reserve in nearshore tropical waters should ensure that it is located, if possible, so as to protect important spawning aggregations. Other means of protection include closing spawning grounds or closing fishing for important species during the spawning season. Most of the few examples of such protection of nearshore tropical spawning aggregations are found in the western Atlantic.

The Role of Marine Protected Areas in Coral Reef Conservation

Tundi Agardy
Conservation International

Marine protected areas (MPAs) serve myriad roles in conserving coral reef biological diversity, creating opportunities for sustainable use and stewardship, and promoting effective management of reef resources. Specifically, these objectives include, among other things:

- Protecting reef habitats from dynamite fishing, cyanide fishing, and other destructive extractive industries
- Developing ecotourism that minimizes environmental costs and maximizes economic benefits
- Providing a means for more effective fisheries management
- Providing sites for research
- Finding means for involving local communities in management and promoting stewardship
- Increasing the perceived value of reef areas in the minds of decisionmakers and investors.

These are worthy targets for conservation, and MPAs serve as invaluable tools for achieving them. In fact, in some areas MPAs may be the only feasible method for dealing with the complex suite of problems affecting reef areas today.

However, it may be that many of our coral reef conservation investments that rely on establishment of MPAs are at risk—in other words, we may in fact be investing poorly. This is for two reasons:

- We tend to treat MPAs as end points instead of starting points—starting points to demonstrate how integrated coastal management may actually be achieved, and starting points for scaling up conservation so that it approaches ecosystem scales that are appropriate to these vast systems. We haven't done a very good job of learning from existing MPA efforts, and we rarely harness the knowledge we have in order to scale up our protection and sustainable use. And unless we do so, and address the context in which these minute islands of protection sit, our investments will prove useless over time.
- We tend to establish MPAs where they are needed least: in relatively pristine areas that have few user conflicts and that are an "easy sell" to the donor community. Though I recognize that we must be realistic and look for conservation opportunities wherever they may occur, we are doing the seas and their biodiversity a great disservice in staying away from the problem areas. Establishing MPAs in relatively trouble-free areas may make conservationists and their supporters feel good about their work, but inevitably this squanders precious resources. It also allows decisionmakers to feel as if they have adequately addressed marine conservation issues, and will eventually lead to a potentially disastrous complacency.

Broadly speaking, one can view the impetus for establishing MPAs as being of three kinds: (a) proactive conservation, in which individual MPAs or MPA networks are established to protect relatively pristine, representative habitats or "hot spots" of biodiversity; (b) interactive conservation, in which MPAs are established to resolve user conflicts and promote stewardship or wise use of ocean space and resources; or (c) reactive conservation, in which MPAs are established to help degraded ecosystems recover from overexploitation and misuse. Networks of marine protected areas are most commonly planned and implemented with proactive conservation in mind—but personally I believe MPAs have greatest value in mitigating existing negative impacts on ecosystems and on the human communities that rely on them.

The benefits provided by MPAs, when they are planned correctly and implemented effectively, go well beyond their usefulness in conserving coral reef resources and biodiversity onsite: MPAs can provide salient examples of how to effectively integrate management, use science as a basis for policy, and involve stakeholders in the management process. Through their demonstration role, MPAs give us concrete, testable models for how we ought to be practicing marine conservation at even larger scales: national, regional, and even global. This additional value of MPAs is often overlooked by those who would judge the effectiveness of any single MPA merely by how well it protects the habitats and species within its boundaries.

There is without question great need for utilizing MPAs fully in all their possible roles, and for creating such demonstration models. We are losing marine biological diversity, irreversibly effecting coastal habitats, and lowering the quality of human life in coastal communities every second. This has consequences not only for ocean advocates and coastal peoples themselves, but indeed for the entire biosphere. Sadly, we are destroying the worlds' oceans even as we come to appreciate their importance.

Three areas come to mind as deserving particular support from multilaterals: (a) efforts to establish individual MPAs or networks of MPAs in places where coral reef conservation is inherently difficult—that is, where user conflicts exist and degradation is already occurring, as opposed to the easy places that are biologically rich but relatively intact; (b) efforts to establish marine protected areas in biologically important places that are currently outside the geographic scope of what most conservation groups consider priority areas (for example, west Africa, parts of Latin America such as the Abrolhos reef of Brazil, and Micronesia); and (c) efforts to move up from small-scale MPA conservation to scales that are appropriate to the ecosystem (for example, national or regional scales).

In the developing world, government agencies must be involved—but should not be relied upon to play the lead role in establishing MPAs. Most governments don't have the institutional framework or capacity to plan or manage MPAs. Parastatal organizations that have representation from traditional government sectors (for example, ministries of parks, wildlife, fisheries, and tourism) are a tried and true means to effective management of MPAs, and such multiparty groups can keep interagency disputes to a minimum. Nongovernmental organizations often play a vital role as honest brokers and can in some cases be relied upon to oversee management or monitoring of an MPA. Academic institutions and research agencies within government also play a vital role in MPA planning, though in management their roles are usually superseded by organizations established specifically to oversee the operation of the MPA. Last, bilaterals and multilaterals can play crucial roles in providing additional support and incentives for MPA establishment.

International agreements such as the Convention on Biological Diversity (CBD) and the multilateral agreements under the Commission on Sustainable Development (CSD) can be harnessed to add even greater support for MPA efforts, but these international forums provide countries with little guidance as to where, when, and how to initiate marine conservation measures. My fear is that countries that are obligated to establish MPAs, or other management measures under such treaties, will do so in places where they are least needed: areas that are largely unthreatened and remote.

One of the great failures of marine conservation is that conservation groups and decisionmakers rarely work to identify root causes of conservation problems in areas that they deem worthy of conservation attention. Most typically, the types of conservation projects undertaken in a particular place will reflect the interests and capacities of the lead institution, not the reality of what is needed to fix the problem. Conservation resources are often wasted when management action and protection are piecemeal.

In order to be truly strategic, conservation initiatives in priority areas will thus have to address the most important root causes of degradation and biodiversity loss. Once root causes and their drivers are identified, those tools most effective in addressing these causes should be chosen from the conservation toolbox that is available. Some of these tools will be local-scale initiatives such as marine protected areas and microenterprise projects. Others will be larger in scale, involving advocacy, education, and work toward bringing about changes in policies.

Yet it is not enough to choose appropriate tools and use them. In order to be most effective, marine initiatives should be undertaken in a synergistic and integrated way. A metaphor for this is borrowed from marine navigation, involving ships, their anchors, and the lines that connect the two. Any strategic reef conservation effort will have to have site-specific elements that act as conservation anchors in priority geo-graphic areas, such as marine protected areas (including biosphere reserves), microenterprise projects, community-based ecotourism, land management projects, and so forth. It will also have to embrace, or at the very least work in synergy with, the larger policy elements. These broad-based policy elements are the ships that the field projects act to anchor. Conservation organizations can and must work to gain maximum leverage from international conventions such as CBD, Law of the Sea (LOS), and the CSD agreements, and should work to build up capacity for regionally coordinated work. There will be additional opportunities to work with industry to develop best practice guidelines and incentive measures for sustainable use, at either local scales or greater. In all these initiatives, however, it will be necessary to explicitly link the anchors to the ships—creating lines where none exist and increasing their potential to leverage influence in either direction. The World Bank and other multilaterals can continue to support local-scale MPA and other projects in coral reef s around the world, but they will be most effective only if they promote the establishment of MPAs in areas under threat, support efforts to scale up from the site-specific to the regional, and work to ensure that regional and global policies are conducive to effective and efficacious marine conservation.

The Reefs at Cancún: A Social Laboratory

Juan E. Bezaury Creel
Amigos de Sian Kaían A.C.

Back in the early 1970s a group of notable islanders from Isla Mujeres, Quintana Roo, noticed that the local reefs were rapidly deteriorating. This was due mainly to overfishing and the increased use generated by the incipient development of the federally financed tourist city of Cancún. These islanders persuaded the Secretariat of Industry and Commerce, which had the responsibility of fisheries management, to create a "marine flora and fauna refuge" named Costa Occidental de Isla Mujeres, Punta Cancún y Nizuc. The presidential decree was published February 7, 1973, specifying that no fisheries, no waste disposal, and no use of explosives could take place within the three specific areas, or polygons (figure 1).

Over 20 years passed, and Cancún became a touristic giant of over 20,000 hotel rooms, receiving close to 2,000,000 visitors a year and supporting a city of over 350,000 people where nothing had existed less than a generation before. As to the foresight that created the refuge, it was clearly a typical case of the "paper park" syndrome. Because of the public's consistent outcry, federal, state, and municipal authorities tried to regulate the highly abused reef areas; however, it was "discovered" that the old presidential decree dealt only with fisheries and pollution and lacked teeth to control tourism, by now the main destructive factor.

Costa Occidental de Isla Mujeres, Punta Cancún y Nizuc, is located almost on the northernmost portion of what has recently been named the Mesoamerican Caribbean Reef System, which originates at Isla Contoy, Quintana Roo, and follows the coast through Belize and Guatemala to the Bay Islands in Honduras. The two most northerly polygons of the park are located within the Northern Quintana Roo Patch Reefs Subprovince; Isla Mujeres has patch reefs mainly at Manchones, and Punta Cancún has patch reefs at Cuevones and Chitales and a rocky "shelf edge" about 1.5 meters high at a depth of 60 to 75 feet that concentrates fish and contains various dive sites. The third polygon of Punta Cancún is located at the northernmost portion of the Northern Quintana Roo Shallow Fringing Reefs Subprovince, presenting a complex reef crest system (locally known as the first, second, and third barriers), and it contains the only spur and groove formations in this subprovince (and the northernmost in the Mesoamerican system). Although each and every area is ecologically unique, the social uniqueness of this area is far more important, since one can find richer and better developed reef ecosystems south of Cancún, but certainly no richer and more diverse interaction between man and the reefs.

Tourist activities are diverse within the area. The Costa Occidental de Isla Mujeres polygon is mainly a snorkeling destination with some scuba diving activities. It presents many contrasts. For example, small, local operators, most of them organized in tourist cooperatives, are the vast majority of stakeholders in this polygon.

They provide for the low-cost end of the tourist demand based in Isla Mujeres and are basically self-employed ex-fishermen who own a boat or two. On the other side of the scale there are the Cancún-based businesses that take tourists from Cancún to Isla Mujeres on various tours, including a state-of-the-art tourist submarine that visits artificial reefs, reef diving, snorkeling/day-at-the beach/shopping, "lobster by candlelight" or "pirate night" dinners on a ship, and a multiple variety of what can be generically termed "booze cruises," which at some point include flippers, a mask, and a snorkel.

Punta Cancún's activities are run by medium-sized to large operators who provide mostly scuba diving trips and two nonsubmersible fish observation vessels that seat people on the ship's keel.

Punta Nizuc contains what we believe is the single most intensely used reef in the world. This small portion of the polygon, located in the first barrier, is no more than 400 meters long and 100 meters wide, or 4 hectares in total area. This section of reef receives an average of 1,700 visitors a day, resulting in over 600,000 visitors a year on 358 double-seated waverunners and 29 large vessels. This situation arises from an unique Cancúnean touristic product named the Jungle Tour, a visitor activity with a high impact. It consists of minifleets of five double-seater waverunners that follow a leading vessel around Nichupte Lagoon, past a mangrove channel, and out to sea; they tie down west of the first barrier of Nizuc, where the tourists snorkel before going back to the marina. Jungle tours account for 80 percent of the visitors to this polygon; the other 20 percent gain access to the reef using the larger vessels. Most of these vessels are used as bases for snorkeling activities, but the largest company has anchored a platform by the first barrier, complete with bathrooms and lockers, a restaurant and bar, a dive shop, a souvenir shop, and a sun deck. This facility is used as a way station for vessels called the Reef Express that run back and forth from the marina to the platform each hour. The platform is also used as the boarding station for four nonsubmersible fish observation vessels. The latest permit application describes an underwater motorcycle for individual use.

As can be deduced from the activities described above, there is no lack of creativity in finding new and innovative ways of placing ordinary couch potatoes in direct contact with the reefs. The impact of all these activities on the first barrier has been devastating for most corals and sponges, but nevertheless, there still exists enough fish life to sustain the place as a tourist attraction.

As for the original presidential decree, prohibiting fishing within the polygons, presently no lobster and very few large edible fish can be readily observed within the area. Local fishermen continue to fish these areas early in the morning before tourists arrive. Additionally, pollution from the great concentration of motorboats has become apparent, and at least in two sites—El Garrafon and the first barrier of Punta Nizuc—reef damage seems to be irreversible.

In 1995 the Subcommittee for the Protection of Nichupte Lagoon (a coordinating forum that includes national, state, and local government; stakeholders; academics; and nongovernmental

Figure 1. Costa Occidental de Isla Mujeres, Puerta Cancún y Nizuc

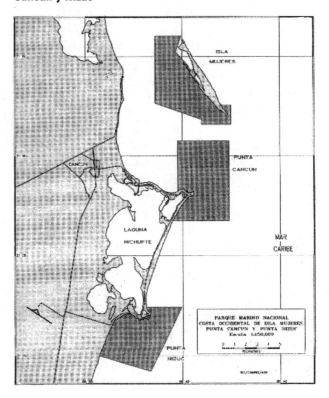

organizations) created a Technical Council for Reefs that worked towards the recategorization of the refuge as a national park. These efforts resulted in the publication by the Secretariat of Environment, Natural Resources, and Fisheries on July 19, 1996, of the Presidential Decree for the Park, with three redefined polygons and a total area of 8,673 hectares. The designated area includes extensive sea grass communities along with the reefs.

By July 24, 1996, through an agreement between the federal government and most of the participants of the Technical Council for Reefs, the park's Planning Council was formed. That same day, a trust fund was established by an agreement signed between the federal government and the tour operators, in which the latter would voluntarily deposit a "maintenance fee" for the park. A park director with 11 staff members established an office with three patrol vessels and minimum equipment, serving to integrate the first effort for operating the park. A management plan is being developed, along with regulations for park use.

Although the park is well on its way to becoming an effective vehicle for natural resource protection and sustainable use of reef resources, some points need further clarification.

First, the issue of environmental sustainability needs to be addressed within a larger context. Some areas of the park are beyond their carrying capacity and are being overused. On the other hand, the overuse of these areas has prevented damage to adjacent sites that receive little or no use (for example, the second and third barriers in Nizuc). An interesting phenomenon was foreseen and later observed with the creation of the park and the enforcement of access to Nizuc only by permit-holding vessels. The ex-pirates overflowed the park and went with their jungle tours farther south, generating the establishment of the Puerto Morelos Reef National Park a year after the one in Cancún was created, to control this overflow.

My personal opinion is that the heavily used areas should be managed in such a way that deterioration does not go further or expand to other areas, in order to keep activities concentrated within a site and not allow them to spill over into other areas, where they cannot be as easily controlled by park staff. To achieve this, trails would need to be designed and constructed using rosaries of buoys and unorthodox park practices—such as fish feeding—would need to be continued, for such places to remain attractive to unsophisticated snorkelers. The better-trained and supposedly more "conscious" scuba divers with more sophisticated tastes would be allowed to spread out as administrative management capacity increases. In short, certain parts of the reef should be managed as "sacrificial reefs" in order to protect others, because of the high demand of reef visits generated by Cancún as a valid conservation strategy.

Second, the financial sustainability of the park needs to be further defined, since not all touristic operators have been diligent in depositing their voluntary maintenance fees for the park, resulting in only a 50 percent compliance rate. At this point, we should analyze the park's potential for income generation.

It has been estimated that close to 1,000,000 people a year visit all three of the park's polygons. The legal entrance fee for all Mexican protected areas is around US$2.75 per person, which means that a theoretical $2,750,000 could be collected just from entrance fees. By law, these funds need to be collected and sent to the Secretariat of Public Financing, since a mechanism for recycling operating funds generated within protected areas has not yet been implemented, but one is still being actively sought. This is one of the main reasons why the voluntary trust fund model was chosen to finance the park.

In this model the number of usable seats for the total number of vessels was first determined (5,227 seats on 589 vessels). A seat cost factor was determined to reach a collection goal for 1997 of $285,000. This factor was differentiated by activity: a higher factor for the most profitable activities, lower factors for inexpensive activities, and the use of the park for nonreef-related activities and to cooperative members. The seat cost factor, per number of seats each tour operator had in its vessels, was the amount to deposit monthly in the trust fund, using two trade associations—one for the Cancún operators and the others for those from Isla Mujeres.

The amount collected through this model, on its first year of application (that is, if fully paid because of its voluntary nature), is equivalent to an average of $0.285 per user, or 10 percent of the legal entrance fee.

Thus, it is obvious that the potential of the park for generating income lies somewhere in between these scenarios. Choosing the full collection model implies enforcement and administrative costs of diminishing return, and that the park has the potential to generate resources not only for its upkeep, but also for management of other areas with less demand from tourists. This is also true for other national parks in the region, such as Cozumel Reefs and Isla Contoy, where tour operators have voluntarily participated in financing programs that charge less than the legal entrance fees, and produce visible management effects from the money spent. Nevertheless, tour operators have been very active in opposing the application of legal fees.

The tour operators in Cancún and Isla Mujeres are fierce competitors in a very competitive market. Because of the diversified nature of their services, they have difficulty in agreeing among themselves on many of the important issues related to park management (including the use of the Punta Nizuc platform, which has become a critical issue). Exceptions exist for those issues that directly threaten their collective interest, such as a collection model that would allow the government to verify their taxable base (like the full collection model). On the other hand, there is an abysmal difference between the financial capacities of tour operators from Cancún and those from Isla Mujeres. Nevertheless, they are the first line of contact with the visitors, and their cooperation and participation—since they are important stakeholders—are basic necessities for the park's well-being.

The economic impact of the park on the communities of Cancún and Isla Mujeres is yet to be determined, but an area that is used by one out of every two visitors must certainly play a significant role in the local economy. On the other hand, the potential for the creation of environmental awareness concerning coral reefs and their importance is very high, and programs should be implemented to make the best of this potential.

The renewed experiment is less than a year and a half old, but it has already generated a stream of new lines of thought and action on participatory protected area management in Mexico. Turning a paper park into a real one is no easy task. Time will tell us if we are able to balance the need to protect the environment with everyday economic necessities. But isn't that what sustainable development is all about?

Entrepreneurial Marine Protected Areas: Small-Scale, Commercially Supported Coral Reef Protected Areas

Stephen Colwell
The Coral Reef Alliance

Marine protected areas (MPAs) are widely acknowledged as having great potential for protecting coral reef habitats and related marine life. Despite this potential, many MPAs in coral reef areas lack sufficient funding and management and therefore do not provide any real protection. This paper explores the current involvement of dive resorts in the creation and management of MPAs and suggests that, in some circumstances, dive resorts, which have a vested economic interest in promoting abundant marine life, can become the primary stewards of small-scale, commercially supported MPAs in coral reef areas.

Background

There is no single, ideal model for creating protected areas for coral reefs. While important management principles have been identified for years, (Kenchington and Hudson 1984) and guidelines created for establishing marine protected areas (MPAs)(Kelleher and Kenchington 1991), the actual structure of a successful MPA is highly dependent upon a variety of local biological, geographic, social, political, and economic factors (Kelleher and others 1995). In certain instances, small-scale, commercially supported MPAs may provide the best form of protection for coral reef areas.

MPAs are widely acknowledged as having great potential for protecting coral reef habitats and related marine life (Eichbaum and others 1996, Sobel 1993). The Global Representative System of Marine Protected Areas (GRSMPA) proposed by the World Conservation Union (IUCN), the World Bank, and others is an ambitious program to create a worldwide network of primarily large-scale MPAs that would ultimately protect 10 percent of all marine and coastal areas (Kelleher and others 1995). A global representative system of MPAs would provide unprecedented protection for marine habitats and inhabitants, thus the efforts to create this system deserve enthusiastic, global support.

Unfortunately, like most ambitious projects, implementation of the GRSMPA poses a number of substantial political, legal, and management challenges: a global system of large-scale MPAs would require agreement among many conflicting resource stakeholders, vast amounts of financing and capacity building, and decades of development to become fully operational (Kelleher 1996).

A simultaneous and complementary approach to the GRSMPA is to create a network of widely dispersed small reserves in addition to the large reserves (Jameson and others 1995). Small-scale MPAs may be especially appropriate in coral reef areas, where nearby reefs can be managed by local communities and nongovernmental organizations (NGOs) (Alcala 1995, White and others 1994). In addition to community-based MPAs, in certain circumstances dive resorts or similar commercial entities can act as the primary stewards of coral reef resources as managers of small-scale MPAs. The key to the success of this approach is to acknowledge dive resorts or other commercial entities as full partners in the planning and management of the MPAs, not just as potential sources of revenue to support the MPA. The lessons of community-based management strategies for coral reef areas apply equally well to commercially supported MPA efforts: without substantial input of all key stakeholders in defining issues, selecting management strategies, and implementing management measures, the best-laid plans for MPA management will fail (White and others 1994).

Entrepreneurial MPAs

In this paper, small-scale, commercially supported MPAs will be referred to as entrepreneurial MPAs to distinguish them from other small-scale MPAs established by governments, community groups, or NGOs. Entrepreneurial MPAs cannot provide the comprehensive protection ultimately required on a global level, but they may perform several valuable functions including:

- Protecting discrete areas that serve as refuges for threatened marine life
- Building local capacity in MPA management
- Acting as test cases for MPA management techniques
- Building public awareness of and support for MPAs
- Providing core areas for larger, slower-developing MPAs.

Entrepreneurial MPAs have the advantage of using existing commercial infrastructure (such as boats and communications equipment) and management structures, making it possible to create these small-scale MPAs more quickly and to institute management regimes more easily than with large-scale MPAs. Thus, entrepreneurial MPAs may have a better chance of providing the success stories that planners and managers need in order to convince a broader audience of the value of MPAs. The ultimate goal of this approach is to create an expanded network of small, locally run MPAs that use tourism or other commercial support to achieve long-term economic and environmental sustainability.

Dive Resorts and MPAs

Dive resorts in a number of coral reef areas already serve as de facto stewards of local marine resources. MPAs have proved to be effective tourist attractions (Agardy 1991); the increased marine life found in MPAs is a magnet for scuba divers, snorkelers, glass-bottom boaters, and other marine enthusiasts. There are a number of examples where resorts have become active participants in the management of existing MPAs or the moving forces behind the creation of new MPAs: At the El Nido Resort, Palawan, Philippines, frequent use of the surrounding area by the resort's diving boats (staffed by deputized rangers) has proved to be the most effective method of enforcing the local restrictions on destructive fishing practices. The Sandy Bay/West End Reserve, in Roatan, Honduras, was started in 1991 and financially supported for four years by one local resort; local NGOs, other hotels, and dive operations have joined to expand the scope of the reserve. The Kungkungan Bay Resort, Lembeh Straits, Indonesia, is in the early stage of creating an MPA, but it has already been successful in attracting government support for dismantling an enormous fish trap that was decimating the local marine life, and thus reducing the area's attractiveness for marine tourists (Colwell forthcoming). In each case, the resort owners and managers determined that protecting the local coral reefs was the best way to protect the long-term financial viability of their resorts.

Strategy for Creating a Network of Small-Scale Entrepreneurial MPAs

While tourism is often cited for its potential to fund MPAs (Kelleher and others 1995) there is very little focus on the potential of a commercial enterprise to be the primary manager of marine resources. Scientists, conservationists, governments, and local communities all have their own reasons for hesitating to surrender control of an MPA to a commercial entity: there is great potential for abuse of power by a resort or other commercial entity that has profit as its primary motive and does not answer to a public constituency. Nonetheless, the demonstrated potential of resorts to serve the public good through MPAs while pursuing private goals seems to justify exploration of whether more functional MPAs can be created and managed by private enterprises. While it is essential to guard against surrendering too much authority to commercial entities, this must be balanced by efforts to create a framework where the management potential of commercial partners is utilized. As with any partnership, choosing the right partners and creating a working relationship that explores and incorporates the interests of all parties is the best guarantee of success. CORAL (the Coral Reef Alliance, a nonprofit conservation organization in the United States) is instituting a pilot program to promote small-scale coral reef MPAs in developing countries. One element of this program is focused on entrepreneurial MPAs. The basic plan is to work with dive resorts, scientists, educators, governments, conservationists, and experts in MPA and community-based management to:

- Develop educational materials on MPA creation and management designed for dive resorts and similar commercial enterprises.
- Use networks of scientists, NGOs, governments, the tourism industry, and others to identify opportunities for creating small-scale, sustainable marine protected areas with local commercial partners.
- Determine with each local partner the need for technical and material assistance and provide necessary training and consultation to increase local capacity.
- Establish a clearinghouse for information on materials needed by commercial partners to create and manage MPAs (from mooring buoys to communications equipment).
- Provide microloans of $3,000 to $15,000 per year from a Coral Reef Conservation Fund to support entrepreneurial MPAs. A parallel microgrant program will support community-based management of small-scale coral reef protected areas. The fund would be created and replenished by grants, contributions from CORAL members, other private donors, and the dive/tourism industry, as well as by repayment of microloans.

- Build a network of small-scale MPA operators to share experiences and form a possible basis for joint marketing of MPA resorts.
- Evaluate the progress of each MPA and share lessons with potential local partners in other communities that might consider establishing their own protected areas.

It should be stressed that the entrepreneurial MPA approach is not intended to compete with either GRSMPA or community-based efforts to build MPAs. In fact, integration with other MPA programs and networks will be critical to the success of this program. Further, this strategy will work only in limited circumstances. Most notably, it will work only in coral reef areas that have sufficient marine resources and are accessible enough to attract a steady, paying clientele of scuba divers and snorkelers to help offset the costs of the MPA (Colwell 1995). The selection of entrepreneurial MPA sites would be primarily market-driven rather than based on the priorities developed for the GRSMPA. Nonetheless, even the best-financed entrepreneurial MPA will need to adhere to most of the management principles recommended by the GRSMPA as well as develop local community support if it hopes to be sustainable in the long run.

There are a number of other potential problems with small-scale MPAs (whether community or commercially based) such as concern that the area they protect may be too small to provide real benefits in preserving biodiversity. Although small-scale projects may not provide the same total ecosystem protection offered by a large-scale MPA, many countries have small reefs only, therefore regional or national administration of these MPAs is less practical (Alcala 1995), and even very small coral reef reserves (from 1 to 3 square kilometers) have been successful in increasing the abundance and size of fish and other marine life (Roberts 1994). From a management perspective, the most successful MPAs in developing countries have been small-scale projects that include local stakeholder input and accountability (White and others 1994, Alcala 1995).

Ultimately, for entrepreneurial MPAs to be truly successful they must be a part of a more integrated management approach that takes into account causes and effects outside the MPAs' boundaries; entrepreneurial MPAs must be tied into a network that includes traditional, national, and international coastal and marine managers. The initial step, however, is to help create enough entrepreneurial MPAs so that the basic models can be tested and improved. Many entrepreneurial MPAs will not fit the GRSMPA criteria for model MPAs; but rather than waiting until an ideal MPA can be created, it may be more effective to create MPAs that can achieve local objectives for marine conservation (Kelleher 1996). As long as funding and expertise are not being drained from other MPA projects, the entrepreneurial MPA approach offers a chance to increase the number and variety of MPAs at a fairly low cost. Variations on the entrepreneurial MPA strategy, such as co-management of the MPA with a local NGO, or the creation of new community-based dive resorts, expand the potential benefits of this approach.

Conclusion

Flexible and creative approaches to MPA management are needed in order to approach the goal of protecting at least 10 percent of the world's marine and coastal areas. A network of small-scale, commercially supported MPAs would provide a useful complement to the GRSMPA. In certain circumstances, private enterprises, such as dive resorts, may be able to provide the financial resources and management capacity to create and operate small-scale MPAs, particularly in coral reef areas. Many of these entrepreneurial MPAs will suffer from the lack of the careful research and planning that are recommended for the establishment of MPAs in the GRSMPA. On the other hand, some of these smaller, entrepreneurial MPAs will achieve their potential, mature more quickly than large MPAs, help develop local capacity, and provide some of the success stories and lessons in MPA management needed to make the goal of increased marine and coastal area protection a reality.

References

Agardy, M. T. 1990. "Integrating Tourism in Multiple Use Planning for Coastal and Marine Protected Areas." Woods Hole, Mass.

Alcala, A. 1995. "Protective Management of Small Coral Reef Areas." In Final Report, the International Coral Reef Initiative Workshop, Dumaguete City, Philippines.

Colwell, S. D. 1995. "Ecotourism, Scuba Diving and Coral Reefs." In Final Report, the International Coral Reef Initiative Workshop, Dumaguete City, Philippines.

———. Forthcoming. "Entrepreneurial Conservation: Private Sector Management of Small-Scale, Coral Reef Marine Protected Areas." In Proceedings of the 8th Global Biodiversity Forum Workshop on Incentives, Private Sector Partnerships and the Marine and Coastal Environment. Montreal, Canada.

Eichbaum, W. M., M. P Crosby, M. T. Agardy, and S. A. Laskin. 1996. "The Role of Marine and Coastal Protected Areas in the Conservation and Sustainable Use of Biological Diversity." *Oceanography* 9, 1: 60–70.

Jameson, S. C., J. W. McManus, and M. D. Spalding. 1995. "State of the Reefs: Regional and Global Perspectives." International Coral Reef Initiative Executive Secretariat Background Paper. Washington, D.C.

Kelleher, G. G. 1996. "A Global Representative System of Marine Protected Areas." Marine and Coastal Workshop, IUCN World Conservation Congress, Montreal.

Kelleher, G. G., C. Bleakley, and S. Wells, eds. 1995. "A Global Representative System of Marine Protected Areas." The Great Barrier Reef Marine Park Authority, the World Bank. and the World Conservation Union (IUCN), Washington, D.C.

Kelleher, G. G., and R. A. Kenchington. 1991. "Guidelines for Establishing Marine Protected Areas." IUCN, Gland, Switzerland.

Kenchington, R. A., and B. E. T. Hudson, eds. 1991. *Coral Reef Management Handbook.* Jakarta, Indonesia: UNESCO.

Roberts, C. M. 1994. "Marine Reserves: A Brief Guide for Decision Makers and Users." UN Global Conference on Sustainable

Development of Small Island Developing States, Barbados.

Sobel, J. 1993. "Conserving biological diversity through Marine Protected Areas: A Global Challenge. *Oceanus* 36: 19–26.

White, A. T., L. Z. Hale, Y. Reynard, and L. Cortesi, eds. 1994. *Collaborative and Community-based Management of Coral Reefs: Lessons from Experience.* West Hartford, Conn.: Kumarian Press.

Various Factors in Coral Reef Protection in Jamaica and the Role of the South Coast Conservation Foundation

Peter Espeut
South Coast Conservation Foundation

In Jamaica, the main threat to coral reefs is nutrient pollution leading to eutrophication of nearshore waters. These nutrients are not generated within the marine space, but are land-based in origin: from sewage and agricultural and domestic runoff in the watersheds. Also, a significant amount of nutrient pollution can be traced either to ships that discharge near protected reefs or from sources upstream in the marine current. The second main threat to Jamaican coral reefs is sedimentation caused by soil erosion and deforestation in the watersheds above the reefs (an exogenous source). The reefs get buried in sediment, and even slight particle suspensions significantly reduce light for photosynthesis by the symbiotic algae inside the coral polyps.

The boundaries of marine protected areas or marine management areas do not usually contain enough of the watershed for the main threats to the health of coral reefs to be managed. Therefore, in my view, both approaches are inadequate for the problems coral reefs face in Jamaica. This is likely to be so elsewhere.

The whole watershed approach to coral management (and marine management in general) is to be preferred. In islands, especially small islands, this approach is quite feasible, and is being tried in Jamaica and elsewhere. In larger islands and continental systems, this may be unworkable, as the watersheds are too extensive to be included in marine protected areas. In these cases, efforts need to be made to reduce nutrient discharge throughout the large river-

systems, possibly through a system of riverine protected areas.

The third major threat to coral in Jamaica comes from overfishing and destructive fishing practices, which must be distinguished, although they are related. Jamaican waters are the most overfished in the Caribbean because fishing effort—in terms of number of fish, number of boats, number of traps, and mesh size—is just too high. Practices that were innocuous in earlier years, with smaller numbers of fishers, led to overexploitation of fish resources when the number of fishers increased. Layoffs in the private and public sector over the last 30 years have led to significant increases in fishing pressure, as displaced workers invest their severance pay in fishing boats and equipment. Clearly, alternatives to fishing have to be identified. There has been little success in this direction, as the Jamaican economy has been under pressure and few efforts at diversification have been competitive.

In Jamaica, destructive fishing practices such as dynamiting and drag netting (such as beach seines and trawl nets) contribute to overfishing, but they also destroy habitats, reducing the total capacity of the system to produce, and these practices result in declines in total catch over time.

It is now a cliché that coral reef management is not the management of corals, but of the actions of people. The people whose actions have a negative impact on coral reefs may be near the reefs in the marine space or they may be miles away in a forest or on a farm. Some culturally acceptable framework must be found within which human impacts on marine resources, including coral reefs, can be managed.

The government of Jamaica, through the natural Resources Conservation Authority (NRCA), intends to declare 15 parks and protected areas on land and sea by the end of the decade. The NRCA does not intend to manage any of these, but will delegate the management to non-governmental organizations (NGOs) and community-based organizations (CBOs). The NRCA has already begun doing so, delegating the management of the Montego Bay Marine Park to the Montego Bay Marine Park Trust, and the management of the Blue/John Crow Mountain National Park to the Jamaica Conservation and Development Trust.

The South Coast Conservation Foundation (SCCF) expects to be delegated the management of the Portland Bight Area—200 square miles of land and 550 square miles of marine space. It is a multi-use area, with two ports, eight fisheries landing sites, and several industrial entities, including two power installations, a feed mill, a bauxite-alumina plant, and two sugar estates. At the same time it contains Jamaica's largest remaining mangrove stands, the most important turtle nesting sites, many important coral reefs and sea grass beds, the last remaining iguanas, and more than 150 square miles of bird habitat. The waters in Portland Bight support about 4,000 fishers (about 25 percent of Jamaica's fishers). The protected area is named the Portland Bight Sustainable Development Area (PBSDA) and should be declared late in 1997; delegation should follow soon after.

The SCCF is an environment and development NGO dedicated to implementing the principle of co-management, where all stakeholders collaborate to set management policies and oversee their implementation and enforcement. The intention is that the PBSDA should be managed through a series of resource management councils, each consisting of representatives of the stakeholders in that resource.

One such entity, the Portland Bight Fisheries Management Council (PBFMC), is already in existence. It had its first meeting on Petitions Day (June 29) 1997, and has met monthly ever

Table 1. Membership of the PBFMC

Type		Total
Eight artisanal fisher organizations	(2 each)	16
Two fisher cooperatives	(1 each)	2
The umbrella group of fishers' co-ops		2
Two sportfishing organizations	(1 each)	2
The NRCA		1
The government Fisheries Department		1
The government Port Authority		1
The government Infrastructure Development Agency		1
The government Co-operative Development Agency		1
The Jamaica Coast Guard		1
The Jamaica police		2
The SCCF		2

since. It has 32 members representing all of the stakeholders in the fisheries, as given in table 1.

The membership agrees that the present composition adequately represents the stakeholders in the fishery.

Over the last two years, the PBFMC has agreed on a set of fisheries management regulations (with penalties for breaches) to apply within the PBSDA. These are currently before its member organizations for ratification. After consensus has been reached, the final draft will be sent to the Minister of the Environment for signing into law. The proposed penalties include a ban on drag nets, minimum mesh sizes for nets and traps, a series of eight fish sanctuaries, a ban on the use of scuba and *hookah* gear for fishing, and a system of limited entry of new fishers into the PBSDA.

Several conflicts between resource users within Portland Bight have been resolved in the PBSDA. Most notable has been the damage to seven fishers' nets by a tug and barge carrying fuel from the oil refinery in Kingston to one of the power plants in Portland Bight. The council was able to obtain redress from the petroleum company for the fishers.

The PBSDA is currently preparing regulations for the management of the coral reefs, turtles, manatees, and coral cays within the PBSDA. It is also making preparations for implementing the fisheries management regulations it has drafted.

For the first few years, the PBSDA will not be financially self-sufficient, as capital expenditures, it is hoped, will be funded through grants. The plans for sustained funding of the PBSDA in terms of recurrent expenditure include user fees (approximately 10 percent of total recurrent budget), nature tourism (30 percent), merchandizing (30 percent), and the income from a trust fund (30 percent) that has been established.

The nature tourism efforts will include an ecoheritage trail, two mangrove tours, a salt marsh tour, two bird-watching walks of differing difficulty, snorkeling tours, picnics on the coral cays, and tours of the sugar estate. This is a major part of the SCCF development program in the PBSDA, as it not only will provide revenue for management but will also provide employment for local people, which will contribute to raising the standard of living of the community (which is quite low, on average).

This cutting-edge effort needs to be supported financially and with technical advice, and must be continually evaluated. Possibly the World Bank might be interested in helping.

GREEN GLOBE: The Tourism Industry and Sustainability

Carolyn Hill
GREEN GLOBE Americas, World Travel & Tourism Council

As concluded at the Earth Summit in Rio, sustainable development is the global priority, and all parts of society—governmental, intergovernmental, nongovernmental, private, and public—are responsible for their actions regarding sustainability. The private sector, especially the travel and tourism industry, is an essential component of sustainable development.

There is no getting around the fact that tourism is huge. Already touted as the world's largest industry, tourism is expected to double over the next 10 to 15 years, moving nearly 1 billion international visitors per year and generating more than 100 million new jobs. The tourism industry:

- Profoundly influences the environment, especially through the use of resources, trading patterns, and marketing that creates consumer demand.
- Provides direct and indirect employment for 212 million people, one in every nine workers worldwide; by 2005 it is expected to provide nearly 340 million jobs.
- Is responsible for 10.9 percent of direct and indirect world gross domestic product (GDP), generating more than US$3.4 trillion of gross output.
- Generates up to 30 percent of investment, GDP, and jobs in tourism-dependent regions like the Caribbean.
- Accounts for 11.4 percent of all consumer spending.

- Will continue to be a dominant development force in the 21st century.

Local communities and countries with few other comparative industrial advantages look to tourism as the source of foreign revenue. Private sector resources for development far outweigh other financial flows into developing countries (for example, over US$260 billion flowed from Organisation for Economic Co-operation and Development economies to developing countries in 1995, compared with US$56 billion in official development assistance).

Because of its size and scope, the tourism industry faces inherent environmental challenges, such as:

- It is resource intensive and congestive.
- It has effects on local populations.
- It depends on infrastructure whose development is often out of the tourism industry's hands.
- Tourists increasingly venture into formerly remote regions and fragile ecosystems.
- Tourism's greatest impact is felt in marine and coastal environments—already at risk from disproportionately high urban sprawl, nonsustainable consumptive patterns, industrial and chemical wastes and pollution, and extractive industries such as offshore oil and gas, sand mining, and fisheries.

Humans need water, and this is reflected in tourism patterns. For example:

- Cruise ship tourism is the fastest-growing part of the industry.

- Island destinations receive the most tourist arrivals (for example, the Caribbean, the Pacific, the Indian Ocean, the Mediterranean, and the Atlantic). The Coral Reef Alliance tells us that:
  - One hundred thousand divers visit the Caymans per year, and "Stingray City" generates US$1 million per year.
  - Three thousand retail dive centers train over 800,000 scuba divers each year.
  - Divers spend approximately $1.8 billion dollars in the Caribbean each year.
- GREEN GLOBE figures show that:
  - Four million visitors take part each year in whale watching in the USA and Canada, 375,000 in Australia and New Zealand.
  - In Europe over 200,000 whale-watching holidays are sold each year, and 150,000 people visit Ireland each year to watch dolphins.
- And the World Conservation Union (IUCN) tells us that the majority of resort-based tourism concentrates around marine and coastal environments, and is booming in Asia.

Beaches are the primary destination for 30 percent of Costa Rica's and 37 percent of Mexico's visitors. The Galapagos Islands are the major tourist attraction in Ecuador; the seaside is the most popular destination for holiday travelers in the United Kingdom; and many big city tourism destinations are coastal, such as Sydney, San Francisco, Miami, and New York.

The sheer numbers of tourists create a major socioeconomic phenomenon in coastal destinations. For example, 100 million visitors join the 170 million Caribbean residents each year; 100 million vacationers summer along with the Mediterranean's 230 million coastal inhabitants. We have already begun to witness the destruction caused by unregulated and excessive tourism:

- Beaches are being closed because of toxic effluent from hotels and resorts (the Surfrider Foundation says that 3,500 beaches were closed in 1995 because of pollution and toxicity levels that made it dangerous to swim).
- Marine life is being destroyed by boats and souvenir hunters.
- Development runs unregulated and unchecked in many parts of the world.
- Indigenous cultures are struggling to maintain their identities and integrity, and national parks are being trampled to oblivion.

The tourism industry has not always been sensitive to its impact on the environment. It has really only been since the Rio Earth Summit in 1992 that the industry has acknowledged the fact that a clean, healthy environment is the core of its business, and that the tourism industry plays a unique and leading role in sustainable development and the implementation of Agenda 21.

The World Travel & Tourism Council, a global coalition of industry chief executives, is committed to sustainable tourism as one of the four principal tenets of its Millennium Vision. The mechanisms that WTTC has developed to bring the sustainable tourism vision into reality are:

- The Agenda 21 for the Travel and Tourism Industry
- Eco-Nett, the European Community Network for environmental travel and tourism
- GREEN GLOBE, a systematic, comprehensive, environmental management program for companies and destinations.

As demonstrated by the actions outlined above, the tourism industry is taking on more responsibility for safeguarding natural, cultural, and historical heritage while at the same time contributing to economic growth and development. Innovative environment and tourism programs such as GREEN GLOBE are springing up in many countries. While GREEN GLOBE is certainly not the only environmental initiative in the travel and tourism industry, it is the only program that:

- Provides a systematic approach to improving environmental practices for companies of any size, in any sector
- Offers a comprehensive destination management program
- Demonstrates the tourism industry's commitment to the environment through a universal brand that is central to public awareness

- Supports existing ad hoc environmental programs and efforts.

GREEN GLOBE is a vehicle through which the travel and tourism industry can move toward sustainability. However, GREEN GLOBE faces great challenges, many of which reflect the challenges faced by other sectors. To move toward a new paradigm of sustainability requires:

- Appropriate and enlightened policy and regulation.
- Open communication and dialogue between all sectors.
- Education at all levels.
- Financial support and incentives from, and for, all sectors.
- Development of partnerships and alliances, particularly among sectors and industries that have not previously collaborated.
- A change in attitude:
  - Take responsibility for our individual actions.
- Be willing to go "out of the box."
- Exchange of technologies, information, and resources.
- Internationally accepted standards or criteria. (GREEN GLOBE has recently formalized a partnership with SGS / ISO 14000, the world's largest independent certification and accreditation firm. GREEN GLOBE and SGS have recently established environmental criteria for the tourism industry, and SGS will take the responsibility of certifying and monitoring.

GREEN GLOBE Members and Destinations

The World Travel & Tourism Council is committed to overcoming these challenges, and move the tourism industry toward sustainability as part of its Millennium Vision. We welcome ideas and support from our global partners in all sectors in order to achieve this goal.

Environmental Responsibility and Tourism on Tropical Islands

Richard C. Murphy
Jean-Michel Cousteau Institute

The diving industry in many tropical areas has made great strides in protecting coral reefs by creating boat moorings, banning spearfishing, and educating divers about coral reef protection. Comparable advances have not been made in the development and operation of resorts and other coastal facilities. Energy and water conservation programs are seldom employed. When sewage is treated, very little attention is given to reducing the resultant nutrient impact on reefs. Recycling and waste management programs are rarely implemented, and pesticides and other toxic products are commonly used. On a broader scale, mangroves are often cut; coastlines are altered, increasing suspended sediment loads; landscape biodiversity is reduced; and local food self-sufficiency is seldom considered.

In light of the many ecological connections between the terrestrial and marine environments, it is obvious that effective protection and management of coral reefs must address these on-land issues.

An Experiment in Responsible Development

The Jean-Michel Cousteau Fiji Islands Resort comprises 20 individual housing units, called bures, a restaurant/bar, conference area, and dive operation. The resort is located at the end of a peninsula on the island of Vanua Levu in the Fiji Islands. On the seaward side of this peninsula is a fringing reef and inside the bay are patch reefs of varying sizes.

In attempting to minimize the impact of the resort on the environment, I have used the metaphor of a coral reef's functional characteristics to guide the environmental systems we have implemented. A reef ecosystem runs on solar power, without the luxury of stored energy reserves. The reef is relatively efficient in the utilization of essential materials, such as nutrients, recycling at both the micro level (corals-zooxanthellae) and at the macro level (detritivore and bacterial remineralization of organic matter). Biodiversity is important where a greater variety of species provide alternate and redundant ecological functions. And finally, ecological connections between diverse species contribute to an integrated, and presumably sustainable, whole.

Energy

The resort uses the sun's energy to heat water. We have no air conditioning and have installed thatched roofs that breathe, high ceilings, and louvered walls. The shade provided by natural vegetation also helps to cool the air. Although we currently utilize inexpensive city power, an evaluation of diesel generator versus photovoltaics has proved that photovoltaic power has advantages because the true cost of diesel power generation was three times the cost of the diesel itself. This added cost was due to maintenance expenses, generator replacement, fuel transport charges, and cleanup costs from unavoidable spills.

Efficiency and Recycling

By the end of the year, the resort will be using constructed wetlands to treat our wastewater. We are doing this for the following reasons:

- To treat sewage
- To reduce nutrient leaching onto the reef
- To provide nutrient-rich water for irrigating the landscape and fruit trees.

We compost, or use for animal food, 80 percent of our garbage, recycle paper and metal, and have reduced packaging materials and containers previously destined for a dump by 70 percent. Our initial attempts at recycling were quite a challenge because the volume of wastepaper was so small that the recycling company, which is located on another island, was unwilling to work with us. This has been resolved by encouraging other resorts and businesses in the local town to combine wastepaper. This effort has not only solved our problem but has also stimulated community-wide interest in recycling, which had not existed before.

Biodiversity

We have designed a functional landscape where diversity is not only aesthetically appealing, but productive as well. Our "edible landscaping" provides fruit for the kitchen, flowers for decorating guest rooms, (which also attract pollinators for the nearby gardens), shade for cooling, and a more diverse habitat to attract a variety of birds and insects, which serve as pest predators.

Integrated Systems

Pesticide use has been reduced by 90 percent through an integrated pest management system. In addition to the benefits from a greater diversity of pest predators, breeding habitats for mosquitoes have been reduced. We have converted temporary puddles, which were the major breeding grounds for mosquitoes, into permanent ponds and have filled the ponds with indigenous biota from local streams. Simply altering this hydrological feature and creating a more ecologically complex ecosystem has reduced the number of larvae by a factor of 50. We have also eliminated other breeding sites by cleaning up discarded containers, cutting up open coconuts, and filling tree stumps where water stands. Finally, we introduced mosquito parasitoids, which are selective predators on mosquito larvae only.

The previous owners of this property had cut almost all the mangroves and then, some years later when the ecological function of the mangroves was lost, were faced with severe shoreline erosion. Today, we solicit the help of our guests to bring back seedlings during organized nature tours to intact mangrove systems. We now have over 90 mangrove trees in various stages of growth. As soon as they begin to stabilize the erosion problem, we will be able to remove the existing unsightly cement barriers.

The fruits and some vegetables of our edible landscaping are irrigated with recycled water, enabling us to make use of what would otherwise be a pollutant. In this way nutrients, in the food served to guests, pass through them and into the sewage, which is then treated, enabling the nutrients or fertilizer to be returned to the plants to begin another cycle.

The resort does not exist alone in the region and cooperates with the local human community as much as it is integrated into the adjacent ecological communities. Our staff biologist organizes programs with local schools, which bring classes to the resort on field trips twice each month. We offer slide shows, guide them through our educational CD-ROM on coral reefs, host beach or mangrove walks, or present a live audiovisual dive adventure. The uplink program involves a diver and videographer on the reef, outfitted with a communications system that enables the divers to speak and hear and transmit images to an audience in the resort's lounge. Through a walkie-talkie, the audience can communicate with the divers. This live, two-way communication system has proved an extremely effective way to share the wonders of the reef with our nondiving guests and local school groups. In addition, our biologist regularly visits schools, villages, and town council meetings to discuss local coral reef issues.

This outreach effort has been critical in establishing a local marine reserve. We also monitor the reefs, participating in Reef Check, the Global Coral Reef Monitoring Network, and ICLARM's Global Database. Many of our more experienced divers have responded well to the ICLARM program, and it serves as an important focal point for discussions on reef ecology and management.

The Jean-Michel Cousteau Fiji Islands Resort has hosted a few scientists, and we are building a small dormitory and wet and dry lab for students and researchers to study our reefs. Our most recent guests included a team from Australia and the United States, which took core samples from large Porites colonies to measure carbon and oxygen isotopes as indicators of temperature and salinity, which are indicative of past climatic conditions. Select corals were stained for future sampling to provide data on contemporary climate change.

Although the resort, like any other, is dedicated to recreation and relaxation, we have infused all our activities with an educational or environmental message. Critical to this has been our on-site staff biologist, who not only provides the guests with an interpretation of the natural environment but also ensures that they understand the resort is trying to operate in the most environmentally sound manner possible. We emphasize our use of the free services of nature as a means of saving money and integrating ourselves with the natural environment: "Terrestrial vegetation and mangroves are living machines which provide shade for cooling and coastal protection. Edible landscaping gives us a pleasing environment as well as food. Constructed wetlands convert waste into a resource (nutrient rich water for irrigation) and minimize nutrient impact on the reef. Biodiversity and integrated pest management help us control mosquitoes without toxic chemicals."

We hope this modest experiment in what I call "applied ecology" will serve as a model whereby others can learn from our successes and avoid our mistakes in developing their own environmental programs.

Discussion

Bob Johannes, R.E. Johannes Pty LTD: I have been studying spawning aggregations of reef fish for some years, and recently, I and a group of colleagues have been studying grouper spawning aggregations in Palau. During those studies I have scoured the literature, and to my great amazement, although one reads in virtually every review on the value of marine protected areas in the tropics that the primary value is the protection of spawning stock biomass—that phrase is used over and over again—I find virtually no evidence outside the Caribbean and Bermuda, and even there on a limited extent, that people who are designing marine protected areas are paying any attention whatsoever to the existence of spawning aggregation sites.

Now for those of you who are not aware, let me explain briefly what they are: A great many reef fish, particularly larger ones over about 25 centimeters aggregate at very specific locations and times—times in terms of moon phase and in terms of season—in order to spawn. In Palau, the three groupers that we studied (the three most important [commercially] there) all spawned (aggregated in large numbers to spawn) at the same locations, the same moon phases, and in overlapping seasons. Moreover, we observed during our studies the spawning of more than 50 other species of fish there. Now some of those fish spawn in small numbers all along the reef, and they just happen to be there; but others, including the most important single species of food fish in Palau, spawned there by

the thousands and several other important food fish did also. The point I'm making is that there are certain locations where a lot of different reef fish spawn—often at the same season, and fishermen have capitalized on this fact for centuries in some cases. There's a lot to capitalize on for managers and researchers, and yet rather few of us have done so. And I think it's most unfortunate that particularly from the Indo Pacific there is virtually no evidence, except in Palau—and maybe one case I can think of in the Philippines—that anybody's paid any attention to this phenomenon. Particularly since there are predictable places where it occurs. Because a lot of important fish choose these same spots, to pay no attention to them when you're designing marine reserves—drawing the boundaries doesn't make much sense to me, and since this kind of information I'm giving you has, in fact, been in the literature for over a decade, I'm [inaudible] when it suddenly occurs to me that nobody has been paying attention to it.

Richard Kenchington: I'd like to take that one up—I applauded Bob's comment about data-free management this morning, and one of the things that we did with advice from Bob was to zone a couple of reefs [inaudible] on the basis of their anecdotal spawning site importance. Judging by the squeals we had from the fishermen, I suspect that we hit the right target. The problem, of course, is one of enforcement. My overall summary on that is that it does seem to take now about 20 years to get a human generation of attitude change. We are now getting fishing industry people, particularly the younger ones, saying that they want this sort of thing to happen. Twenty years ago they would have killed us over the exercise.

Herman Cesar, World Bank: I'd like to ask a question of self-financing marine parks. It seems that if Callum is right—that it takes three to five years before you actually see the real increase in fish yields in the surrounding areas—you have a real management problem in actually starting with it in the sense that you need to give alternative income generation, or money, or whatever, to the fisherman in that specific time frame. So if you develop a project, you need to do something in that time frame. Your tourists won't come too soon because they like to come more when the bigger fish are there as well. So I'd like some of the speakers to give some ideas of how you want to address that intermediate period in which you have established the no-take zone, but the fisherman haven't benefited yet, and how do you take that and make the fisherman better off in the interim period so that they will agree to the no-take some in the first place?

Callum Roberts: It's a credit to fishermen in many parts of the world that they have gone along with the establishment of no-take reserves without having any form of compensation, other than the promises of managers and scientists that things will get better sometime down the line. Now I think that the only reason why they've been willing to do this is because they can very much relate to that kind of management. They understand that if you do protect things then they can reproduce and that reproductive output will somehow benefit them through increased catches down the line. There are very few cases that I know of where people have done a process of compensating fisherman to begin with in reserve creation. I think that where there is not the obvious contrast between those who are getting much, much better off very quickly from tourism and those who are suffering as fisherman. Fishermen are used to

suffering—they have done it a long time—then you don't find that increase in social conflict that I talked about in St. Lucia to such an extent. The trouble is that throughout large areas of the world, there is now tourism and impoverished fisherman very close together. That's when I think compensation programs will prove to be a mechanism of getting people over that hump. In other cases, such as parts of the Philippines where they've been establishing these no-take areas, there are other ways of motivating a community to tighten their belt even more over that short-term hump than compensation, and I can't give you any new answers of how to compensate.

Jan Post: I think that's really the big question—is how to compensate the fishers for the benefits forgone for not fishing. It's not so much a matter of money. Studies have shown that the willingness to pay in the ecotourism business is tremendous, and probably from an economic point of view, a live grouper on a reef in the Caribbean is worth a lot more than on somebody's plate. It's a matter of how we make this mechanism work, and we're actually working in the World Bank to try and solve this problem.

Teri Marsh, NOAA/National Marine Fisheries Service: I have a question for Juan Bezaury. We've heard from some of the other panelists concerns that we're not good at ecosystem conservation—we need to learn from our successes and our failures in certain other marine protected areas. There are a number of paper parks given lack of effective management and the importance of the connection between the land and the sea. I'm wondering about the Great Meso-American Reef Initiative. It seems like it could be a very exciting proposal, and if you could just comment on your perspective of its potential for addressing those concerns and being a successful, and maybe self-financing, marine park?

Juan Bezaury: The idea behind this initiative is to have a globally important ecosystem—large enough to be globally important, but small enough to be manageable—and to try to manage it. This is using the coral reef as the charismatic microfauna as a pretext for this because you can't protect coral reefs by themselves. Coral reefs are part of the coastal system, so you are speaking about an integrated coastal management project for the four-country region. That might sound like much, but it's no more than 800 to 1,000 kilometers long. So the whole idea is to get the region to cooperate in doing this. For instance, Guatemala has almost no reef, but they play a very important part in this system since they are the largest watershed—it's in the Montagua system. So if you don't take them into account, they might not have reefs, but Belizian reefs will suffer from the stress created in this watershed. So the whole idea is to get a large ecosystem, but small enough to prove that cooperation can manage. On the other side we have the advantage of a low population, and a lot of tourist potential. So I think the table is set for a project that can show success. And one of the things you have in demonstrating the project is to show success so that others can take the lessons learned from that project.

Sandy Zicus, Consultant: I'm a science and environmental education consultant. I'm not sure if there is an answer to this question, but as I'm listening to people talking, and I'm hearing about alternative ways of making a living—cutting down on the fishing and increasing tourism and bringing in more money that way, or shifting the reef fishing to the pelagic fishing, it seems like we're ignoring the fact that we've still got the basic problem that people need to eat. We're not lowering the number of people, we're not lowering the amount of food that needs to be produced and consumed. So I'm just wondering if you have any ideas on this; it's one thing to say we can shift it from here to there, but are we going to be overfishing the pelagic areas? If people are going to be earning their money through tourism rather than fishing, they're going to have to purchase food from somewhere, and where is that going to come from?

Callum Roberts: What shifting fisheries from one sector can do —for example, the inshore reef fisheries to off-shore plastic fisheries, such as

putting in fish aggregating devices—is to buy a little time to get you over that period where setting up no-take zones is providing you with no net benefit. In fact, you're into losses. So if there are alternative areas which are not being exploited in a place, then it can buy you the necessary time to get over the most difficult time just after [no-take zone] establishment. So there is a good reason for trying to exploit different parts of the fisheries sector in places where they're not exported to any great extent.

Jeremy Woodley, University of the West Indies: I wanted to mention a small example of another way to compensate fisherman in the establishment of a protected area. An example from Discovery Bay in Jamaica, where the protected area is a fisheries reserve with little potential for tourism. But thanks to the generosity of a local industry, there is funding to support the establishment of this reserve, and fishermen and relatives of the fisherman are employed in patrolling the site.

John McManus, ICLARM: I'm following up something that Steve Colwell brought up, which was the idea of looking for resorts and so forth that have a stake in an area, and helping them. I think that's an excellent idea, but it may be more excellent than people think, because what that means is you have a wonderful opportunity to start turning around some of the attitudes of the tourist resort owners. In crowded coastal areas, where you have a tourist operation, and where you set up a marine protected area, you're creating a resource conflict. A crowded coastal area generally has full use of its resources. People fish everywhere that there are fish and it is worthwhile fishing. And those places that are worthwhile fishing are generally the places you want tourists to go. It's also the places where you want to put in the marine protected area. So the resort owners have to be turning some of the profit back to the village somehow, and there's a number of mechanisms to do this. And if there's a marine protected area that goes in, and if there's going to be any successful, peaceful way of maintaining it with respect to the village, the village has to have decided to put it in, not a resort owner. The other problem with the tourist resorts, in general, is that if they're right next to the coral, very, very few tourist resorts have any sewage processing. The idea of the septic tank has spread throughout the world. The idea of emptying the septic tank has not. And so after a year or two, most resorts will be directly polluting their coral reef—the coral will turn green. And most resort owners don't seem to understand this. So we do find the occasional opportunity that when resort owners says, "Well, how can I fix my reef?" The first thing we say is, "Well, it's going to die anyway if you don't do something about this, and you're going to always have trouble with people poaching and so forth, because you put in the reserve as opposed to the villagers." I know Steve has thought about this, perhaps he has some other ideas?

Stephen Colwell: You're absolutely right, John, there's no way to go through and have it be imposed by a resort, and I wouldn't propose that. But where you have people like Richard Kenchington, sitting to my left, and a number of other people have looked at—what are the essential qualities of good MPAs? In a number of cases you can find those characteristics in an area where you have tourist resorts. It doesn't mean there isn't a conflict—you're right, there will be. But if you can use the basic criteria to look at how you would manage it, and you can use the existing capacity, you have a much better chance of creating something successful— because it's market-driven. We could go out and set up as many MPAs as we want, but unless there is a funding mechanism, they're going nowhere, and that's been proven all over the world. So I don't at all propose that as the overall solution, but in certain cases where you do have a sustainable market, and you can enforce the kind of things you're talking about, such as treatment of sewage, it's an alternative that will work. One of the things that wasn't discussed here that's very important is the IUCN/World Bank/Great Barrier Reef Marine Park Authority initiative on the Global Representative System of Marine Protected Areas, and we don't have time to discuss it here, but that's another network where people working together can share ideas and, I think, can hopefully create more of these successful things in different parks.

Summary: Jan Post: Our task ahead is daunting, to say the least, and not even unique to the marine environment. I'm an ecologist and I also follow the terrestrial debate. Most of the issues in the terrestrial biodiversity preservation initiatives are the same as here. We've talked about this for the last 40-45 years or so. I think what we should try to do here, and the next stage in this process, is the breakout session, and to limit ourselves— not forgetting that there's much more to the issue—limit ourselves to a few main themes, and come up with recommendations. And I invite all of you to have your input tomorrow afternoon to try and come up with something that is really useful and practically implementable. It has really amazed me here in this institution—in the World Bank— that often, money is not the issue. Money is around. Money is around for conservation, and money is around, lately, for marine conservation in much larger quantities, because there is a real focus now on marine conservation—people are waking up. It's just a matter of writing it up into something that the higher-ups can deal with, which fits within a bureaucratic structure, and is understandable to the layman. And that will probably be our biggest challenge for the next day. Thank you.

PANEL FOUR

MARINE INFORMATION AND EDUCATION

Session Chair: Marea E. Hatziolos, World Bank

ReefBase: Status and Plans

J. W. McManus
International Center for Living Aquatic Resources Management (ICLARM)

ReefBase is a global database on coral reefs and their resources that serves as the official database of the Global Coral Reef Monitoring Network. It is a joint project of the International Center for Living Aquatic Resources (ICLARM), the World Conservation Monitoring Centre (WCMC), and the University of Rhode Island. Its major activities are the extraction of data from existing publications and the production of standardized digital maps of the world's coral reefs. Increasingly, ReefBase has become a host system for data from prior and ongoing field data collection activities. Objectives include the investigation, definition, and analysis of coral reef ecosystem health at global, regional, and national levels. The ReefBase Aquanaut System involves training scuba divers to collect ecological information about coral reef health through an international certification system. The Rapid Assessment of Management Parameters (RAMP) system is an integration of field protocol and database structure aimed at social, cultural, and economic analyses relevant to coral reef uses. Ongoing ReefBase activities include the estimation of coral reef fish harvest and coral reef area and, in collaboration with the World Resources Institute, the determination of probable levels of reef degradation by country. ReefBase is released annually on CD-ROM. The current version, ReefBase 2.0, has information on over 7,000 coral reefs and serves as a vital tool for facilitating coral reef management at all scales.

Background

It is widely believed that many, if not most, of the coral reefs of the world are in various states of degradation (UNEP/IUCN 1988, Wilkinson 1992, Ginsburg 1994, Jameson and others 1995, Maragos and others 1996, Eakin and others 1997). This decline in the quality of reef resources has serious consequences for tens of millions of dependent people, particularly those who fish on coral reefs (McManus 1996, 1997). However, it has been difficult to assess the extent of the degradation and its effects with any reasonable degree of certainty. Indeed, even the locations and global coverage of coral reefs are poorly known (Pennisi 1997). Recent debates on the global warming issue have clearly demonstrated that effective, long-term action on the part of the governments and intergovernmental bodies of the world must be based on high-quality scientific evidence and analysis (see Knowlton, these proceedings, pp. 183–87).

The development and implementation of management strategies for specific reefs has often been inhibited by the difficulty of gaining access to relevant information. Most coral reefs are in developing countries, and most of the policymakers and managers tasked with protecting coral reefs have little access to major coral reef publications because of a paucity of reasonable libraries in these countries. In cases where useful biophysical and socioeconomic information has been gathered for a particular reef, this information has often deteriorated in filing cabinets, been lost on unreadable computer media, or been reported in publications with little or no distribution in the countries from which the data originated.

ReefBase is a project for which a primary objective is to consolidate and distribute information on the coral reefs of the world through a user-friendly database to a wide audience. It directly addresses the need for information on the status of coral reefs and their dependent peoples, and facilitates coral reef management at local, national, regional, and global scales.

History

The idea for ReefBase was a response in 1988 to requests from the media for information on the global status of coral reefs (McManus and Ablan 1996, 1997). While very useful and relatively well substantiated information existed for rates of loss of the world's rain forests, no such information was available for coral reefs. In 1992, ReefBase was a priority topic in an international workshop on coral reef research needs held at the Australian Institute of Marine Science (Munro and Munro 1994, Froese 1994). The project was initiated with two years of funding from the European Commission beginning in late 1993. It involved ICLARM in database design and implementation, and the World Conservation Monitoring Centre in digitizing maps of coral reefs from around the world. Initial planning efforts included international workshops in the United Kingdom and Luxembourg, and a planning meeting on socioeconomic aspects at the University of Rhode Island in 1994.

By early 1995, the database had progressed enough to produce major inputs for the "State of the Reefs Report" (Jameson and others 1995). These included maps showing the locations of most of the shallow reefs of the world, and several point maps illustrating the distributions of major sources of reef degradation, including blast fishing, cyanide fishing, coral bleaching, sedimentation, and pollution. The report served as the background document for the global workshop of the International Coral Reef Initiative (ICRI) held in the Philippines in mid-1995.

The ICRI resulted in a "Framework for Action," which was endorsed by acclamation initially by representatives of 39 countries, and later through regional workshops by at least 85 countries. Others involved in the development of the framework included the World Conservation Union (IUCN) and major funding agencies such as the World Bank and the Asian Development Bank. Among the priority actions called for in the framework were the strengthening of efforts to provide for the dissemination of information to facilitate reef management.

ReefBase 1.0 was released in mid-1996 (McManus and Ablan 1996), and was followed a year later by ReefBase 2.0 (McManus and Ablan 1997).

Coverage

ReefBase 2.0 contains information on over 7,000 coral reefs, including ecological information on corals and fish communities for 2,700 reefs, coral reef fisheries and mariculture activities for 2,500 reefs, reports of stresses affecting 2,000 reefs, dive tourism information for 850 reefs, and descriptions of management practices and legislation for 500 marine protected areas. The 196 standard digital maps from the WCMC maps include most of the charted reefs of the world in global, regional, and subregional maps, and many selected reefs in detail. Linked to particular coral reef records are 883 aerial, underwater, and terrestrial photographs of reefs, showing their uses and misuses. Indexes include information on over 1,600 coral reef experts, monitoring programs, and institutions involved in coral reef research. A dictionary defines 191 terms related to coral reef studies. The reference section includes over 6,500 references on coral reefs from conference proceedings, technical reports, and informal articles.

Nearly half of the structure of the database is devoted to the Rapid Assessment of Parameters (RAMP) system. The RAMP system was developed to provide an integrated system for the collection, storage, and retrieval of information on the cultural, sociological, legal, and economic factors affecting people associated with coral reefs. The system was designed primarily by Dr. Richard Pollnac of the University of Rhode Island. The variables are linked in a hierarchical system and chosen so as to facilitate multivariate analyses of factors relevant to management decisions regarding the reefs.

Because charted reefs tend to be those that represent hazards to navigation, they generally omit the large areas of coralline ecosystem existing below 10 meters depth scattered across the shelves and subsurface sea mounts of the tropics. In order to estimate the extent and location of these areas, Dr. Joanie Kleypas of the National Center for Atmospheric Research determined where reef corals were likely to grow around the world, based on a variety of environmental parameters (Kleypas 1995, 1997). One of the resulting REEFHAB maps (the most conservative) is available in ReefBase 2.0 as a global map into which the user can zoom for greater detail.

The ECOPATH system is a standardized approach to ecosystem modeling that permits the calculation of a wide range of useful ecosystem parameters and facilitates meta-analytical studies leading to generalizations about ecosystem structure and dynamics. At least five coral reefs around the world have been modeled using the system. The current version of the model, ECOPATH 3.0, is included on the ReefBase CD-ROM as a tool for coral reef researchers. Included as well are the parameters to allow the researcher to reconstruct and experiment with each of the published ECOPATH models of coral reefs.

Distribution

Approximately 500 copies of the ReefBase CD-ROM are distributed each year. About half of these are donated to developing country research institutions, and the others are sold at cost. In addition to the CD-ROMs, several key tables from ReefBase have been made accessible through the Internet. More of the database will be put onto the Internet as software advances facilitate the conversion to Internet-compatible formats.

Facilitating Current Management

ReefBase is designed to make optimal use of the vast body of information that has been or is being gathered on coral reefs around the world. Needs addressed by ReefBase include data archaeology, archiving, repatriation, distribution, standardization, meta-analysis, and gap identification.

Data archaeology is the locating and reintroduction to science of data sets from previous research efforts. ReefBase provides a focal point for data archaeological efforts, including, for example, the digitization of data from mimeographed reports from the 1970s and earlier. All data in ReefBase are archived on CD-ROM. The reproduction in hundreds of copies and continual upgrading to new software and hardware requirements helps to ensure continued accessibility in terms of decades.

A major problem in past studies of coral reefs has been related to the fact that much of the research on reefs has been accomplished by expatriates. The resulting data and reports have often been relatively inaccessible to researchers from the developing country with jurisdiction over the reefs. ReefBase provides such researchers with access to this data in a very usable, quantitative, and standardized form. The combined distribution of data via CD-ROM and Internet far exceeds the original data distribution for most of the included studies, in which data were usually confined to a few diskettes, disk drives, computer tapes, and reports of very limited circulation.

Standardization is approached in two ways in ReefBase. First, researchers read through all reports, converting data into standard units wherever possible, while screening for probable reporting errors. In some cases, substantial data sets are recalculated from raw data. Second, ReefBase as a project is involved with the standardization of methodologies for collecting data. This activity was a response to numerous requests for guidance on what type of data ReefBase needed from people planning trips to coral reefs. This led to the development of the ReefBase Aquanaut Survey Method (McManus and others 1997) described below, and the

RAMP protocol described above. ReefBase personnel are routinely consulted by groups developing reef-sampling standards. The presence of the database tends to encourage the development and widespread acceptance of data-collecting standards. Standardization, the quantitative nature of the database, and features built into the system to produce data tables from user-friendly queries all contribute to the acquisition of information through meta-analysis. These features also facilitate the identification of critical data gaps and needs, thus providing a basis for prioritizing research efforts and preventing redundant research.

ReefBase has an "encyclopedic aspect," in which it provides information about individual reefs to those who would develop improved management strategies or conduct further research. In many cases, existing data on a reef are relatively inaccessible to reef managers. For example, a manager concerned that a recent construction project may be damaging a coral reef through siltation may not be aware of studies showing that high levels of silt from deforestation were present long before the construction project. ReefBase makes this type of information available, including quantitative data about the problem whenever possible. Without this information, managers must either commission new studies or base their decisions on inferences from factors such as the presence of deforested hillsides. In all such cases, the lack of access to prior studies limits understanding of trends over time, thereby lowering the certainty of management predictions. Where previous studies exist, ReefBase makes the data accessible to those who must evaluate trends affecting the reef as a basis for informed management. Because of the early stage of research on coral reef ecosystem health, analysis of trends in variables such as hard coral cover is often the only reliable indicator of the state of a given reef and of the need for corrective management action.

The "summary aspect" of ReefBase is equally important. The maps of reefs and of stresses affecting reefs produced by ReefBase for the "State of the Reefs" report (Jameson and others 1995) strongly influenced those developing the

Framework for Action of the International Coral Reef Initiative. The locations of reefs compiled and carefully verified in ReefBase provided a basis for the calibration of the REEFHAB model described above, which in turn plays a major role in discussions concerning the role of the oceans in global warming. ReefBase has provided information for recent reports summarizing the status of coral reefs (Maragos and others 1996, McManus 1997, Eakin and others 1997). These in turn provide a basis for the prioritization of funding for coral reef conservation.

Reef Ecosystem Health Studies

Ecological studies of coral reefs began prior to 1800, and became particularly prominent after the first publication of Charles Darwin's paradigmatic study on reefs (Darwin 1851). However, most coral reef research has been focused on basic concerns such as niche interactions and the description of general biogeochemical cycling. Applied and strategic research has focused principally on fisheries (Munro 1983, Johannes 1981, Munro and Williams 1985, Polunin and Roberts 1996, McManus 1997), and specific degradative problems such as sedimentation and organic pollution (Johannes 1975, Johannes and Hatcher 1986).

Recent concern about the global environment has led to the rise of the field of ecosystem health, which focuses specifically on the status of ecosystems with respect to human use and management (Rapport and others 1981, Costanza and others 1992). This field is concerned with managing ecosystems from a holistic, pragmatic view, analogous to that of modern medical practice. A good definition of a state of ecosystem health is "one whose parameters do not vary outside predetermined limits from a predetermined level within a given period of time" (Jakarta Mandate 1997).

The relevance of the holistic, health approach to the management of coral reefs can be seen in the recent debates concerning coral reef degradation in Jamaica. Hughes (1994) reported that coral cover in coral reefs of northern Jamaica had declined from mean values of greater than 50 percent to current values of less than 5 percent over the previous decade. This change was explained principally in terms of :

- The reduction of populations of herbivorous fish through overfishing
- The destructive effect of a hurricane
- The proliferation of macroalgae
- The subsequent proliferation of herbivorous sea urchins
- The rapid decline of sea urchin populations
- The dominance of reef substrate by macroalgae, which prevents the settlement of corals.

Some of the assumptions of the explanation were later challenged. In particular, some researchers have suggested that fisheries may have had less to do with the overgrowth by algae than organic pollution from the highly populated coastline of Jamaica (for example, Hodgson 1994, Ogden 1994). The general feasibility of the Hughes conclusions, as well as the alternative explanations, highlights the need for management-oriented studies of coral reefs to treat the system holistically. Thus, a coral reef ecosystem health approach is warranted.

The ecological components of ReefBase have been designed specifically to facilitate progress in coral reef ecosystem health by providing a basis for the identification of the predetermined levels and limits called for in the Jakarta Mandate. An example is the recent analysis of 205 well-studied reef slopes showing that 40 percent is a reasonable expected value for hard coral cover on reef slopes among a given (large) set of reefs (McManus and Ablan forthcoming). As data matrices in ReefBase are filled in over time, increasing efforts will be directed toward applying multivariate analysis to the development of functions relating variables to healthy versus degraded coral reefs. Ultimately, parsimonious sets of variables will be recommended for monitoring and use in the identification of reefs under stress, based on such functions. This will also greatly facilitate the development of corrective action plans, the evaluation of their effectiveness, and the implementation of adaptive management (McManus and others 1988).

The need for blocks of "solid" data (nonsparse matrices—those with more data than missing values) necessitates action beyond the passive activity of summarizing existing reports. Coral reef studies have involved researchers with substantially different objectives using a very wide variety of approaches. Data needed for reef health analyses should cover a limited range of variables and be gathered under a limited number of standards. Thus, ReefBase has been active in collaborating in the implementation of the Global Coral Reef Monitoring Network (GCRMN). It has also produced the ReefBase Aquanaut Method described above, which permits nonspecialists as well as scientists to gather data compatible with the standard methods of the GCRMN.

Current and Future Activities

The continual development of ReefBase involves the conduct of associated research projects designed to generate new information from a variety of data sources. Research associated with ReefBase 3.0 (to be distributed in July 1998) includes country-level estimates of coral reef fish production, coralline area, and coral reef degradation.

Past estimates of global, regional, and national fish production from coral reefs have generally been based on estimates of reef area multiplied by catch rates per unit of area (Munro and Thompson 1973, Smith 1978, Munro 1996). Fish statistics reported to and by the United Nations Food and Agriculture Organization (U.N. FAO) have often involved general categories, such as "grouper," which do not indicate the catch by species and give little other indication of the habitat source. ReefBase is currently weighting the reported categories by proportion expected from reefs, to arrive at estimates of coral reef fish production at global, regional, and national scales. A set of regional experts is reviewing the weightings and they are being adjusted as appropriate. The resulting estimates will be useful in a variety of policy decisions concerning fishery production and coral reef management.

The REEFHAB model described above provides estimates of reef area geographically around the world. However, the assignment of these coralline areas of the ocean shelf to individual countries requires analysis within the framework of the International Law of the Sea. This process is ongoing, and will result in estimations of reef area by country based on the predictions of the model and the estimation of shelf area of responsibility of each country.

A major objective of ReefBase is to provide a basis for the assessment of coral reef degradation by country and region. Doing so empirically requires very large amounts of data, because of the extreme variability of coral reefs and of the types of studies currently available to provide the data. Thus, reliable empirical predictions are expected to be possible only after a few more years of research (depending on levels of funding, the activity levels of the GCRMN and Aquanaut program, and other factors). However, the 2,000 reefs for which stresses have been reported do provide a basis for calibrating and refining models designed to determine the likelihood of stress problems on large scales. Thus ReefBase is collaborating with the World Resources Institute in the development of a global situation report based on factors such as distances from population centers, fishing pressure, likely levels of sedimentation, and other variables. The variables are interrelated in a Geographic Information System (GIS) and adjusted with respect to known stress reports. The procedure incorporates multiple consultations with regional and tropical experts.

The growth of the GCRMN is being accompanied by a rising concern for the establishment of regional and national databases. All aspects of ReefBase are provided in the public domain, including the structure and code. ReefBase makes these available to minimize the labor and cost involved in establishing new databases. Advice and training in database development are also available from ReefBase.

A recent effort within ReefBase is the development of a set of recommended standards for the processing of satellite imagery for inclusion in the database. With assistance from the government of the Netherlands, ReefBase is reviewing and testing existing analytical approaches for inclusion. The resulting product will incorporate the suggestions and contributions of a set of remote sensing experts from around the world.

Conclusions

ReefBase is far more than a traditional database. It is a set of research initiatives designed to facilitate the evaluation and management of coral reefs. It is an effective means of data archaeology, archiving, repatriating, standardizing, and distributing that facilitates a wide range of coral reef investigation, including meta-analysis across sets of coral reefs. More important, it is a physical end product of the efforts of coral reef scientists, managers, and users around the world that returns information in value-added form. This physical entity then serves as a rallying point for enhanced, targeted efforts in the conservation and management of coral reefs.

Note

This is ICLARM Contribution Number 1417.

Acknowledgments

I thank all those who have made ReefBase possible, in particular M. D. Spalding, L. A. B. Meñez, Jr., B. M. Vallejo, Jr., C. F. Cabote, M. C. A. Ablan, M. L. G. Gorospe, K. P. K. Reyes, S. G. Vergara, I. D. Uy, G. U. Coronado, M. L. D. Palomares, R. Pollnac, J. Kleypas, Z. N. Alojado, P. Ziegler, L. Halmarick, H. R. Montes, Jr., C. J. Cabalang, M. Edwards, C. Ravilious, J. Rhind, A. Lee, I. Wheeldon, A. Grenfell, S. Hirsh, J. Hughes, S. Frade, J. Rogers, M. Noordeloos, J. L. Munro, S. Wells, D. Pauly, R. Froese, M. J. Williams, P. Gardiner, and R. Luxmoore. ReefBase has been sponsored by the European Commission, Government of the Netherlands, U.S. Agency for International Development, the Swedish International Development Authority, and ICLARM Core Funds from various donors. Funding for the development of the ReefBase Aquanaut System was provided by the Winslow Foundation.

Bibliography

Costanza, R., B. G. Norton, and B. D. Haskell. 1992. *Ecosystem Health: New Goals for Environmental Management.* Washington, D.C.: Island Press.

Darwin, C. 1851. *Geological Observations on Coral Reefs, Volcanic Islands, and on South America.* London: Smith Elder and Company.

Eakin, C. M., J. W. McManus, M. D. Spalding, and S. C. Jameson. 1997. "Coral Reef Status around the World: Where Are We and Where Do We Go from Here?" *Proceedings of the Eighth International Coral Reef Symposium,* 1: 277-282.

Froese, R. 1994. "ReefBase: A Global Database of Coral Reef Systems and Their Resources." In: Munro, J. L, and P. E. Munro. 1994. (eds.), "The Management of Coral Reef Resource Systems." ICLARM Conference Proceedings. 44: 52-63.

Ginsburg, R. N. (compiler). 1994. "Proceedings of the Colloquium on Global Aspects of Coral Reefs: Health, Hazards, and History,. 1993." Rosenstiel School of Marine and Atmospheric Science, University of Miami.

Hodgson G. 1994. (letter). *Science* 266: 1930-1.

Hughes, T. 1994. "Catastrophes, Phase Shifts, and Large-Scale Degradation of a Caribbean Coral Reef." *Science* 265: 1547-1551.

Jakarta Mandate, 1997. Convention on Biological Diversity, First Meeting of Experts, March 1997, p. 26.

Jameson, S. C., J. W. McManus and M. D. Spalding. 1995. "State of the Reefs: Regional and Global Perspectives." International Coral Reef Initiative (ICRI) Secretariat Background Paper, U.S. Department of State. Washington, D.C.

Johannes, R. E. 1975. "Pollution and Degradation of Coral Reef Communities." In E. J. F. Wood and R. E. Johannes, eds. *Elsevier Oceanogr.* 12: 13-51.

———. 1981. *Words of the Lagoon.* Berkeley, Calif.: University of California Press.

Johannes, R. E., and B. G. Hatcher, B.G. 1986. "Shallow Tropical Marine Environments." In Soulé, ed. *Conservation Biology: The Science of Scarcity and Diversity.* Sunderland, Mass.: Sinauer Associates, Inc.

Kleypas, J. A. 1995. "A Diagnostic Model for Predicting Global Reef Distribution." In O. Belwood, H. Choat, and N. Saxena, eds., PACON Intl. and James Cook University.

Kleypas, J. A. 1997. "Modeled Estimates of Global Reef Habitat and Carbonate Production since the Last Glacial Maximum." *Paleoceanography* 12(4): 533-45.

Maragos, J. E., M. P. Crosby, and J. W. McManus. 1996. "Coral Reefs and Biodiversity: A Critical and Threatened Relationship." *Oceanography* 9(1): 83–99.

McManus, J. W. 1996. "Social and Economic Aspects of Reef Fisheries and Their Management." In N. Polunin and C. Roberts eds., *Coral Reef Fisheries.* New York: Chapman and Hall.

McManus, J. W. 1997. "Tropical Marine Fisheries and the Future of Coral Reefs: A Brief Review with Emphasis on Southeast Asia." *Coral Reefs* 16, Suppl.: S121-S127.

McManus, J. W., and M. C. Ablan, eds. 1996. *ReefBase: A Global Database of Coral Reefs and Their Resources. User's Guide.* Metro Manila, Philippines. ICLARM.

McManus J. W. and M. C. Ablan, eds.) 1997. *ReefBase 2.0: A Global Database of Coral Reefs and Their Resources. User's Guide.* Metro Manila, Philippines. ICLARM.

McManus, J. W., and M. C. Ablan, M. Forthcoming. "ReefBase: a Global Database of Coral Reefs and Their Resources."

McManus, J. W., M. C. Ablan, S. G. Vergara, L. A. B. Meñez, B. M. Vallejo, K. P. Kesner, M. G. Gorospe, and L. Halimarick. 1997. *The ReefBase Aquanaut Survey Manual.* Metro Manila, Philippines. ICLARM.

McManus, J. W., E. M. Ferrer, and W. L. Campos. 1988. "A Village-Level Approach to Coastal Adaptive Management and Resource Assessment (CAMRA)." *Proceedings of the Sixth International Coral Reef Symposium,* 2:381-386.

Munro, J. L. 1996. "The Scope of Coral Reef Fisheries and Their Management." In N. Polunin and C. Roberts, eds., *Coral Reef Fisheries.* New York: Chapman and Hall. New York.

Munro, J. L., ed. 1983. "Caribbean Coral Reef Fishery Resources." *ICLARM Studies and Reviews* 7, Metro Manila, Philippines: ICLARM.

Munro, J. L, and P. E. Munro, eds.. 1994. "The Management of Coral Reef Resource Systems." ICLARM Conference Proceedings, 44.

Munro J. L., and R. Thompson, R. 1973. "The

Biology, Ecology, Exploitation and Management of Caribbean Reef Fishes." Part II. The Jamaican fishing industry, the area investigated, the objectives and methodology of the ODA/UWI Fisheries Ecology Project. Res. Rep. Zool. Dept. Univ. West Indies. 3. 44.

Munro, J. L, and P. E. Munro, eds. 1994. "The Management of Coral Reef Resource Systems." ICLARM Conference Proceedings 44, 129.

Munro, J. L. ed. 1983. "Caribbean Coral Reef Fishery Resources." *ICLARM Studies and Reviews* 7, Metro Manila, Philippines, ICLARM.

Munro, J. L., and D. McB. Williams. 1985. "Assessment and Management of Coral Reef Fisheries: Biological, Environmental And Socio-Economic Aspects." *Proceedings of the Fifth International Coral Reef Symposium.* 543-578.

Ogden, J. C. 1994. (Letter). *Science* 266: 1931.

Pennisi, E. 1997. "Brighter Prospects for the World's Coral Reefs?" *Science* 277: 491-3.

Rapport, D. J., H. A. Regier, and C. Thorpe. 1981. "Diagnosis, Prognosis and Treatment of Ecosystems under Stress." In G. W. Barrett and R. Rosenberg, eds., *Stress Effects on Natural Ecosystems.* New York: Wiley.

Smith S. V. 1978. "Coral Reef Area and the Contributions of Reefs to Processes and Resources of the World's Oceans." *Nature* 273: 225-26.

UNEP/IUCN. 1988. *Coral Reefs of the World.* (vols. 1-3). Gland, Switzerland, and Cambridge, United Kingdom. K./UNEP, Nairobi, Kenya, IUCN.

Wilkinson, C. R. 1992. "Coral Reefs of the World Are Facing Widespread Devastation: Can We Prevent This through Sustainable Management Practices?" *Proceedings of the Seventh International Coral Reef Symposium,* 1: 1121.

Coral Reefs: Harbingers of Global Change?

Phillip Dustan
University of Charleston, South Carolina, on behalf of the Cousteau Society

Evolution produces a very few new species every million years. If we are to assume that nature can cope with our feverish developments, it is probable that mankind would be submitted to the fate of the dinosaurs. Destruction is quick and easy. Construction is slow and difficult.

—*J. Y. Cousteau, 1973*

Coral reefs form in the tropical, equatorial waters of the world's oceans and are the marine analogs of tropical rain forests. They are the oldest, most diverse and productive ecosystems in the sea. Coral reefs are a reservoir for much of the ocean's biodiversity, providing an estimated 10 percent of the world's fisheries, and their productivity fuels intense biogeochemical activity linking them to the global carbon cycle. Complex reef structures house some of nature's most amazing creatures while protecting miles of coastline from the full fury of the sea.

Coral reefs develop to their greatest expression in clear tropical waters under extremely nutrient-poor conditions. Abundant solar energy fuels photosynthetic activity, which is transferred to the food web by a host of grazing herbivores (animals that eat plants). This lush development of reefs under extreme oligotrophic conditions created a "paradox of reef" among scientists until the role of symbiosis was fully recognized. Now we know that the high productivity of reefs results from the evolution of many symbiotic associations, mainly coral-algal

(zooxanthellae), that increase the retention of limiting nutrients, primarily nitrogen and phosphorus. Reef corals are functionally both animals and plants. Ironically, the same intricate patterns of survival that have developed over an immense span of evolutionary time make the reef vulnerable to changes in environmental conditions, especially temperature, sediment, and nutrient concentrations.

Anthropogenic stresses are thought to be contributing to the decline in coral reef ecosystems, notably in the Caribbean and the western Atlantic. Driven by the engine of ever-increasing human population, more and more land has been converted from its natural state. Generally, terrestrial ecosystems tend to be conservative and export little in the way of nutrients, carbon, and sediments. But, agriculture, urbanization, and deforestation reduce the capacity of terrestrial ecosystems to trap and retain materials. Development has altered the ecological characteristic of watersheds, overloading rivers with sediments, and nutrients, and adding toxic chemicals. Simple runoff has become an effluent that can have a significant deleterious influence on water quality. The addition of fertilizers, organic carbon, and urban and commercial dumping further enriches the watershed's effluent as it flows into the sea. When these ecological variables pass some threshold, the species composition of the reef community becomes reorganized.

The addition of sediments or nutrients triggers a set of ecological processes that alter the selective pressures facing corals. In disturbed areas, increased loading of sediments and nutrients often co-occur, making it difficult to isolate their individual effects. Generally, increased sediment and nutrient loading favor the growth of macroalgae over corals. Suspended sediments reduce light levels to the corals and coat their soft tissue surfaces. Algae strip nutrients from the water column, quickly enabling them to grow faster than stony corals.

Excess sediment, coarse or fine, smothers coral tissue, impeding diffusive gas exchange through the tissues while also reducing the amount of light available for photosynthesis. Since corals work best when their surfaces are sediment-free, their metabolic efficiency diminishes. Energy spent on housekeeping is not available for prey capture, growth, or reproduction. As the sediment load increases, the tissues cannot maintain their status and tissue death occurs. Microbes quickly claim the freshly exposed skeleton, which is followed by a successional process ending with an algal turf or macroalgal community. Tissue losses increase when, through fishing and collecting, levels of herbivory are reduced or at least altered. Such reefs change from coral gardens to algal-covered rocks, in precisely the type of trend that is one of the key problems facing coral reef ecosystems in the Caribbean and western Atlantic today.

Curiously, luxuriant reefs can be found naturally in areas with high sediment loading, such as could be found near the mouths of tropical rivers along the north coast of Jamaica. The difference is that these reefs developed under these conditions rather than being subject to dramatic environmental shifts after becoming established. Reef corals that have developed under one set of conditions may not possess the necessary flexibility in their physiology or genetic makeup to cope with the added stress of rapid environmental change.

The death rate of coral tissue from sediment necrosis increases when algae grow in close proximity to corals. Macroalgae can shade coral tissue, causing bleaching and eventually tissue necrosis. Large algal colonies can also abrade the soft coral tissue as they wave in the surge. Microalgal filaments at the edge of corals form effective sediment dams that prevent corals from clearing sediment off their surface, slowly suffocating the live tissue. This process, termed edge damage, is a functional disease and appears to be a significant source of coral tissue mortality. Additionally, any lesion increases susceptibility to opportunistic pathogens that can kill a colony in less than 1/100 of the time it takes to grow. In the Florida Keys in 1974, I observed the process on reefs that had increased amounts of fine sedimentation. The condition became much more prevalent after the mass mortality of *Diadema antillarum* greatly reduced levels of herbivory. Today, throughout the Florida Keys and the Bahamas, almost anything that lives on hard substrate is being overgrown by algae. It is abundant, almost metastatic, on the outer reefs of Key Largo. Molasses Reef, the most heavily visited reef in the world, has thick ruglike algal mats, while Carysfort Reef has mats with finer filaments. Both types of algal communities trap sediments and the finer particulate organic snow, which shade, smother, and rather quickly kill coral tissue.

The reefs in many parts of the Caribbean and western Atlantic are showing signs of decreasing vitality; coral cover is decreasing while algae are increasing. Coral regeneration is slowing, and the increased levels of algal biomass may be, in part, responsible for reduced levels of coral larvae settlement. Signs of stress appear most evident on coastal reefs near population centers. In the Florida Keys, one of the most dramatic sites, I am frequently asked which single factor is responsible, sediments or nutrients? My perspective is that the factor may actually be the accumulation of a series of nested stresses that are as local as the fisherman; as regional as the landowner, sugarcane field, or village; and as global as deforestation in Amazonia, the ozone hole, and the greenhouse effect. Each factor compounds the rest, a synergy leading toward death for the reef.

Locating the sources of increased levels of nutrients and sediments, and other stressors, has proved as elusive as defining the nested levels of stress. In the Florida Keys, the effluent of cities, towns, farms, a watershed too vast to control, slowly bleeds into the sea through canals, rivers, and coastal bays. The origin can be either a steady and well-defined point source stream or an effluent that seeps from the land with each rainfall. Both push sediments, nutrients, and contaminants into the sea. More of it upwells from injected sewage; some leaches from shallow septic tanks, urban lawns, agricultural lands, or vacant lots. Some washes into the sea along the west and east coasts of Florida, the Everglades, the Mississippi, and lands that are farther downstream. Bits and pieces from a diffuse array of sources contribute to a pervasive level of adverse stress for the reef.

The changes we are witnessing in reefs are echoes of the increased levels of harmful algal blooms in coastal waters, beach closings, and the general global decline in fisheries. The impact of man is extending into the seas. Watershed effluent, runoff from increasingly urbanized landscapes, an unprecedented manipulation by humans, is thought to be responsible for increased levels of nutrients and sediments, but the definitive data are not yet in. The data are elusive because reef community metabolism has evolved to rapidly take up and sequester the very nutrients signal we are trying to detect. Increases in algal biomass are thought to reflect increased nutrients but do not constitute proof. Carbonate sediments are almost as hard to follow, so at this time we are left with correlation rather than causality. It is my belief that the declining vitality of reefs is a metric for the health of the oceans, analogous to the coal miner's canary in the cage. They are the fragile harbingers of change warning us of declining oceanic health.

Coral reefs, rain forests, and human civilization are the three most complex communities on earth. The first two are the most productive natural communities, while humanity, is rapidly encroaching on the entire planet. Reefs are the oldest, having existed since there were organisms with skeletons in the sea. Modern coral reefs date from about 250 million years before the present. Like rain forests, these communities have evolved an ecological logic that allows them to flourish and persist on a planet that is forever changing.

Over enormous spans of evolutionary time, very sophisticated relationships emerge and form the core of biodiversity. The most elaborate ecosystems tend to be found in places that are old, benign, predictable, and frequently rich in solar energy. These ecosystems are very proficient at elemental recycling, so that the living portions of the habitat are richer in nutrients than their surrounding soils or seas. Both reefs and rain forests develop to their highest expressions in habitats that seemingly cannot support luxuriant growth. The soil of rain forests is extremely poor, and the clear, warm tropical seas that bathe reefs have nutrient levels at or below the minimum level of detection. In this case, more is not always necessarily better.

Human civilization is undergoing an unprecedented population expansion coupled with an economy driven by consumption and profit, as opposed to efficiency and recycling. Humans treat biological resources like agricultural systems in which net production is maximized rather than managed for sustainable yields. Such systems are inherently unstable. They require a constant input of nutrients, very little of which are sequestered in the standing stock, or "body," of the ecosystem. They grow at the expense of other systems and greatly increase the entropy of surrounding areas. But since the earth is finite, this approach cannot continue without increasingly severe degradation of the biosphere.

One long-range vision for the future of humanity suggests that the incorporation of the logic of natural systems into our mode of living might, perhaps, enable civilization to persist as long as coral reefs and rain forests. Given humanity's commerce-driven dominance of ecosystems, the environmental and long-term costs of economic activities need to be reflected in market prices. We must change our present practices, lest we leave only our wastes for future generations.

The very first diving expedition of *Calypso* was to the Red Sea, beginning the modern study of coral reefs using the Aqualung. It was there that Jacques Cousteau became astounded and entranced by the splendor and the extravagant beauty of the coral world. In time, his concern grew for the careless destruction that our unchecked technological development is spreading into the oceans. His legacy to us is a greater understanding and appreciation for the marvels of life.

Recommendations for the World Bank

Recognizing that coral reefs may be indicators of oceanic health and that their decline may forebode the decline of the oceans, the World Bank should assume a leadership role in the global conservation of coral reefs for a sustainable future by undertaking the following:

- Establish an international interdisciplinary working group composed of scientific, technical, and policy experts to ascertain the state of knowledge of coral reef ecosystems and make recommendations concerning their sustainable future.
- Establish collaborations with international space agencies to develop a global capability to map and monitor the distribution of coral reef communities, to ascertain their health and identify potential hazards to their future.
- Support a climate of stimulation for existing activities and fund scientific programs on the health and vitality of coral reef ecosystems, and support efforts to implement sustainable fisheries practices at all levels.
- Recognize the dynamics of population growth in coastal areas and focus attention on protecting the ecology of the land-sea margin and watersheds of coastlines and rivers. Address land-based sources of marine pollution, including nutrient and chemical inputs, soil erosion, and forest and agriculture practices.
- Support the development of an industrial/technological ecology focused on both remediation and an end to pollution of the seas, and develop new environmental management techniques integrating ecology, economics, technology, and social sciences ("Ecotechnie") with the goal of significantly reducing pollution in coastal areas, remediating ecological harm, protecting human health, and enhancing human welfare.
- Expand support for small-scale projects designed to eliminate destructive fishing (such as the use of cyanide and dynamite), implement reef surveys and monitoring activities, and protect reefs from physical harm. Work at the national and international level to address fisheries that exploit children, and implement certification programs for aquarium fish to ensure they are caught in a nonharmful manner. Explore the use of microcredit loans for small-scale entrepreneurial activities to promote the sustainable use of coral reef resources.
- Ensure that the knowledge and means for management are transferred to tropical developing nations where most of the world's reefs are located, and assist in developing the capacity of local communities to manage and use these resources in a sustainable manner.
- Support the establishment of marine protected areas and particularly sensitive sea areas (PSSAs) to ensure the conservation of marine biodiversity.
- Support the full implementation of the Jakarta Mandate on Marine and Coastal Biodiversity, and the development of a Protocol on Marine Biodiversity Conservation to the Convention on Biological Diversity.

The Global Coral Reef Monitoring Network: Communities, Governments, and Scientists Working Together for Sustainable Management of Coral Reefs

Clive Wilkinson
Global Coral Reef Monitoring Network

Bernard Salvat
GCRMN Scientific and Technical Advisory Committee

The declining status and health of coral reefs around the world stimulated the formation of the Global Coral Reef Monitoring Network (GCRMN), a component of the International Coral Reef Initiative (ICRI).

Formation of the GCRMN

The GCRMN was established under sponsorship by the Intergovernmental Oceanographic Commission of UNESCO (IOC), the United Nations Environment Programme (UNEP), and the World Conservation Union (IUCN) and is co-hosted by the Australian Institute of Marine Science (AIMS) in Townsville and the International Center for Living Aquatic Resources Management (ICLARM) in Manila.

The GCRMN commenced in March 1996, when the IOC appointed a coordinator using U.S. State Department funds. The GCRMN is governed by the sponsors, hosts and ICRI forming the Management Group. Advice is provided by a widely representative GCRMN Scientific and Technical Advisory Committee (STAC), with the chair sitting on the Management Group. The first major task was to produce a "Strategic Plan," which is available at this meeting.

GCRMN Strategies

The GCRMN will develop partnerships with local users and other stakeholders, government departments, scientists, and resource managers to implement a global program of reef monitoring. The GCRMN will function as an association of independent networks (or nodes), within regions based on the UNEP Regional Seas Programme. The size and composition of nodes will depend on the number of countries, geographical range, distance, language, culture, religions, and political affiliations. Central coordination will diminish to a role of preparing reports and assisting in funding nodes.

Regional nodes will identify major stakeholder groups to train and involve in local area monitoring, as well as conducting country-wide monitoring. Specific emphasis will be placed on involving fisher cooperatives, women's organizations, and schools. The objectives of the monitoring are twofold: to gather data on the status and trends in coral reefs, and to raise awareness amongst all stakeholders, as well as decision-makers, on the current rates of reef destruction and causes. These objectives feed directly into the ICRI programs of integrated management and capacity building.

GCRMN Regions and Nodes

Regions and nodes will be effectively independent with their own budgets and reporting, coordinated through a central office, usually the UNEP regional office. Nodes will be staffed by a coordinator and staff able to train in biophysical and socioeconomic monitoring, plus be responsible for in-country monitoring. Each node will produce annual reef status reports, based on data from participating countries, and ensure the wide dissemination of reports. The regions are:

- *Middle East.* Countries bordering the Red Sea and the Persian Gulf, which held their first ICRI Regional Workshop in September 1997.
- *Western Indian Ocean and Eastern African States.* The ICRI Regional Workshop in the Seychelles, April 1996, recommended a Western Indian Ocean node to assist Comoros, Madagascar, Mauritius, Reunion, Seychelles, based in Mauritius and supported by the Indian Ocean Commission; and an Eastern African node assisting Kenya, Mozambique, Tanzania, South Africa (and possibly Eritrea, Somalia) hosted by the Kenya Marine Fisheries Research Institute in Mombasa.
- *South Asia.* One node for India, the Maldives, Sri Lanka (Bangladesh, Pakistan) was designated at the Maldives ICRI Regional Workshop, November 1995. The node is supported by the Department for International Development, UK, and hosted at IUCN and SACEP in Colombo, with Jason Rubens appointed as the interim regional coordinator.
- *East Asian Seas.* Five countries (Indonesia, Malaysia, the Philippines, Singapore, and Thailand) will be independent nodes. One node is planned for Cambodia, Myanmar, and Vietnam; another node is envisaged for North Asia, with the Okinawa Coral Reef Conservation and Research Center of Japan assisting China, the Republic of Korea, and Hong Kong (China). These were decided at two ICRI regional workshops—Bali, March 1996, and Okinawa, February 1997.
- *Pacific.* Six nodes will serve the countries and states within the South Pacific Regional Environment Programme (SPREP). These were decided at the GCRMN meeting in Fiji in July 1997. The nodes are Hawaiian—for Hawaii, U.S. Line, U.S. Phoenix and Wake Islands, based at the University of Hawaii, the East-West Center, and the Bishop Museum; Polynesian—at the Ecole Pratique des Hautes Etudes/Centre de Recherches Insulaires et Observatoire de l'Environment

(EPHE/CRIOBE) station on Moorea, assisted by the government of French Polynesia and Université Française du Pacifique, to include the Cook Islands, Tokelau, Niue, Wallis, and Futuna; Northwest Pacific—based at the University of Guam and the Guam Coastal Management Program and incorporating Palau, the Federated States of Micronesia, and the Northern Marianas; Central Pacific—based in the Marine Studies Center, University of the South Pacific, in Suva, Fiji, and including American Samoa, Samoa, and Tonga; Pacific Atoll—based in the USP Atoll Research Unit in Kiribati for the Marshall Islands, Nauru, and Tuvalu; Melanesian High Islands—for New Caledonia, Papua New Guinea, the Solomon Islands, Vanuatu, and Australia, hosted probably at ICLARM in Honiara.

- *Caribbean and Tropical Americas.* There will be many nodes based on the expertise within the CARICOMP network of interacting marine institutes, with some coordination through the UNEP regional offices in Jamaica.

GCRMN Program and Progress

- *Planning.* Initial interagency support has been obtained to establish the GCRMN and fund coordination. The Strategic Plan, Biophysical Manual, and Protocols are being distributed. A manual of social, cultural, and economic parameters is currently being drafted. The GCRMN Pilot Monitoring Project is under way with more than 50 institutes or individuals signifying interest. A manual for tourist and volunteer divers is being planned by the East-West Center in Hawaii, to include existing projects like Aquanaut and Reef Check.
- *Negotiation.* More than 80 governments participated in the six ICRI Regional Workshops; most requested participation in the GCRMN. These workshops determined the problems for their coral reefs and established action priorities. Many scientists and resource managers participated and are willing to assist.

- *Node formation.* Approximately 16 nodes in four regions have been formed around strong centers; approximately 12 remain to be designated. Coordinators have been selected for most nodes and funding is assured for the establishment of the South Asian node, and five independent country nodes in Southeast Asia will seek their own funding. Funding proposals are being developed for the others.
- *Training.* Initial training has started in the Western Indian Ocean, South Asia, Southeast Asia, and the Pacific. Full training should commence within nine months in most regions. Likewise the socioeconomic manual will be simultaneously tested in all regions.
- *Devolution.* The next step, after country monitoring has started, is to train and involve communities in monitoring their resources, with the view toward developing local management plans.
- *Reporting.* The GCRMN will produce two reports (results of pilot and initial regional monitoring, and assessments by expert scientists and resource managers) for the International Year of the Ocean and presented at ITMEMS, an international coral reef management conference in November 1998. A major status report will be presented at the International Coral Reef Symposium in Bali, 2000. Specific reports by communities and countries should commence by June 1998.
- *Over to ICRI.* GCRMN country and community activities will constitute the basis to achieve ICRI goals of integrated management and capacity building.

Specific Anthropogenic Problems and Solutions

The ultimate cause of coral reef degradation derives from greater use of resources by increasing populations, which are driven to overexploitation by poverty and a lack of control over these resources. Solutions to these problems operate at a larger scale than the GCRMN; but we intend to assist in tackling the direct causes of most coral reef degradation. In this paper, we consider two levels of anthropogenic damage:

- That which can be controlled by communities (localized overfishing; damaging fishing; overharvesting of sand and rock; immediate pollution by sediment, sewage, agricultural and small industrial effluents)
- Large-scale impacts imposed on reefs from outside the system (catchment area pollution, oil and large-scale industrial pollution, global climate change and sea level rise).

The GCRMN is focused on the first—assisting communities in developing awareness of the problems facing coral reefs and educating users about the connections between human activities and reef damage. The impacts listed below that are directly controllable by local communities are marked ($). Solutions to some of these are treated in detail elsewhere in these proceedings.

- Sediment pollution:
  - Deforestation ($)
  - Stripping of mangroves ($)
  - Coastal and catchment development ($)
- Poor agricultural practices:
  - Dredging for mariculture ponds ($)
  - Dredging for ports
  - Land reclamation
  - Dumping of spoils at sea
  - Mining in the catchment area
  - Coastal mining (for example, tin dredging)
- Nutrient pollution:
  - Runoff from cleared land ($)
  - Sewage wastes ($)
  - Agricultural wastes and fertilizers ($)
  - Intensive animal husbandry ($)
  - Intensive mariculture, such as shrimp ponds ($)
  - Wastes from food and paper industries
- Overfishing:
  - With fine mesh traps and nets ($)
  - Fishing with spearguns ($)
  - Commercial fishing with compressed air ($)
  - Destructive fishing—nets and trawlers($)
  - Cyanide fishing ($)
  - Poison, such as bleach ($)
  - *Muro ami* fishing ($)
  - Blast, or dynamite ($)
  - Anchor damage ($)
- Engineering: building of groins, harbors, and walls; building of airports, ports, marinas.

Sediment and nutrient pollution can be controlled by integrated management of watersheds directed by local populations and assisted by central government. Many developmental and agricultural practices can be managed to reduce sediment loss, such as clearing land during the dry season, green tillage, building bund walls around coastal developments. Nutrients can be reduced by the target application of fertilizer, use of sewage wastes in agriculture, installation of basic sewage treatment for towns and agricultural industries, sustainable stocking rates for grazing. The development of crops requiring less fertilizer is needed for coastal communities.

Combating overfishing and damaging fishing practices will require coordinated action to reduce poverty by providing alternative employment through industries like tourism. Fishers are usually the poorest of the poor. The reliance on wild-caught fish must be reduced by improved mariculture and cage culture, using larvae and juveniles caught in traps or nets or on artificial reefs.

Above all are the major efforts required to reduce population growth, combat poverty, provide alternative employment, ensure that local people have greater control over their resources, and improve information, awareness, and education into the causes of problems and possible solutions. This will require some funding, but at low levels (for example, US$3 million to 5 million) across the globe. The GCRMN is specifically targeted at providing communities with the information and understanding necessary to take greater control of these resources, but by pursuing the goals, the GCRMN will form networks and provide them with some tools to tackle the larger problems.

Marine Information Management and Environmental Education

Janine M. H. Selendy
HORIZON Communications

To effectively and expeditiously protect and preserve coral reefs, marine information and environmental education efforts must be undertaken, reaching people throughout the world to heighten awareness of problems and dangers and to provide answers: solutions that can be and are being undertaken from environmentally sound fishing and extraction practices to controls on trade and tourism. To help achieve this goal, on the 15th of October, HORIZON Communications, a not-for-profit international research, film production, and development organization based at Harvard and Yale Universities in the United States, is launching its CORAL REEF ODYSSEY: QUEST FOR SURVIVAL project. This effort, consisting of television programs, books, and other multimedia materials, is designed to help increase public understanding of the importance of coral reefs, of the threats to their survival, and of the efforts that can be and are being undertaken to protect them.

HORIZON is embarking on a new symbiotic relationship between research and the media. The ODYSSEY, will take audiences on a research expedition through the major coral reef ecosystems of the world with a group of dedicated marine biologists led by Dr. Walter Adey, Director of the Marine Systems Laboratory of the Smithsonian Institution. The quest will be threefold: (1) to find new organisms which may be a source of future medicines and other biochemical products, both addressing the newly growing practice of bioprospecting and necessary precautions to avoid hurting the reefs and showing how environmentally friendly bioprospecting is benefiting local communities without harming the reefs; (2) to heighten public appreciation of the beauty and complexity of these extraordinary ecosystems and of the interdependence of man and coral reefs; and (3) to provide examples of successful reef protection and management practices.

The many problems confronting the reefs will be played against the story of efforts to protect and preserve these fecund oases of biodiversity. The media coverage will reach people throughout the world.

Environmental education needs to be culturally and politically sensitive and to reach children as well as adults. Television and all media available in a region should be employed, along with hands-on training of local people who are or can be involved in protective measures. Whenever possible, local participation in the media coverage itself should be factored into information packages. This can be done without much extra expense by adding segments produced by and with local individuals depicting their situations. Adding material to existing educational videos can be achieved using simple camcorders. In order to make their additions to the productions particularly effective, integration of their segments into the body of existing tapes should be done. This can be achieved by providing them with special edits of the

ODYSSEY, for example, in which blank sections are left into which they can cut a segment produced locally. In regions where they do not have access to cameras and video equipment, the equipment and training could be provided, adding to learning skills and direct involvement in preservation efforts. HORIZON has had a long experience in creating documentaries composed of detachable segments which can be seen in sequence or can be worked into news programs, reaching audiences not only through major broadcasters such as PBS, but also appearing in whole or part in major news programs on ABC in the United States and in Burkina Faso, China, Germany, Lebanon, Mexico, Pakistan, Peru, Poland, Thailand, and other countries.

The World Bank can benefit fisheries and coral reefs around the world by encouraging research, education, and environmentally sound consumer demand. It can play a very meaningful and effective role by incorporating, as part of the Bank's long-range ecological objectives, support for education, disseminating knowledge of successful models of conservation with profitable development. Thus, the Bank can help provide a foundation of knowledge on which people can act. What better resource to focus on than coral reefs, where the stakes are so high and the promising initiatives so compelling.

The fact that the diversity of coral reef life has great scientific and economic potential needs to be spread in environmental education. The work of Dr. William Fenical of the Scripps Institution of Oceanography serves as such a model, representing the promise of medicines from coral reef organisms and of market incentives. In the Bahamas, successful bioprospecting work begun under Dr. Fenical is under way. There a treelike gorgonian, *Pseudopterogorgia elisabethae*, is being harvested by local fishermen who carefully cut only a few branches from the gorgonian, which then regenerates. Substances derived from the branches are used by a major cosmetic company and are being studied for use of its powerful anti-inflammatory properties. The Bahamian government is receiving hundreds of thousands of dollars in export taxes from this resource.

Uneducated Consumers

Tourism is a rapidly growing industry throughout the coral reef areas of the world. Uncontrolled or inadequately controlled tourism is resulting in coral reef destruction, often by unwary divers who mean no harm. Education and controls are essential. In Bonaire, a wonderfully successful coral reef preservation effort, and an excellent example of effective ecotourism, is working and has been under way for more than 20 years. Videos are employed to teach divers the do's and don'ts before they can receive their diving permits. The production of the ODYSSEY will commence this month with filming of the Bonaire effort, including how this ecotourism effort came about and why the ecotourism effort is so successful, not only in terms of protecting the reefs, but also in economic terms.

Environmental education and marine information management need to address boaters, pleasure fishing, reef treasure hunters, amateur and professional archeologists, other explorers, and pleasure divers. There is vital interdependency between fisheries and coral reefs about which not many people seem to be aware. *Time* magazine of August 11, 1975, provides a good example of how major media coverage can help. Its article on fisheries draws attention to their fragility, helping to increase public awareness of fish losses from excessive catches. The article presents startling facts about fish popular among chefs in the United States, such as the orange roughy. They grow extremely slowly, live for more than 100 years, and take 25 years to reach sexual maturity. The consumer sitting in a restaurant may never have thought about the fact that consuming an orange roughy was encouraging overfishing and depletion.

Time offered a section on "What Consumers Can Do," providing lists of what is OK to eat sparingly and what is not OK to eat. For example, the grouper, a resident reef fish which is easily caught, is being targeted in many tropical waters. They are most often taken at a crucial point in their life cycle—when they gather by the thousands to spawn. *Time* reports: "In some places, fishermen have wiped out nearly an entire generation of reproducing adults in just a few seasons." Many have heard of a single grouper commanding a price of $10,000 in Southeast Asia, where the economic boom is generating wealth that is too often encouraging plundering of such resources. Mass education is needed to alert people to the consequences. Grouper in the Caribbean are facing imminent danger, according to some marine scientists. They are concerned that there will be uncontrolled poaching of grouper during their forthcoming spawning season, wiping them out. This situation needs attention. Media can alert people and inform them about actions they can take, such as avoiding catching and consuming grouper.

Recommendations for Future Actions

1. Sustainable Practices and Private Entrepreneurs

People who are drawn into poisoning and dynamiting for fish need to be educated about alternatives. Daniel Pelicier of Mauritius provides an excellent example of environmentally friendly aquarium collection, in both his techniques and his reasoning. By sharing knowledge of his approach in the media, he will heighten awareness of how one can make immediate money while providing for long-term availability of resources.

2. Bank Staff and Policymakers

Media can help alert people to illegal and harmful fishing and extractive practices and can be very effective in bringing about major policy decisions. If the world knows about what is being done, the force of the public can make the difference. For instance, it could be tremendously helpful for the media to bring to attention the loss of fisheries and coral reefs along the heavily populated coasts of Indonesia. Professor Paul Dayton of the Scripps Institution of Oceanography says that 112 million Indonesians living along the seaboard depend on fish. "Pirates have destroyed their entire resource." Can pirating be stopped? It may go on if there is not enough of a public outcry. That outcry comes from knowledge of the cause. People recognize

that illegal taking of fish and destruction of coral reefs is theft. It is theft from local communities and from their livelihoods, theft from the interdependent species that are hurt or killed: theft from our global capital. When the message gets out that our global capital is being lost to pirates on the coast of Indonesia, people will wake up and realize that it affects them, whether halfway around the world or on the Indonesian coast. It puts the situation in a perspective that everyone can relate to. Hence, it generates action. Similarly, it is important that the World Bank take into account not only local and regional considerations when financing a development, but also global capital. Will the development cause depletion of global capital? Will the development harm or destroy global capital with pollutants? Will the development have negative long-term consequences on our global capital? The Bank's new "outplacement" policy begun by President Wolfensohn benefits both the Bank staff who can expand their knowledge and experience and the organization with which they are collaborating. It could be made more liberal with time and Bank resources.

3. Reef Managers

The World Bank and other entities could help with the establishment and operation of training programs with education and certification of coral reef managers, using media to illustrate problems and best practices. There needs to be more power of enforcement than now exists in many areas, and stronger infrastructure from which to work. Effective education programs incorporating visual material for coral reef reserve managers can help to effectively and quickly generate an understanding of the long-term consequences of failure to enforce the controls over poaching or other harmful activities. A striking example of conservation enforcement was presented in the *Economist* of September 20, 1997, one I am not advocating: In order to help the black rhinos in Zimbabwe, their national parks "are protected by a new and fiercer force. If guards and game rangers come across anybody who might be a poacher, they now have the right to shoot first and ask questions later."

The *Economist* states, "Its effect was immediate—and salutary."

4. Educators

Educators in various fields should incorporate an understanding and appreciation of the biodiversity of coral reefs and of the interdependent relationships of fisheries and coral reefs, mangroves, and sea grasses. Symbiotic relationships showing caring, understanding, and mutual protection and support provide striking examples which can be effectively incorporated into education and marine information management programs. The images and stories of symbiotic anemones and clown fish, gobies and pistol shrimp, symbiosis crabs on sea feathers, porcelain crabs with their delicate translucent plankton nets, and many other magnificent examples will make people better understand the complexities of coral reefs. Interdisciplinary studies need to be fostered to increase understanding of coastal related influences on coral reefs such as agricultural runoffs, sewage, and industrial processes that cause pollutants.

5. Scientists

Members of the scientific community can build on knowledge of interconnected influences causing reef degradation and destruction such as weakened conditions due to toxins and increased algal blooms leading to newly emerging viruses and death. Scientists, fishermen, and coral reef communities can all play an essential role by sharing knowledge of spawning and breeding grounds, knowledge of crucial times for corals and fish, such as fertility cycles, breeding grounds needing protection, and symbiotic relationships between various species of fish and corals. To provide an understanding of long-term consequences, this information then needs to be made widely available through all multimedia forms, reaching into even the smallest community.

To further facilitate local and regional coral reef protection efforts, HORIZON, in collaboration with the United Nations Environment Programme, Development Programme, Population Fund, UNICEF, the International Development Research Centre of Canada, and Harvard and Yale Universities, will be sharing solutions in easily accessible case studies on its "Solutions Site" on the HORIZON Web page. We welcome participation in this site, for which case studies will be checked for applicability and feasibility by HORIZON's Scientific Review Board, Coral Reef Advisory Board, and other experts. The information will be made available in newsletters and other means as well as on the Internet. Please visit HORIZON's Web page for more information on the CORAL REEF ODYSSEY: http://www.yale.edu/horizon and to share your ideas with us in our guest book.

Discussion

Stephen Colwell, Coral Reef Alliance: There are dozens, actually hundreds, of organizations that are not here today, all of whom have participated in getting out the very information we are talking about [the International Year of the Reef], and the reason I'm saying this is that there's often people who are saying, "We need to create this or that." A lot of it is out there, a lot of it is done. It's important to tap into that so that we don't spend all of our time creating, and we put a lot of resources into distribution. There are exhibits, like the Smithsonian Tropical Research Institute's, Nuestros Arecifes, which is going through the Caribbean; there are NOAA's programs this year, which they have done for "52 Stories," which has been picked up by newspapers around the world; there are Web sites. In fact, if you look at the International Year of the Reef Web site, you can see hundreds of people in over 50 countries have set these things up. And you should tap into those, particularly since 1998 is the Year of the Ocean. We really have a chance to use this momentum. I was taking a shuttle to the airport in New York, and had the cab driver say, "Oh, coral reefs, aren't they really in trouble? Really bad things are happening in Indonesia, right? " It's out there—we can build on it, particularly with all the resources that the panel and other people have developed, I think we have an obligation right now to carry this momentum through to 1998.

John McManus: Thank you, Steve. You have broadened the picture—that was extremely important. We're also very supportive of ReefCheck—a very successful move to get a lot of people in the water in a hurry to get some sort of immediate feedback about coral reefs, but also to get a lot of people involved in looking at coral reefs. There's going to be a press conference [October, 16, 1997], in Hong Kong about the initial results. I was actually one of the people on the first ReefCheck. They have the advantage that you can train somebody in three hours and get them in the water, and gather some sort of information. And we have just agreed that ReefCheck will be seen as some sort of a two-level thing. After ReefCheck—if people want to go through three or four days training at the Aquanaut program, then that becomes stage two. There's a number of other volunteer programs around the world that we're very happy about including the reef program with fish watching, so there's lot of things going on around the world.

Silvia Earle: I wanted to quickly respond to something that Janine [Selendy] was alluding to, which I guess you could sum up with just referring to the distillation of this Black Sea Conference, which was a curious mix of religion, environment, scientists, economists. It was really something—the idea being trying to pull people together from various disciplines that normally don't talk to one another, and to see if we could find the common ground. I had the fun of trying to come up with some of the essence of what it was all about. And it seemed to me that you could say that some of the things you learn as a little kid about "doing to others what you would have them do unto you"—this is the ethic that we grow up with no matter what culture we come from. And no matter what culture we come from there are certain guidelines for living, such as "thou shalt not kill, and thou shalt not steal." And as you were saying, Janine, about theft of things that go beyond taking things from one another's backyard. In a sense, this is our backyard, but we haven't yet quite extended the ethic to an environmental ethic of "thou shout not kill the environment upon which you and your neighbors depend. You shall not steal from the future generations by killing the environment upon which we all depend." And I think that is one of the things at the end of this discussion, whatever else we go away with, if we can come together with a new ethic of caring, a new understanding that the Napoleon wrasse—even if it's worth $10,000, once as a gourmet feast—if left in the ocean as a part of that system can be worth $10,000 month after month—a priceless value. In fact, you can't put a price tag on its value as part of the system—what it generates in income, but also what it generates in terms of the health which we cannot replace.

Richard Jordan, Inter-Faith Partnership, UNEP Regional Office, North America: I, too, was on the Black Sea, and I mentioned a term in Japanese: *Mottainai,* which means "humble sense of awe," and that certainly was put forth very well in the videos. But what I would like to do in building upon what Clive [Wilkinson] and Jack [Sobel] mentioned, in building on your partnerships and outreach to other organizations and networks, please include the religions. Religions are extremely good at developing and spreading this idea of the humble sense of awe, and I can certainly tell you that the Inter-Faith Partnership at UNEP, which has existed for 10 years, will certainly disseminate the results of this conference, and will perhaps help you in doing that. Thank you.

Clive Wilkinson: Thank you very much for that comment, and I'd like to talk with you afterward about that. Certainly in areas where I'm familiar, the local priest is a very important person in the community to get the message across about conservation of protecting reefs. And we're hoping in the year 2000, at the International Coral Reef Symposium, to hold a special symposium on the role of religion in conserving coral reefs, and I've been talking to Graham Kelleher about that, so please talk to me later.

Barbara Ornitz, Shellman and Ornitz: I want to address this to Jack [Sobel] and to Phillip [Dustan], because we had a meeting about this the other day. When we talk about the power of one, we—each of us in this room sitting in Washington, D.C., today—can do something, and I want wanted to let you know, and ask Jack and Phillip how they feel about this? There are some letters on my exhibit table that deal with three pieces of legislation—resolutions that are now sitting in the Senate and Congress. It's the first time that we've had, in principle, the proposal for stewardship for coral reefs that our Congress is looking at. My question—the letters are out there. Each one of us can sign one of these letters; we can send it to our senators, we can send it to our congressmen, and we can say, "We are exercising our power to ask you to support reefs." One of the resolutions deals with just a general stewardship call. The second resolution deals with cyanide and dynamite fishing practices as we have been talking so much about in this conference. And the third deals with funding—for projects for science and monitoring, community work—which we have also been talking about. So I guess my question would be: these are beginnings, but we—each of us—can take the step to sign onto these letters and send them on, and I would ask the panel members, particularly Jack and Phillip, if you would endorse that, or if you have comments about that, and then I would urge you to please pick up these letters and send them in.

Phillip Dustan: I think, unequivocally, I endorse that, and I know the people I have spoken to within the Cousteau Society endorse the idea.

I'm going to take the letter back and take it to my child's preschool and get the little kids to write letters, too, because my son wants to form an earth-saver's club.

I'd like to make one other comment about this that hasn't really come up—here we are at the World Bank—the value of the world's ecological goods and services, the kinds of things that reefs do for us has been valued at $33 trillion. That should make any banker take notice. And that's stuff we don't have to pay the world to do; it just does it for us. So maybe somewhere that should find its way into this educational process. It is an extremely conservative figure.

Marea Hatziolos: We have used that figure to try and educate our own senior management.

Jack Sobel: If I could just also comment on that—a couple of thoughts. First of all, we [Center for Marine Conservation] certainly endorse that. We think that taking personal action, whether you're a government person, whether you're an NGO representative, whether you're a scientist, whether you're a fisher—is really important. When I first came to Washington, D.C., I worked on "the Hill" [the U.S. Capitol], and the one thing that the Hill really convinced me of is that democracy does work if people participate. And writing letters and contacting your representatives and government makes an enormous difference. The other thought I have is that, in an international setting like this, I think it's still worth supporting that, but we shouldn't forget that there's a lot of people here who are not Americans, but there are similar [issues]—the same role of letter writing and individual participation is important. And because there's a fair number of people here who in one way or another are leaders in various communities, it's not just important to take personal action in terms of writing your own letter, but you have much greater impact if people go beyond that and encourage others, particularly when they have opportunities to speak publicly in open forums, to encourage other people to do that. I think you can really multiply your impact—in not only taking individual action, but also encouraging others to do the same.

Alexander Stone, Reef Keeper International: I would just put two things on the table for consideration at your work. One with regards to public awareness: we think it's real important to undertake focused awareness efforts that reach coastal user groups. And by that I mean the owners and managers of the reef that have outfalls that are dumping the sewage into the water. How do we target, or create public awareness efforts so we make sure we are getting the right message to that kind of a person? Or to the cab driver in the U. S. Virgin Islands that asks me: "Well, what's the big deal with those rocks that out there?" or the maid in Cozumel that tells me her family has lived in Cozumel for generations, and never has had the chance to look at a coral reef. How do we get to them? That's question, or point number 1. Point number 2 has to do with reef monitoring efforts. Particularly, I am addressing this to Clive [Wilkinson] and to John [McManus]: [inaudible]…we want to connect with you. And somehow we have spent a year wanting to connect, and we're still not touching. So I'm saying, let's develop some sort of a process to do that, because time continues to roll long and our reef monitoring efforts are growing and so are yours, and we don't want them to be too divergent for too long. Thanks.

Clive Wilkinson: I think the point is the power of one. I have salary until next February. John [McManus] is running out of money. We need a few more "ones" to make a team. But one thing you said about communication—I want to make one point; it is an anecdote that Jim Porter from the University of Georgia made. He was appearing before the Congress, or the Senate or some committee, and he had his best scientific presentations—graphs, histograms, pie diagrams—the lot. And they nodded [fell asleep]. And then he showed some before and after photographs. "Gee, it's that bad? We didn't realize it was that bad!"…So, we've got to learn to communicate.

John McManus: Yes, I'll just quickly add to that. What we've been doing with other groups is that we've been putting a bit of the onus on the other group, because especially initially, we had to be very cautious not to look like a threat to other groups. There were some groups that were nervous, so we've been more responsive than we have been aggressive toward getting information. The other problem is that there is only one of me, and Sheila Vergara, who is our team leader is out there, and her job is to figure out what we do at what time, and who actually puts it in, so please communicate directly with her if you have any trouble getting responses back from me.

Jack Sobel: It also sounds like, perhaps, taxi drivers are a particularly important constituency for us to reach out to [laughter]. I say that partly in joking, but the Reverend Bill Ballentine, for people who have worked on no-take marine reserves, has been one of the most forceful and effective advocates for reserves—in New Zealand and elsewhere—makes a point of wherever he goes, and I've traveled with him some and seen him do this—to talk with to everybody. And he, too, points out taxi drivers, because they talk to a lot of people. And it's the one-to-one thing of talking to taxi drivers; he doesn't limit it to there, he also he spends a fair amount of time in bars, and in bars he also reaches out to the bartender, and the person sitting next to him. And I think that is another way—there are a lot of constituencies. And the point I made earlier about who are the stakeholders? Everyone is a stakeholder in coral reef conservation. Some of them realize it already; some of them don't. And I think we need to reach out to a much broader and much more diverse group of people than we have so far been successful in reaching out to.

PANEL FIVE

ECONOMIC VALUATION OF CORAL REEFS

Session Chair: Maritta Koch-Weser, World Bank

Economic Values of Coral Reefs: What Are the Issues?

John A. Dixon
World Bank

Our concerns for the inherent values of coral reefs—both biological and economic—are central to their conservation and use. There has been much discussion at this workshop about the importance and values that people assign to coral reefs. However, at the same time we see that coral reefs are being destroyed around the world and that reefs are not being managed in a sustainable manner.

If something is recognized for its beauty, its biological richness, its opportunities to provide goods and services to individuals and societies, why is the same resource not being better managed? Earlier this week I had a visit from Matthew Wright from Jamaica, who is doing some very useful work on the Negril coral reef system in his country. He discussed the analysis being done on the importance of the reefs to the tourism industry and the Jamaican economy, and yet there is no money from the government for protection and management

Why is this? Why do we see this dichotomy—on the one hand, the widespread expression of interest in coral reefs and their conservation and protection, and, at the same time, the lack of resources to provide even minimum levels of management?

Part of the explanation for this state of affairs is the difference between economic values and monetary prices, and understanding that people and governments are often responding to monetary price signals. Economics can help explain this dichotomy. Coral reefs have been called the rain forests of the sea, and they face many of the same problems that rain forests face. We talk about the values associated with healthy rain forests and the importance of sustainable management and protection, yet we see the same widespread use of destructive practices and lack of resources for management.

Valuing the Known

A major problem, both for tropical rain forest's and for coral reefs, is that we tend to place values on what we can easily identify or see. The unknown is often assigned a value of zero—hence market forces reflect that portion of the goods and services that we can identify and can buy or sell. However, for both the rain forest and the coral reefs, there may be important values that we do not even know about yet, or ecosystem services that are only incompletely understood.

A useful theoretical construct is a concept called total economic value (TEV). This is a simple heuristic device stating that the total value of any resource is composed of different components, and some of these components are easy to identify and value, and others are either unknown or very intangible. As seen in figure 1, the components of TEV range from very concrete and marketable use values (on the left side), to uses that are more indirect, to values associated with mere existence of the resource or the possibility of leaving it for one's children. All

Figure 1. Total economic value of coral reef ecosystems

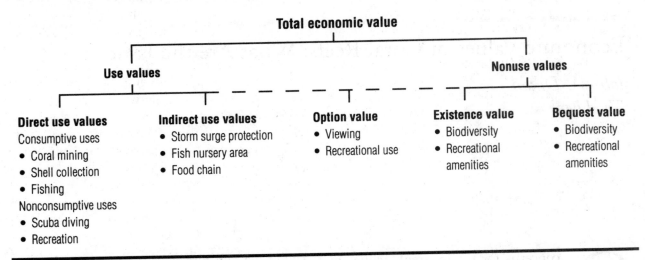

of these values are real; it is just that some are easier to measure and monetize, while others are much more difficult. The direct use values on the left side tend to be monetized and included in most calculations about the "economics" of coral reefs; the harder-to-quantify values on the right are often ignored. The sum of all of these values is called the total economic value, and this number is an economic measure, as opposed to a financial measure.

Components of Value

Think about coral reefs and their economic analysis: most analyses of coral reefs focus on a very small set of these values—frequently on the values associated with direct use of the reef and associated economic activities. These are called direct use values and may be either consumptive uses (such as collecting corals, shells, or reef fish) or nonconsumptive uses (such as recreation—snorkeling or diving—or sailing). In this case, the term *nonconsumptive* merely means that one can use the resource without destroying it; the difference is between observing reef fish as a scuba diver and catching and eating the same fish! In general, direct use values—consumptive and nonconsumptive—are unfairly easy to quantify, and we have learned a great deal about how to place monetary values on these uses. In fact, since direct use values are frequently driven by market forces and the desire to obtain a private financial return, these uses are the easiest to value. Some of these uses are destructive: for example, the collection of shells or mining of coral to produce lime. Other uses are nondestructive: recreational benefits can also be included in the calculation and may be an important form of nonconsumptive use.

In different situations, one form of direct use may be more important than another. For example, Herman Cesar discusses some very interesting results from Indonesia, where the direct use values of coral reefs—for fishing, lime production, the collection of shells, and other things—is considerable. These are all examples of consumptive, direct uses, and he estimates the financial returns to the individuals involved in each activity. In other locations, nonconsumptive uses are very important. Sport diving, a growing industry worldwide, is a nonconsumptive use of coral reefs and their associated habitat. Certain areas of Indonesia are developing into well-known scuba-diving destinations. Nonconsumptive uses have the attraction of allowing many individuals to enjoy the same resource and, with proper management, leave the resource healthy and productive.

In addition to direct use values, there are a number of other use values associated with coral reefs. Indirect use values, the second component of the TEV calculation, are important ecosystem values associated with healthy coral reefs. These include the following: the role of reefs in protecting coastal areas in times of storms; coral reefs acting as a nursery area for reef fish, and healthy reefs serving as part of the food chain for a wider range of sea creatures, including the pelagics. Many of these uses have been discussed here and are well known from the literature.

Most of these indirect uses, however, are usually not easily valued. Markets do not exist for most ecosystem services. Estimates have been made for some of these, however. One can value the catch of reef fish or other fish dependent on the reef. If the cause-effect link can be established, the calculation of monetary values is not very difficult. But what about the protective value of a reef in terms of coastal storm protection? Economic values for this service can be calculated but usually are not included in any analysis of the "value" of a coral reef. Consequently, most indirect use values are ignored when decisionmakers consider alternative uses for coral reefs.

The third type of values listed in figure 1 are option values, which are often difficult to measure. The concept of an option value is relatively straightforward: I want to protect this coral reef so that I may have the option to use it in the future. I do not know if I will or will not use it, but it is worth something to me to protect it and consequently I am willing to pay some amount of money to retain this potential future use. Option values can then be thought of as a form of deferred-use value.

Many nongovernmental organizations have been very effective in capitalizing on these feelings and mobilizing donations based on the willingness of individuals to pay for this option value. Save the humpback whale! Protect coral reefs! Or what have you. It helps, of course, if whatever you are trying to raise money for is attractive. Fortunately for coral reefs, they are beautiful and the phase "rain forest of the sea" is as much a marketing ploy as a scientific statement. Public information (TV specials, museum and aquarium exhibits, the activities of the Cousteau Society) are all very important in raising public awareness and thereby helping to create this option value. It's no coincidence that the

WWF uses a panda, or the Cousteau Society uses the dolphin, as symbols. Perhaps some other species (such as a rattlesnake or sea grass beds) is in fact more important ecologically, but it is not as likely to be as useful in raising money!

The *nonuse values* on the right side of figure 1 include pure existence values and bequest values. These represent the willingness to pay by individuals or societies to maintain a resource for the future, either just so they know it is there, even if they don't plan to use it (existence value) or to leave the resource to their children or grandchildren (bequest values). Since these values are nonuse values, they involve no present-day consumption of the resource, and are therefore the most difficult to measure and value. Usually some form of survey technique is used to identify and quantify nonuse values. These values can be considerable, however, and are important in both rich and poor societies.

The components of this whole suite of values—from direct use, both consumptive and non-consumptive, all the way to existence and bequest values—are all important and form part of the total social valuation of coral reefs. Note, however, that these values do not necessarily say anything about the inherent or intrinsic biological value of coral reef ecosystems as such. Economics is a social science that is anthropocentric and places values based on people's uses (and perceptions) of any resource. Economic analysis does not do a good job of valuing biodiversity per se.

Nevertheless, the economic information contained in a total economic value calculation can be very powerful in making the case to decisionmakers and others responsible for allocating financial resources that the benefits of protecting and managing coral reefs in a sustainable manner are substantial. And since the TEV approach captures both the easily identified financial returns from direct uses of the reefs, as well as the more difficult and often nonmarketed values associated with indirect uses, option values, and nonuse values, it reminds the decisionmaker that much more total value is produced by healthy coral reefs than just those limited uses that can be easily valued using market prices and market transactions.

Minding Our Ps and Qs

The major problem in valuing coral reefs relates to identifying what are the various components of value, and what monetary prices to assign to them. Since economics is based on individuals' expressions of value, the results are usually very site-specific, and one has to be very cautious about generalizing results from one study to other, very different locations.

A recent article by Bob Costanza and colleagues on the value of the worlds' ecosystems included a "value" for the world's coral reefs (Costanza and others 1997). The estimate illustrates the danger in using the "benefit transfer" approach whereby values determined in one study are applied to other locations. In the Costanza study the estimate of the global value of coral reefs was made by taking a per hectare estimate of various use values (the P, or price) and multiplying it times the global area of coral reefs (the Q, or quantity). In this case the Q was 62 million hectares of coral reefs, and the total P was some \$6,075 per hectare. Of this, fully half was attributed to recreational use: US\$3,008/ hectare/year. (The other large item was disturbance regulation, worth \$2,750/hectare/year.) The result of this exercise was a very large estimate of the economic value of the world's coral reefs—a total of \$375 billion per year. Obviously there are locations (such as well-known dive destinations like the Caymans, Bonaire, or the Red Sea) where high levels of revenues from recreational use are generated. Many of the world's coral reefs, however, are remote and little visited and do not generate this level of use (and economic value). Although flawed, this type of analysis does help to raise awareness that there are values associated with healthy coral reef ecosystems. The danger is that any economic estimates ultimately have to pass close scrutiny from the Treasury or Ministry of Planning if the results are to be believed and resources allocated for coral reef protection.

What can economists do, therefore, to make estimates that recognize the range of values associated with coral reefs and are also believable? Here it is important to introduce two concepts. Once concept central to much of environ-mental economics is that of externalities. Externalities are quite simple: they occur when an action that one takes has an effect on someone else, and the affected person is not part of the decisionmaking system. This leads directly to the second concept, the divergence between individual perceptions of value and societal perceptions. For example, in the Philippines, some fishermen use dynamite for blast fishing, which also destroys the reef, thereby harming others who depend on the reef via artisinal fishing or recreational diving. The blast fishing imposes an externality on the other users of the same reefs. But because the others are not part of the management process, they don't have an input into the decision to use blast fishing or an alternative measure, some of which may be much less destructive to the reef. Because of the existence of externalities, there is a divergence between private benefits and costs, and social benefits and costs. Simply put, the search for private financial gains by the blast fisherman imposes much larger costs on society. This divergence between private and social perspectives is the fundamental reason why we see so many perverse and destructive actions being taken in the use of the world's coral reefs.

The existence of externalities is a pervasive problem in the management of coral reefs. Herman Cesar, in his presentation on valuing coral reefs in Indonesia, talks about precisely this issue. He has carefully identified, in the case of Indonesian coral reefs, who benefits and who loses by each use or threat to the coral reefs. By quantifying the economic numbers involved, and the number of persons involved in each activity, he is able to point out those uses that generate large amounts of private benefits for a few individuals and also impose larger social costs on Indonesia because of externalities. By identifying these numbers, it is possible to discuss realistic management interventions. In some cases the private financial benefits are very large (for example, the live fish trade in species like the Napoleon wrasse for the Hong Kong Chinese seafood restaurant market). The number of individuals involved are few; their private gain is large. In other cases, such as coral reef mining to produce lime, the number of individuals involved is large but the per-person return is small. Each problem presents a different management challenge.

Second, the existence of externalities relates to the issue of property rights and who has rights to use coral reefs. In many traditional societies, reefs were part of the community-managed resource base. In Hawaii, for example, the traditional land management unit was called the *ahupua'a*, which was a slice of land that went from the top of the mountain down to the edge of the coral reef. Thus the individual or group who owned the *ahupua'a* owned an entire functioning ecosystem, a self-contained economic and environmental unit. Any externalities were thereby internalized, and the land managers realized that actions taken in the upper watershed (such as agricultural production or logging) would have an affect both on the water quality on the taro fields in the lower watershed well as in the coral reef and the coastal fish ponds. Since all impacts were contained within the system (with clearly defined integrated property rights), decisions were made taking these impacts into account and thereby balancing any tradeoffs involved.

The Hawaiian *ahupua'a* system is the ideal world; it very rarely exists today. Usually externalities are present, and they lead to the results that we observe: mismanagement, overuse, needless destruction of precious resources.

Some Final Cautions

Economics has a very important role to play in making the case for improved management and conservation of coral reefs. Perhaps most important, economic analysis helps to get some of the numbers on the table. Often these numbers are large and they are useful in getting attention. However, be careful in using and presenting these results. Always explain to the minister of planning or finance that the values that are identified are largely related to direct use of the coral reef—both consumptive and nonconsumptive uses—and may also include a few indirect use values.

Because of the nature of economic analysis, these values are anthropocentric and are deter-mined by how people perceive the various benefits and costs. Consequently, those coral reef areas that are heavily visited for recreation, or have an active fishing population living around them, will appear to have much higher values than remote systems. But we also know that the remote areas may be extremely important for the health of the entire worldwide coral reef ecosystem.

Accordingly, one has to be careful not to confuse prices with true value. Economists can do a good job on estimating the prices and economic returns from different uses. However, as economists, we probably do a pretty poor job on estimating the ultimate values—and this is precisely where scientific information is crucial for effective conservation and management of coral reef systems. Conservation of some parts of a reef system can be easily justified on economic grounds—for example, one can market recreational uses. Other reefs, however, may be remote and inaccessible, or buffeted by storm surge on the windward side of islands, and are not good for recreational diving. This does not mean that they do not have values. But these values may be more difficult to estimate using the traditional tools of economic analysis.

There are a few important lessons to keep in mind when using economic analysis to estimate the economic values of coral reefs:

- Coral reef ecosystems normally contain pervasive externalities. There is often no formal connection between those taking an action and those affected by that action. This has to be recognized, because it explains most of the observed management failures. All too often, "win-win" management solutions are not being followed because the same management options are seen as "lose-win" from an individual perspective — I lose so that others can gain. This situation is exacerbated by weak or unclear property rights. And given the open-access nature of most coastal areas, it is politically very hard to assign property rights to a coral reef to any individual or group.
- Prices are often lacking or hard to measure for many of the goods or services provided by healthy coral reefs. Economists can do a

pretty good job of estimating values for some uses of coral reefs; for many others (especially indirect uses and nonuse values), however, it is much more difficult. Economics has done a great deal in the last few years, and there are many more examples of economic analyses of coral reef ecosystems. A number of these have been presented at this conference. However, because of pervasive externalities, and valuation problems, markets often fail. Coral reefs are like terrestrial protected areas. If left to market forces alone, most of the world's reefs and protected areas will be destroyed because of the externalities and weak property rights. It is therefore an appropriate, legitimate area for intervention on the part of governments as representatives of society. Therefore the three Ps are needed: Planning, Pricing and Policies. Unfortunately, without them we will see continued destruction of much of this unique, valuable and precious resource.

Reference

Costanza, Robert, and others. 1997. "The Value of the World's Ecosystem Services and Natural Capital." *Nature* 387: 253–60.

Indonesian Coral Reefs: A Precious but Threatened Resource

Herman Cesar
World Bank

Coral reefs and their associated marine life constitute one of the greatest natural treasures of Indonesia.[1] Both their quality and their quantity are impressive: Indonesia is located at the center of the world's coral reef diversity, and, with some 75,000 square kilometers of coral, it holds approximately one-eighth of the world's coral reefs.[2] Coral reefs form the core of their livelihood for hundreds of thousands of Indonesian subsistence fishers, and are a source of food security in times of agricultural hardship. They also provide a natural barrier against wave erosion, thereby protecting coastal dwellings, agricultural land, and tourism beaches. They are a potential source of foreign exchange from divers and other marine tourists. In addition, because of their unique biodiversity, they are of great interest to scientists, students, pharmaceutical companies, and others. These and many other functions give coral reefs an important and growing value.

Despite this, the quality of coral reefs in Indonesia is declining rapidly. Even remote reefs in unpopulated areas are not free from man-induced deterioration. Anthropogenic (man-made) threats range from destructive fishery practices to pollution, and from dredging to tourism-related damages. At the moment, only 29 percent of Indonesian reefs are in good condition (that is, with more than 50 percent of live coral cover). In Ambon Bay and near the Thousand Islands, off the coast of Jakarta, once-pristine reefs have been transformed into dead wastelands over the last 20 years. Figure 1 shows this deterioration as measured by the maximum depth of live corals in four islands in Jakarta Bay.

The five main man-made threats leading to coral reef deterioration in Indonesia, are:

- *Poison fishing,* in which cyanide is squirted on coral heads to stun and capture live aquarium and food fish, but killing coral heads in the process
- *Blast fishing,* whereby small bombs are detonated in shallow reef areas, killing targeted

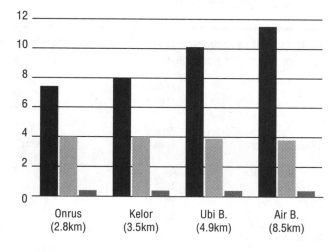

Figure 1. Temporal and spatial comparison of maximum depth of living coral reefs for four islands in Jakarta Bay

Onrus (2.8km) Kelor (3.5km) Ubi B. (4.9km) Air B. (8.5km)

Source: Tomascik and others 1993; references to primary data are given in the article.

schools of fish, but also killing larvae, juveniles, and corals

- *Coral mining,* in which corals are collected and smashed for house construction and lime production
- *Sedimentation and pollution,* as a result of logging, erosion, untreated sewage, and industrial discharges, which smother and kill the corals
- *Overfishing,* which does not destroy corals but reduces abundance and diversity of fish and invertebrates.

Private Gains versus Social Costs

Powerful economic forces are driving the observed destructive patterns of coral reef use, often rendering short-term economic profits, sometimes very large, to selected individuals. Measures for coral reef protection are often presumed to conflict with economic development, and are said to require a sacrifice of economic growth. However, this study shows that this perception stems mainly from a failure to recognize the magnitude of costs to the present and future economy resulting from reef degradation. Table 1 shows estimates of the benefits to individuals and losses to society from each square kilometer of coral reef destruction, providing an economic rationale for preventive or remedial efforts. For coastal protection and tourism losses, we have given both "high" and a "low" scenario estimates, depending on the types of coastal construction and tourism potential. High-cost scenarios are indicative of sites with high tourism potential and coastal protection value. Low-cost scenarios are indicative of sites with low tourism and coastal protection value.

Some of the most important values of coral reefs, such as those to future generations and intrinsic values, cannot be quantified. However, since the economic benefits from reef destruction are often used to justify continuation of these destructive practices, quantifying the costs associated with coral reef degradation is important in making a balanced assessment of the benefits and costs of various threats. The analysis is mainly based on observable data such as the value of the decline of fish catch or expenditures by hotels on groins to temporarily prevent beach erosion. Total costs should thus be interpreted as rough estimates of the lower range of true costs associated with reef destruction. The numbers in table 1 are generated on the basis of available data, using hypothetical examples of sites subject to one individual threat.

Table 1 clearly points out the devastating economic consequences of a policy of inaction. In fact, for none of the threats do the short-term benefits even approach the long-term costs (using a 10 percent discount rate and a 25-year time horizon).[3] For example, coral mining is estimated to yield net benefits to individuals of US$121,000 per square kilometer of reef (in net present value terms), while causing net losses to society of US$93,600 in fisheries value,

Table 1. Total net benefits and losses due to threats of coral reefs
(present value; 10 percent discount rate; 25 year time span; in US$; per km²)

Threat/function	Net benefits to individuals — Total net benefits	Net losses to society — Fishery	Coastal protection	Tourism	Others*	Total net losses (quantifiable)
Poison fishing	33	40	0	3-436	n.q.	43-476
Blast fishing	15	86	9-139	3-482	n.q.	98-761
Coral mining	121	94	12-260	3-482	›67.0**	176-903
Sediment/logging	98	81	–	192	n.q.	273
Sediment/urban	n.q.	n.q.	n.q.	n.q.	n.q.	n.q.
Overfishing	39	109	–	n.q.	n.q.	109

Ranges indicate sites of low and high value in terms of tourism potential and coastal protection value.
n.q. = nonquantifiable
* 'Others' includes loss of food security and biodiversity loss (nonquantifiable).
** Forest damage due to collection of wood for lime processing is estimated at US$67,000.

US$12,000 to US$260,000 in coastal protection value, US$2,900 to US$481,900 in tourism value, US$67,000 in forest damage, and unknown costs due to lost food security and biodiversity. Sometimes, the differences are even larger. For blast fishing in a high-value scenario, the costs are estimated to be more than 50 times higher than the benefits. Note that in the low-value sites, the largest cost to society is forgone fishery income, while in the high-value sites, coastal protection and tourism form the largest losses. Obviously, costs and benefits are very site-specific, and numbers will vary, depending on local circumstances.

Major Threats

Poison Fishing

With Hong Kong, China, restaurant prices as high as US$60 to US$180 per kilo for certain types of groupers and Napoleon wrasse, the wild-caught live fish trade has a gold rush-like character. Though Indonesia has only recently become involved in cyanide fishing, it is now the single largest single supplier of these fish for the Asian food market, holding more than 50 percent of the total share (Johannes and Riepen 1995) and a total value estimated at some US$200 million per year. Both in the restaurant retail business and in the older aquarium fishery, cyanide is nearly exclusively used as the "cost-effective" way of harvesting live fish. If current catch rates continue, the live-caught restaurant fish business will probably collapse economically in about four years (Johannes and Riepen 1995), as rapidly decreasing stocks in Indonesia will make remoter Pacific islands and Papua New Guinea fishing grounds more profitable.

Large-scale poison-fishing vessels operate in remote and unpopulated areas of Indonesia, leaving behind a mosaic of coral destruction. Table 2 shows estimates of costs and benefits of these operations for the whole of Indonesia, under the assumption that this business will become economically nonviable in four years because of a decline in catch rates. Rough estimates of a sustainable alternative in the form of hook-and-line live-grouper fishery, as used in

Table 2. Costs and benefits of all remaining Indonesian large-scale poison fishing and their sustainable alternative
(25-year horizon; 10% discount rate; in US$1,000,000)

	Present (with cyanide)		Sustainable (with hook & line)	
	Costs	Benefits	Costs	Benefits
Direct costs/benefits				
Sales of grouper		475.5		680.8
Labor	108.1		154.7	
Boat, fuel	79.2		204.2	
Cyanide	6.3		0.0	
Scuba/hookah	15.8		0.0	
Side-payment (6.7% of sales)	31.7		0.0	
Subtotal (direct)	241.2	475.5	359.0	680.8
Indirect costs/benefits				
Coastal protection	0.0		0.0	
Forgone tourism	280.2		0.0	
Hospital, mortality	n.q.		0.0	
Biodiversity, etc.	n.q.		0.0	
Subtotal (indirect)	280.2	0.0	0.0	0.0
Total costs/benefits	521.4	475.5	359.0	680.8
Net benefit to society	-46.0		321.8	

Australia and elsewhere, are also presented. Note that even in the absence of any alternative, the large-scale poison fishery creates a net quantifiable loss to Indonesia of US$46 million over four years. On the other hand, a sustainable hook-and-line fisheries option could create foreign exchange for the country, jobs for an estimated 10,000 Indonesian fishers for many years to come, and net benefits of some US$321.8 million (in present value terms).

Blast Fishing

Though forbidden in Indonesia and elsewhere, and despite the inherent dangers, homemade bombs are still a very popular fishing gear used to catch schools of reef fish and small pelagics

Figure 2. Net present value of blast fishing to individuals and associated losses to society per square kilometer of reef

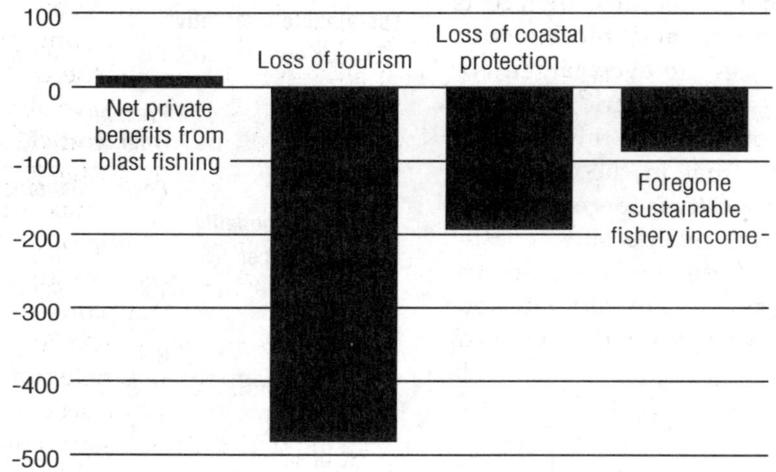

and thereby "earn money the easy way." In the past, the explosive charge came from World War II bombs, though fertilizers and illegally purchased dynamite, often from civil engineering projects, are currently used. The explosion shatters the stony corals and kills fish and invertebrates in a large surrounding area. Over time, blast fishing damages the whole reef and thereby destroys the resource base of many subsistence fishers. The analysis, shown in table 1, illustrates that the costs in terms of forgone sustainable fishery income alone are nearly six times as high as the short-term gains from blast fishing (US$86,000 versus US$15,000). The other losses to society, in terms of forgone coastal protection and tourism, are even higher in areas with high tourist potential or considerable coastal construction. These losses are estimated at US$193,000 and US$482,000 respectively, as illustrated in figure 2.

Coral Mining

Corals have long been used for building material and for the production of lime, as well as in the ornamental coral trade. The lime is often used as plaster or mixed with cement to reduce costs for private dwellings and local administrative offices. Coral mining not only destroys reef flats, and thereby its coastal protection function, but leads indirectly to logging of secondary forests, which furnish wood used for lime burning. The external economic costs of this logging are estimated at some US$67,000 per square kilometer of coral flat mined, as much as the total rent that all the miners get for this area. Coral mining used to be very widespread in Bali, where some hotels are now paying high prices (over US$100,000 a year) to mitigate the resulting beach erosion. Hotel-chain managers have learned from this and state that the status of coral reefs is currently a decisive criterion in site selection for new resorts. Mining activity is still practiced on other islands with large tourist potential, such as Lombok, where total net costs to society are estimated to be 7.5 times higher than the net benefits to individuals.

Sedimentation and Pollution

Sedimentation, both from urban areas and from logging activities, smothers corals as it prevents them from capturing sun light and plankton—their primary sources of energy and nutrition. Pollution, from both agrochemicals and industrial discharges, can also kill corals. These problems are particularly acute close to estuaries of rivers and urban centers. Figure 3 shows the correlation between live coral cover and distance from land for islands near Jakarta. For urban-induced sedimentation, no economic costs have been calculated: typically they vary dramatical-

Figure 3. Relationship between live coral cover and distance from land

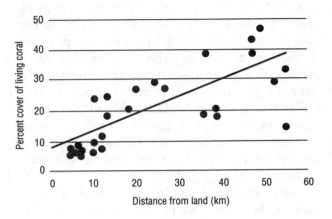

ly with the site, and reduction of discharges often has many other economic benefits (such as sanitary improvements and disease control), making the costs to corals probably minor. Estimates by Hodgson and Dixon (1988) for logging-induced sedimentation damage to a coral reef in Philippines showed costs 2.8 times higher than the associated benefits.

Overfishing

Though not necessarily as destructive as the other threats described above, overfishing does damage coral reefs, mainly through a reduction in fish diversity. It also decreases the value of corals to recreational divers, who are eager to see both large predators and an abundance of small, colorful fish. For the cost-benefit calculation of overfishing, we have abstracted from forgone tourist revenues and only estimated the loss in rent from the fishery at "open access" compared with the "maximum sustainable yield." The present value of this loss per square kilometer is US$ 70,000, as given in table 1. This means that on average, coral reef fisheries could produce an additional US$70,000 in net present value per square kilometer of reef if effective management was introduced.

In general, the necessary reduction in effort to avoid overfishing and achieve optimal sustainable yields is on the order of 60 percent (McManus and others 1992). Alternative income generation, for instance in ecotourism, could be one way of bringing about this reduction in effort. Besides lowering the total effort, fisheries management efforts should also focus on the creation of sanctuaries and the establishment of closed seasons. Figure 4 shows the dramatic difference in yield between a three-year harvesting cycle and a one-year harvesting cycle for mother-of-pearl shells (trochus) in Maluku. Note that the three-year closed seasons ending in 1978 gave an average yield of 3,400 kilograms, or

Figure 4. Yield of trochus (mother-of-pearl) in Noloth (Central Maluku) in 1969–1992
(per kilogram)

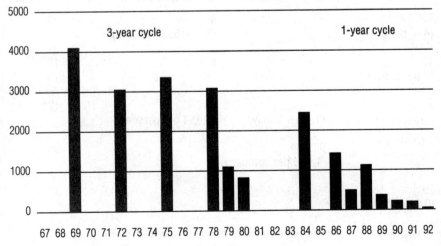

more than 1,100 kilograms per year. In the annual collection pattern followed since 1987, the average yield per year is just over 400 kilograms. Transfer of fishing rights to local communities, as well as reintroduction of traditional rights, such as the *sasisasi* system in Maluku, are other effective ways of dealing with overfishing and destructive fishing practices.

Balancing Winners and Losers

Given the high societal costs created by these threats, the question arises as to why the threat exists in the first place. Two stakeholder issues seem to be of critical importance: the size of the stakes per person, and the location of the individual causing the threat relative to the location of the threat itself. With respect to the first point, the size of the stakes per person, table 3 shows the private benefits that accrue to the various groups of stakeholders as well as to each of the persons/families/boats/companies involved. The total amount of benefit is equal to the value presented in table 1. The column marked 'Others' presents the payments to third persons, sometimes referred to as 'political rents'.

Note that the net benefits per square kilometer to individuals seem to be highest for coral mining. However, if we look at the private benefits per stakeholder (person/boat/company), poison fishing and logging-induced sedimentation have by far the highest private incentives, ranging from US$2 million per company in the case of logging to over US$ 0.4 million per boat in the case of poison fishing (in present value terms). Side-payments are also particularly high, very roughly estimated at some approximately US$0.3 million to US$1.5 million for some receivers of large payments. On the other extreme, coral mining is a very marginal activity for the families involved, though the side-payments are not negligible.

Some major caveats apply with respect to table 3: the stakes per person are calculated on the basis of man-years. For mining, where families are involved nearly full-time with this activity, this approach represents rather well the real stakes per person. But in the case of blast fishing, where many subsistence fishermen use bombs occasionally, the actual stakes involved per person are much lower than the net present value figure of US$7,300 given in table 3. For instance, if blast fishermen use bombs only once a month, rather than every day, the stakes in net present value are less than US$300 per person. A similar story holds for poison fishing, where

---

Table 3. Net benefits to individuals: totals and amount per stakeholder
(present value; 10% discount rate; 25 y. time-span; in 100 US$; per km2)

Threat/individual	Fishermen	Miners, loggers	Others (payments)	Totals per km2
Poison fishing	29 (467 per boat)	–	4 (317–1585 per boat)	33
Blast fishing	15 (7 per fisher)	–	n.q.	15
Mining	–	67 (1.4 per family)	54 (18-54 per person)	121
Sediment/logging	–	98 (1,990 per company)	n.q.	98
Overfishing	39 (0.2 per fisher)	–	–	39

Ranges indicate sites of low and high value in terms of tourism potential and coastal protection value.
n.q. - non quantifiable

Table 4. Size of economic stake and location of stakeholder

	Size of economic stakes	
	Small	**Big**
Insider	**Coral mining, blasting, overfishing** local threat-based approach	**Sediment** integrated coastal zone management
Outsider	**Overfishing** local threat-based approach	**Cyanide, logging** national threat-based approach

Location of the individual causing the threat

divers are often recruited for short periods of time only, a fact that results in significant overestimation of the real stakes per diver. At the same time, the overall picture that incentives differ dramatically per threat remains valid, and types of management interventions differ accordingly. In the case of urban sedimentation, especially when some large industries are involved, the stakes are probably high, though we have not been able to estimate specific stakes per person for this situation.

For the second point, the location of the individuals causing the threat, it is crucially important to distinguish between stakeholders living in the area where the threat is posed (insiders) versus stakeholders coming from elsewhere (outsiders). For instance, in the case of large-scale poison fishing operations, the captain and his crew are outsiders, as is also often the case with logging-induced sedimentation. Overfishing, on the other hand, can come from both local fishermen (insiders) as well as from outside fishermen. Population pressure and open-access problems, respectively, are often responsible for this situation. Mining and blast fishing are typically activities carried out by the local population, though large-scale explosives fishery operations do exist (Erdmann 1995).

The insider-versus-outsider issue and the size of the stakes per person are highlighted in a two-by-two matrix presented in table 4. The boxes in the matrix refer to the specific threats, such as poison fishing in the "big" and "outsider" box. Note that these are general tendencies, and there will inevitably be site-specific circumstances that form exceptions to this framework.

Designing Appropriate Policy Responses

In Jakarta, local stakeholder consultations are not very useful. If the stakes are small and there is one dominant threat, such as coral mining in some locations on West Lombok, integrated coastal zone management (ICZM) may not be necessary: a very direct approach, such as a small-scale alternative income generation project, might be the easiest way to resolve the threat. If there are multiple threats, ICZM will be the preferred solution, although outsider threats have to be dealt with separately. Based on these features, the following three general types of management approaches are defined.

Local Threat-Based Approach

If the dominant threat(s) or threats in a specific site fall under the categories "small-insider" or "small-outsider," a local threat-based approach is probably appropriate. This typically takes the form of community-based management. Examples are villages with a combination of overfishing and some blast fishing. Appropriate options include alternative income generation activities, enforcement of anti-explosives regulation, and establishment of cooperatives or other types of fishermen groups. Re-introduction of traditional common property resource management (for example, the *sasi* system in Maluku) is another possibility. In some situations provincial regulations need to be adjusted to allow for common property resource management. In cases like coral mining, ad hoc solutions might be appropriate. An example is one village in Bali that stopped coral mining completely after a local hotel offered employment as gardeners to all the mining families.

National Threat-Based Approach

In situations where the categorization "big-outsider" applies for the main threat or threats in a specific location, action at the national level is required. The clearest example is large-scale poison fishing operations, which often take place in remote and unpopulated areas. Strong initiatives at the highest national levels, involving the navy and the police, are the only way to stop this threat, as local and provincial officials are powerless in the face of these operations. Likewise, sedimentation from large-scale logging and mining operations can only be dealt with nationally, as it is at that level that the concessions are negotiated.

Integrated Coastal Zone Management

When sites cope primarily with "big-insider" situations, or if the site is confronted with an array of different threats that cannot be dealt with separately, ICZM seems appropriate. This is, for instance, the case in Manado, with a large, thriving dive tourism industry that is more and more endangered by a variety of threats, from sewage to poison fishing. Other examples might include Jakarta Bay and Ambon Bay, also with a variety of threats related to urbanization and population.

Conclusions

Coral reefs are a precious resource, with a variety of functions, such as subsistence fishery, coastal protection, tourism, and biodiversity. The Indonesian reefs are being rapidly destroyed by a number of different threats, especially poison fishing, blast fishing, coral mining, sedimentation and pollution, and overfishing.

The private benefits to individuals involved in these destructive practices are often considerable. However, the costs to society are much larger, up to a factor of 50 times higher in the case of blast fishing in tourist areas. The divergence between private benefits and social costs implies a highly inefficient outcome that calls for decisive government action to stop these threats.

The policy response to be used differs with the type of threat. In cases where the immediate stakeholders are outsiders and the stakes are

big, such as large-scale poison fishing and logging operations, a national threat-based approach is called for. With large stakeholders that are mostly insiders, integrated coastal zone management will be optimal. When the stakes are small, a local threat-based approach would give the most immediate results, typically in the form of community-based management, assisted by appropriate property rights legislation and enforcement.

Notes

1. This paper, authored by Herman Cesar, Carl Gustaf Lundin, Sofia Bettencourt and John Dixon, was reproduced courtesy of the Royal Swedish Academy of Sciences, *Ambio* 26 (6), Sept. 1997.
2. The coral area of Indonesia is commonly estimated at 50,000 to 100,000 square kilometers.
3. Some claim that a lower discount rate than the opportunity cost of capital is called for, given the intergenerational character of the problem, However, this would not qualitatively change the results. Note that a 10 percent discount rate does not imply that all stakeholders will have this rate of time preference; the discount rate is only used for the welfare economic analysis.

References

Cesar, H. 1996. "Economic Analysis of Indonesian Coral Reefs." World Bank Environment Department Paper, Environment Economic Series. Agriculture Operations, Country Department III, East Asia and Pacific Region and Environment Department. Washington, D.C.

Erdmann M. 1995. "The ABC Guide to Coral Reef Fisheries in Southwest Sulawesi, Indonesia." *NAGA: The ICLARM Quarterly*.

Erdmann, M.V., and L. Pet-Soede. 1996. "How Fresh Is Too Fresh: The Live Reef Food Fish Trade in Eastern Indonesia." *NAGA: The ICLARM Quarterly*.

Hodgson, G., and J. A. Dixon, 1988. "Logging versus Fishing and Tourism in Palawan: An Environmental and Economic Analysis." Occasional Paper No. 7. East-West Environment and Policy Institute, Hawaii.

Hutomo M. 1987. "Coral Fish Resources and Their Relation to Reef Condition: Some Case Studies in Indonesian Waters." *Coral Reef*

Management in Southeast Asia, 29: 67–81.

Johannes, R. E., and M. Piepen., 1995. *Environmental, Economic, and Social Implications of the Live Reef Fish Trade in the Asia and Western Pacific.* Jakarta: The Nature Conservancy, Jakarta.

McManus, J. W. 1994. "The Spratley Islands: A Marine Park?" *Ambio* 23: 181-86.

Post, J. C., and C. G. Lundin, eds. 1996. *Guidelines for Integrated Coastal Zone Management.* Environmentally Sustainable Development Studies and Monograph Series No. 9. Washington, D.C.: World Bank.

Tomascik, T., Suharsono, and A. J. Mah., 1993. "Case Histories: A Historical Perspective of the Natural and Anthropogenic Impacts in the Indonesian Archipelago, with a Focus on the Kepulauan Seribu, Java Sea." *Proceedings of the Colloquium on Global Aspects of Coral Reefs: Health Hazards and History.* University of Miami, Florida

Cost-Effectiveness Analysis of Coral Reef Management and Protection: A Least-Cost Model for the Developing Tropics

Richard Huber
World Bank

The primary research question that is being asked by this project is: "What is the most cost-effective means for achieving a given level of coral reef health?" The research asks a supplementary question that recognizes the operational realities of applying such analyses in the developing tropics. Notably, the research addresses the question: "How can the limited ecological data available in developing countries be used most efficiently in identifying least-cost solutions?"

Many coral reef areas in the tropics are deteriorating under heavy pressure from human and economic activities. There are many practical issues in devising cost-effective policy interventions to manage and protect coral reefs. There is also a key conceptual barrier: a lack of quantitative models to facilitate a comprehensive economic and ecological analysis of the effects of economic activity on coral reefs. This lack has made it difficult to develop a ranking of policy and investment interventions by cost-effectiveness, and thus to develop least-cost plans to manage and protect coral reefs. The central focus of this research is to develop a least-cost model of coral reef management and protection.

A key output of this model will be an optimized cost function, relating marginal costs of reef conservation to coral reef quality. The cost function can be used to identify a set of least-cost interventions for any given target of coral reef quality.

A prototype model is developed that is capable of measuring the cost-effectiveness of single policy interventions, though it is not yet capable of developing an optimized set of interventions. In the prototype model, cost-effectiveness is derived in three steps. First, a baseline is established by developing annual forecasts of economic activity and implied pollutant levels for 60 years and, on the basis of the pollutant levels and oceanographic and biotic conditions, developing annual forecasts of coral reef health. The measure of coral reef health is *coral reef abundance*, the percentage of the reef covered by live coral. Second, the total cost (as a present value) of a policy intervention is derived, along with annual pollutant levels and coral reef abundance after the policy intervention is in place. Finally, the cost-effectiveness is estimated on an annual basis, taking into account improvements in reef health over the entire period, but giving greater weight to early effects. The measure of cost-effectiveness is the unit cost of the impact of the intervention (the cost of a 1 percent increase in coral reef health).

Preliminary estimates of unit costs have been prepared for 10 policy interventions, using data loosely based on Montego Bay, Jamaica. In this case of a poor reef with potential for improvement, the key factors believed to be responsible for deterioration of the reef are sediment and nutrient loads. The most cost-effective intervention is a sewage outfall and pump station that takes the sediment beyond the reef edge. Other case studies include the south coast of Cuaraçao and the Maldives.

The dissemination strategy focuses on in-country workshops and seminars for user groups and stakeholders, government agencies, and private and nongovernmental organizations involved in coastal zone management. It also includes activities to foster cooperation among countries on coordinated environmental policies, strategies, and action plans in the coastal zone, and to provide a consultation mechanism for formulating, strengthening, harmonizing, and enforcing environmental laws and regulations. Workshops were held in Montego Bay, Jamaica, in November 1995 and March 1997, and in Curaçao in November 1995 and April 1996.

This study is complemented by another research project, Marine Resource Valuation: An Application to Coral Reefs in the Developing Tropics (ref. no. 681–05), which is deriving improved estimates of coral reef benefits to be used in conjunction with the cost function.

Responsibility

Latin America and the Caribbean, Country Department III, Environment and Urban Development Division—Richard M. Huber (Internet address rhuber@worldbank.org). With H. Jack Ruitenbeek, H. Jack Ruitenbeek Consulting; Frank Rijsberman, Resource Analysis; and Steven Dollar and Mark Ridgley, University of Hawaii. The Netherlands Environment Consultant Trust Fund, the Norway Consultant Trust Fund, and the Swedish Consultant Trust Fund are contributing funding for the research.

Reports

Huber, Richard, Jack Ruitenbeek, Steve Dollar, Mark Ridgely, Frank Rijsberman, and Subodh Mathur. 1996. "A Least-Cost Model for Coral Reef Management and Protection, Phase I: A Prototype Model." World Bank, Latin America and the Caribbean, Country Department III, Washington, D.C.

Resource Analysis. 1995. "Costs Model for Waste Water Treatment, CORAL." World Bank, Latin America and the Caribbean, Country Department III, Washington, D.C.

Rijsberman, Frank, Richard Huber, Susie Westmacott, and Danielle Hirsch. 1995. "Cost-Effectiveness Analysis of Coral Reef Management and Protection: A Case Study of Curaçao." World Bank, Latin America and the Caribbean, Country Department III, Washington, DC.

Westmacott, Susie, Frank Rijsberman, and Richard Huber. 1996. "Cost-Effectiveness Analysis of Coral Reef Management and Protection: A Case Study of the Maldives." World Bank, Latin America and the Caribbean, Country Department III, Washington, D.C.

Marine System Valuation: An Application to Coral Reefs in the Developing Tropics

This project is working to develop improved methods for deriving estimates of coral reef benefits. Such estimates can be used in conjunction with the cost function being developed in a related study (Cost-Effectiveness Analysis of Coral Reef Management and Protection, ref. no. 680–08) to help in identifying an optimal set of interventions for improving coral reef health.

The project adapts and refines existing valuation methods so that they take account of the key characteristics of coral reefs and derive more accurate estimates of coral reef benefits for selected sites. To keep the analysis tractable, the study focuses on three methods for valuing the benefits: direct use valuation, contingent valuation, and marine system biodiversity valuation. The study will apply and refine each of these valuation methods and then develop a synthesized benefits function. It will also identify appropriate policy and institutional reforms for improving the capture of resource values associated with coral reefs in developing countries, and the potential role of the World Bank and other development assistance agencies in helping to effect these reforms.

The study applies direct use valuation to provide a baseline analysis of the direct use benefits accruing to the coral reefs at Curaçao and Montego Bay, Jamaica. Well-established techniques are available for estimating easily quantifiable values associated with direct consumptive and nonconsumptive uses of reefs (such as tourism, demersal fisheries, and mariculture). The study will use contingent valuation to monetize amenity and other noninstrumental uses for the coral reef site in Montego Bay, Jamaica.

The project's work on marine system biodiversity valuation will be more involved. It will require identifying appropriate physical or biophysical indicators in marine systems to which economic values might be attached, and appropriate, quantifiable indicators of biodiversity. It also will require identifying appropriate methods for marine system valuation, based on methods used for terrestrial systems, and for imputing values to natural products. Once the study has identified potential methods for marine biodiversity valuation, it will evaluate them for policy relevance, methodological soundness, operational tractability, and data availability. Up to three of the methods will then be subjected to a preliminary field test.

The dissemination strategy will focus on in-country workshops and seminars targeting those involved in coastal zone management. The workshops will provide training in conducting the contingent valuation survey and in analyzing and collecting data.

Responsibility

Latin America and the Caribbean, Country Department III, Environment and Urban Development Division—Richard M. Huber (Internet address rhuber@worldbank.org. With H. Jack Ruitenbeek, H. Jack Ruitenbeek Consulting; Daniel M. Putterman; Clive Spash, Cambridge University; Nick Hanley, British University of Stirling, Scotland; and Montego Bay Marine Park Trust. The Netherlands Environment Consultant Trust Fund is contributing funding for the research.

Completion date: December 1999.

Report

Huber, Richard M., H. Jack Ruitenbeek, and Daniel M. Putterman. 1997. "Marine Resource Valuation: An Application to Coral Reefs in the Developing Tropics." World Bank, Latin America and the Caribbean, Country Department III, Washington, DC.

Discussion

As we move toward the discussion, let me add a few of my own questions to maybe fuel the discussion we're going to have. Going from local examples, like Indonesia, Bonaire, or Jamaica, to the global scene, how does the world community value coral reefs? This is really an interesting question, because it seems that in some environmental scenes, we get from economic evaluation to action quite significantly. Take biodiversity: the GEF movement as one example, and in other cases we seem to have a harder time. So my question to you is—and I'll illustrate it very briefly, and then we'll move toward the discussion—why is it that not all environmental needs are treated equally? Some of the reasons, of course have to do with understanding, but I submit there are other reasons. And you may find this a bit absurd, but I'm saying let's look at CFCs—at ozone depletion, and why did ozone depletion get such attention, and why do we have less of the same quality of attention when it comes to coral reef and marine issues?

Let's look very briefly at some of the parallels as I would see them. We're dealing with global commons. Nations cannot go it alone, and we're dealing with something where people—in the ozone case even more so than in the marine case—had their doubts about science and was it real? Was it really relevant to us? But we got somewhere. The Montreal Protocol is one of the few, albeit small, first successes where the world community got together, found what the problem is, found a way to start addressing it throughout the world, and we're beginning to see some results. The challenge is similar, there's a time clock taking away—on ozone as on coral reefs. We need to turn this around in a few years or else we shall have lost immensely.

Now, with the CFCs, there is a recognition that the phaseout requires industrial restructuring. People were building the wrong refrigerators and air conditioning systems using the wrong gases, and you had to help them remodel their production line. Now coral reefs and marine issues facing very similar issues. They also have industries that, in a sense, drive them. There are industries that build fishing boats in certain numbers—and they sort of push into the market. There is of course the tourism, and there are the land-based sources of marine pollution. Those industries also need looking at. It's not just the nature of what's being produced, but the quantities that are wrong. But you have an entire production system that is built on this and you have an entire, very large group of people that have bought this equipment—borrowed from the banks, and need to pay back their loans. And unless there is some solution for them, unless they go fishing, they have a very hard time getting out of something which—they will real realize—in the long run is unsustainable. So my question is: Why, in your further discussions, not apply some of these positive parallels—like the Montreal Protocol, to the marine discussion and see what is driving the degradation in this particular case?

So to sum up my question, Is there a reason to discuss what is the magnitude of phaseout of the wrong marine practices? Is there a reason to discuss similar strategies as has been found in other cases? And if so, you may find it worthwhile to discuss some of this now, or in your afternoon sessions. With that let me open for discussion.

Charlotte de Fontaubert, Center for International Environmental Law: I have a question for both John Dixon and Herman Cesar about valuation of coral reef. Herman, I couldn't help but notice the big question marks in your cost-benefit analysis with regards to intrinsic value, biodiversity value, and the food security value. Whilst I'm sympathetic to the fickle nature of measuring nonuse values and option values, my question is, By not integrating these values, are you not missing a whole set of arguments that you could use with policymakers in order to give them an extra incentive to take remedial action?

John Dixon: Charlotte, you point out a very important dimension of the problem. As Herman said: what we frequently have to do is start with the most concrete and most directly measurable impacts, partly because you have a better chance, frankly, of convincing the minister of finance in the five minutes you have that it's an issue. I think you should always point out the other dimensions of value and say we know that these are very important, and we do have studies in other settings which indicate some of the magnitude of some of these values. But separate out those values that are quite concrete, and that you can measure. For the other values, we put them in qualitatively, or sometimes quantitatively. Remember you've got to convince someone who's got a lot of demands on their time and attention, and on their budget. And so we start with those uses and values that are the easiest to communicate, but always recognizing that these are only part of the whole.

Herman Cesar: The question is, Where do you stop? There are a lot of functions that we are very bad in measuring. And if you can make your point with a couple of things that are easy to measure, you might actually make a stronger point to the minister of finance than if you try to measure everything. And I agree with what John says—what you do with the others, you say: "These are other functions that are extremely important, but are very difficult to quantify, to monetize." Sometimes you can already make your point by just one or two functions and measuring them. A minister of finance is interested in tourism dollars; is interested in fisheries because that is often related to social stability of coastal communities; is interested in coastal protection because if that is destroyed that often costs a lot of money for next budget in order for the government to restore that. So those are very concrete things that he can think of in terms of his own budget line items Biodiversity, intrinsic values, and all kinds of other things—which I really believe are much more important—might not be the type of things that would help a lot in convincing the minister. So that's why you sometimes need to pick out a couple of functions that are easy to measure and that already make the point.

John Dixon: Remember that the people we are trying to convince are intelligent people, but they are skeptical too. Look at these values assigned to 62 million hectares of coral reef worldwide by Costanza. Disturbance regulation: $2,750 per hectare per year; waste treatment: $58; biological control: $5; food production: $220, recreation: $3,000. Added together you get a big number quickly—over $6,000 dollars per hectare. When you multiply that times 62 million hectares you get a very big number—over $370 billion per year. But you're talking to the minister of planning in Indonesia, or the Philippines, and he looks at these numbers and says: "Do you really think we're getting the magnitude of benefits? We have thousands of hectares of reefs that are not even visited or used at all. And you say we're getting recreational benefits—how do you know that?" If you're going to make an economic argument, make one that's reasonable and sound, and base it on realistic data. Herman Cesar tried to do this in Indonesia, where he looked at actual use values, actual practices, and gave a range of values. You can make up big numbers easily, and they will just as quickly be dismissed and then you lose your whole argument. So start with estimates that are local, concrete and add the other dimensions as appropriate.

Bill Kiene, Smithsonian Institution: This question is probably more directed to education than an economist, but it is something I've wanted to ask an economist. As a marine scientist I have studied a lot the movement of biological and geological products through reef ecosystems. And in doing so, you have direct analogies that relate to economies. I've used some of that to try and understand the way these materials function in an ecosystem, and also used it in presentations to try and describe reefs to people. The question is: Is there a potential, tangible value in using economic models—not only to try and understand how coral reefs work and understand some of the problems they are undergoing—but also potentially use the way coral reefs function as a way to understand the way economies work, and potentially use this to communicate the value of reefs to finance ministers, or CEOs, or the general public as well?

John Dixon: Economy and ecology come from the same root, *Eco*, and they are obviously linked. Getting information—whether you use a fancy model or a very simple model— is not really the issue. It's trying to present it clearly. If you think about the issue of stakeholders—of the private and social perspectives—and the externalities that exist and present the situation in a straight-forward manner, it can be very powerful. When you go in and the minister of finance asks, "How important, how valuable are our coral reefs?" and you say, "Very valuable," that doesn't get you very far. If you say: "Mr. Minister, there are ten thousand jobs in this area dependent on direct use, indirect use, consumptive/nonconsumptive uses, these are threatened," these numbers strike home.

And remember: don't confuse measures of economic value with intrinsic, ultimate values—that's a separate issue. We're economists, we look at a subcomponent of the whole, although it's an important one and can be very powerful

in making a case for increased resources for coral reef management.

Mary Kasha, Student, New College of Florida: I have a question about the economic value of ecotourism. Yesterday we had a panel speak to us on the various merits of ecotourism as a tool for conservation. Today, Mr. Dustin showed us some of the damages in the Florida Keys that have resulted from that type of tourism. Given that this is a use that's only renewable if we properly managed it, I wanted to ask the panel what they thought of the economic value of this type of tourism, and whether it was applicable to all regions, or whether it was region-specific?

Richard Huber: The three countries—Costa Rica, Belize, and Dominica—which are really making a go of this ecotourism, utilizing marine ecosystems are definitely sharing the benefits, and I think it's one of the several—bioprospecting is another new one that has come on the horizon like ecotourism—which are giving us more apparent economic reasons for preserving these ecosystems.

Dwight Shellman, Shellman and Ornitz: I would like to interject something that has been dawning on me through this whole series of seminar speakers. The actual improvement of the ability of economists like the panelists, to identify externalities—I think there's a missing element, and I would like to engage with other disciplines in maybe exploring it. But the problem that I see is that if we continue to permit externalities to remain external, this will continue to be a public policy discussion. Mr. Cesar's overlay makes an excellent point, and that is, one way to deal with these externalities is to internalize them. And the discipline that is missing here is the legal discipline.

If you look at the people taking the losses—if an American trial lawyer, or an ambulance chaser would look at that scenario, what you would see in many cases is a clientele who has sustained a damage of huge magnitude. And probably, some participants in creating that damage, which would likely be American or multinational corporations who are buying products, that would have deep pockets that would be available to reimburse the losers. And I would suggest that one way to connect the linkage here of internalizing what are now externalities, is to find a case where the taking—that is, demonstrated by those externalities from some population is actually charged back to a corporation to where it either shows up in their balance sheet as a real liability, or as a contingent liability, or as reflected in their insurance policies. So I throw that out as something that I would be happy to explore with others, but I think the state of economic science is improving very rapidly.

Vaughan Davidson: He's right. The first part of my life I was a CPA with Arthur Andersen, involved in audits on a global basis. The last four years I've been on sabbatical. I have a foundation. I'm a trustee with a couple of other people. What I see here is that no one's accruing these costs at the front end. The numbers of plain present value—they don't work in this kind of transaction. Anytime you play with present value, you bring in a number—it's going to be almost zero so many years out. The cost that your creating or occurring the moment you [inaudible] into the river—it's over. So you've got to stop it at the front. The cost should be accrued in total up front, because there's no plan to cover it. What I would contend is like he indicated, we've got to accrue the expenses to match the revenue, otherwise as a value analysis it's bogus. You're not matching costs and expenses. And all the financial statements in the world play with costs and expenses and revenue matched up. That's how the market works, that's how the valuation works. This case is the first time I've ever seen—sitting here this morning—you're not matching costs. You've got bogus numbers. Somebody's missing a big piece here. It's amazing.

Richard Huber: The question, of course, is the value to whom? Not just spatially according to various countries, but in terms of generations into generational value. And it seems to me that that part of the exercise—of being able to increase sophistication of the ability to make these kinds of evaluations is, and part of the charge to economic institutions such as the

World Bank—is to include longer-range planning. These may be costs to you, maybe not today, but sometime in the not too distant future.

Maritta Koch-Weser: Just as a clarification, when you say "cost to you," do you mean individual governments, or do you mean the global community?

Richard Huber: I would say both.

Audience question: I'm a marine biologist. I've been reading this work of Dr. Dixon and many others. My question is related to certain observations reported here from Jamaica, also Indonesia. It seems to me that there's a lot of information, scientific data is coming into this calculation. I think that's the right thing, that without that without proper, accurate scientific data it is not possible to valuate a resource, in fact, in economic terms. My question is that how far, and in what way is the data, which has been reported on sedimentation (in the Indonesian case) in pollution (in Jamaica) has been accumulated, gathered. Is there any closer interaction, or are the economics just based on published data—whether it is related to the economic activity or based on previous data—whether the scientific data is related to the economic activity in terms of time and space. I have also noted that contingent valuation and other methods have been used to come to certain valuations. Economic value, particularly in the case of the Jamaican waters, Montego Bay—how far has contingent valuation have considered to be, in economic terms, really reliable?

John Dixon: Many issues were raised by the previous speakers—a number of them will be discussed in more detail in the afternoon session. Basically, the economic analysis presented here included costs and benefits as they occurred—this is the correct way to do it, and it was done correctly. I want to respond to Maritta's original question. If we could mobilize the world community to control CFCs, why not for coral reefs? There are parallels—both are global commons. But the big difference is the number of actors involved for CFCs where you have a dozen producers worldwide. And you can pay them off, because it doesn't affect anything. Whether I make a foam cup using a CFC or something else doesn't matter because I get the product I want. Whether my refrigerator uses CFCs or more ozone friendly product doesn't matter—I get the service I want. But when you're dealing with coral reefs, you've got people who are living, existing off of their management—catching fish, mining the coral. And as Herman Cesar very clearly pointed out in his study, the magnitude of benefits to individuals can be very high. And so the management challenges are much harder. A global effort may well be needed, but it's a lot more difficult to affect ten thousand Indonesian coral miners, or a million artisanal fisherman than it is to negotiate with twelve producers of CFCs worldwide.

Herman Cesar: The reason for economic analysis or economic valuation as I see it is two. One is to show some numbers and show that destructive practices often, from a true economic point of view, don't make sense. And if you look at the impact of John Dixon and Greg Hodgson's study on Palawan in the Philippines that was done in 1988, in the Philippines the impact of this study—in terms of actually having shifted some of the political agenda and the political will—is still enormous. All of the NGOs there still talk about the study, not because the numbers were correct, but because it was so instrumental in trying to get a very simple point across. And secondly, the reason is to actually look at the individual stakeholders and what is driving the system, and that is crucial information if you want to go to an actual management plan. You want to know who is

gaining now and how much, and it also comes back to Maritta's point. Maybe it is wrong that there are all these fishing boats, but they are there, and these people are paying off their debts, and you damn well take that into account in your analysis if you want to get to a system that makes everyone better off, and that's the only way to change something. That gives an idea of what you have to do for which people for your management plan. So I see those as the two key issues, and whether everything is taken into account or not, that is, to me, a much less relevant point.

Richard Huber: Relative to empirical data—absolutely—if we don't have empirical data, if we're not going in with good data that the coral reef biologists [use]— the transects, the species diversity, the abundance and percent recruitment—what we're doing is just folklore; it's worthless. So most of the modeling that we've been talking about is basically gathering significant information from local stakeholders, and coral reef biologists, putting this together into an economic model. And without that, for example in Montego Bay [Jamaica], we had a wealth of data—the Nature Conservancy had recently done a rapid ecological appraisal. Rolf Bak, one of the world-renowned coral reef experts, in Curaçao has spent his life specifically looking at those reefs, so we've had volumes of data, and that's extremely important if any of this is going to be meaningful.

Is contingent valuation reliable? That's a good question. It's a really useful tool; I'm glad we have it. There's a lot of skeptics out there. I think we can continue to refine it, and it will be very valuable for us in the future for valuing the benefits of marine ecosystems.

SUMMARY

Hard Decisions and Hard Science: Research Needs for Coral Reef Management

Nancy Knowlton
Smithsonian Tropical Research Institute

The proceedings of the International Coral Reef Symposia provide illuminating snapshots of how coral reef professionals spend their time. Of the 179 papers from the Miami meetings published in 1977, less than 5 percent explicitly focused on the role of man or management.[1] Twenty years and five symposia later, over 25 percent of the 318 papers published for the Panama meetings addressed these themes.[2] This enormous growth reflects the belated recognition that reefs worldwide are in trouble.[3] Although this crisis provides no cause for celebration, coral reef science will benefit from the attention that management issues receive—more informative remote sensing, development of coral culturing techniques, and otherwise undoable manipulative experiments (known as marine protected areas) are but a few examples that emerged from the Panama meetings.

Is reef science, then, just a parasite of management? To be sure, most of the problems reefs face come down to the problem of managing people rather than corals.[4] Nevertheless, I will argue here that many crucial pieces of information are missing, and that any politically unpopular but necessary measure is doomed without good science to support it.

Models for Reef Management: How the Simple Becomes Complex

The Intersection of Biology and Economics

In order to defend reefs economically, the marginal costs of reducing stress on reefs must be less than the marginal benefits associated with so doing. Calculating the economic costs of treating sewage, not fishing, or not building are fairly straightforward, and have been used for years to support policies that are detrimental to reefs. More recently, economic analyses of the benefits associated with maintaining or improving the health of reefs have made important strides.[5] To use such analyses, however, we must make biological as well as economic assumptions. For example, we can estimate the economic costs of improving water quality or the economic benefits of increasing coral cover, but we also need to understand the biological relationship between water quality and coral cover to determine if an increase in income from tourism will cover the costs of water treatment facilities (figure 1). While it is tempting to assume simple biological relationships, such assumptions are rarely if ever justified.

Thresholds and the Precautionary Principle

Humans preferentially think of the world in linear terms: if changing the thermostat setting by five notches changes the temperature by five degrees, we expect 10 notches to result in a 10-degree change. Nevertheless, "the straw that breaks the camel's back" is also a well known phrase. The camel teaches two important lessons: the effect of any single straw cannot be

Figure 1. Interrelationship between economic and biological analyses

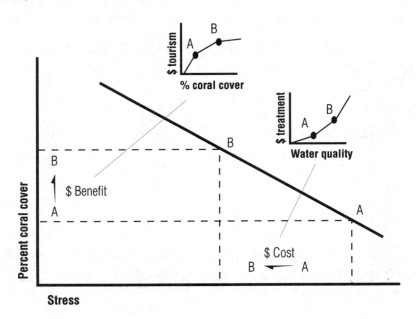

Note: Gaining support for reef-friendly policies. Improving the status of reefs typically involves demonstrating that the cost of reducing stress on reefs is justified by the benefits associated with improved coral cover. For example, should a community invest in wastewater treatment in order to improve water quality, in order to to enhance coral growth, in order to increase tourism? To decide, one must know the economic cost of achieving different levels of water quality (small graph to right), the economic benefits from tourism from improving coral growth (small graph to left), as well as the biological relationship between water quality (or stress generally) and coral cover (main graph).

predicted from the effect of the previous straw, and simply removing the back-breaking straw does not solve the problem of the crippled camel.

The biological world (and for that matter the physical world, such as climate) is dominated by such nonlinear relationships and their resulting thresholds and multiple stable states (figure 2).[6] The history of reefs on the north coast of Jamaica provides a vivid example of what can go wrong when we ignore this fact. These reefs have been severely overfished for centuries, but until recently the corals themselves looked quite healthy.[7] Those of us doing our PhDs during the 1970s recognized and regretted the absence of grouper and snapper but did not worry about the future of the staghorn coral *Acorpora* or the star coral *Montastraea*. We were wrong to be complacent, for overfishing almost certainly prevented normal recovery from two natural disturbances in the 1980s: a major hurricane and the demise of a dominant sea urchin herbivore because of disease.[8] Low densities of urchins

and the resulting replacement of corals by algae have persisted well beyond our initial expectations, for reasons that remain unclear.[9]

The implications of these basic realities should make managers and the public nervous for several reasons. First, removing a stress does not automatically lead to recovery, so that damage once done is often not readily undone. Second, even if one has perfect information about the present (that is, where one is on the curve of figure 2), not all stress is under human control. Synergy between natural acute disturbances and chronic human stress makes living on the precipice an extremely risky strategy. Finally, it is not easy to tell scientifically where on the curve one currently sits. We know that so called pristine reefs with their prehuman component of large predators and herbivores no longer exist,[10] but when does the relationship between overfishing plus eutrophication versus reef health reach a critical point? Simply monitoring the abundance of corals is unlikely to pro-

Figure 2. Threshold effects

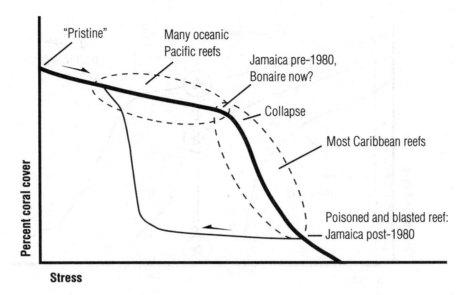

Note: The relationship between reef stress and coral cover is typically nonlinear. Consequently, coral cover is often a relatively insensitive measure of stress for many reefs, and a small increase in stress level can result in a large decline in reef health. Moreover, the response of reefs to increasing stress (thick "collapse"line) is not necessarily the same as the response to decreasing stress (thin "recovery" line), so subsequent recovery is often more prolonged than initial collapse.

tect us from disaster, since once the corals themselves start to collapse in numbers the game may well be over. Thus the precautionary principle[11]—stay away from the precipice—is as relevant to the management of coral reefs as it is to the design of bridges. Unfortunately, we know vastly more about the physics underlying bridge safety than about the biology underlying reef safety.

Ecological Externalities

The theory of metapopulations provides sobering albeit preliminary indications of what might be in store. Stated simply, organisms persist thanks to a patchwork of environments, to which they recruit and from which they go extinct. If you substantially reduce the number of patches, then the number of species will automatically decline. One clear prediction of these models is that species that are ecological dominants but poor recruiters will be particularly hard hit. As a consequence, the future of major Caribbean

reef builders such as *Montastraea* and *Acropora* looks far from secure. Moreover, it takes time for the entire process to play itself out, so that we already owe an "extinction debt" of unknown size because of past reef destruction.

Lessons of the Ozone Hole

The Montreal Protocol provides a striking, even if imperfect, example of what can be achieved in environmental protection when parties agree. Why have we as a planet responded to the threat of ozone depletion, but failed to protect reefs (and natural resources generally)? Clearly the scale of the potential threat to health, the limited number of producers of ozone-depleting chemicals, and the relatively modest per person cost of reducing their use are a big part of the explanation. But the role of science cannot be underestimated. Models and eventually data clearly identified the nature of the threat and what was needed to mitigate it; in the absence of this information, I would argue, no action would have been

Figure 3. The effect of ecological externalities

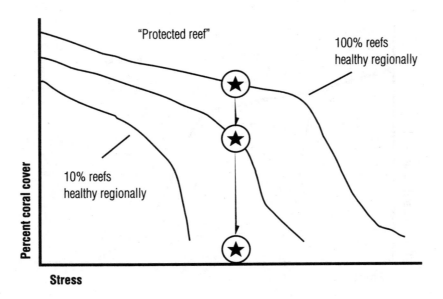

Note: Even excellent local protection from overfishing and eutrophication may not be enough to protect reefs if they are imbedded in regionally catastrophic reef loss.

taken. We may be reaching a similar point in climate change policy.

Marine scientists have recently argued that no-take marine reserves need to be increased from the current 0.25 percent to 20 percent of ocean surface area. They are almost certainly right, but we currently lack the numbers to support such an estimate. Without such support, costly proposals will be dismissed as the ecological equivalent of "voodoo economics," even taking the precautionary principle into account. The shrinkage of marine reserves within the Florida Keys Marine Sanctuary from the 10 percent originally proposed to the 0.5 percent eventually enacted is a clear example of this point. Doing something now is clearly much, much better than doing nothing, so this is not an argument for inaction. But we should also be wary of fooling ourselves with success stories that buy time but are ultimately doomed to failure. Hard decisions require hard science, and successful long-term management without it is an illusion.

Almost all of these points have been made before in the context of coral reef management,

but they apparently bear repeating. There are currently no plans to include the role of scientific research in the inaugural International Tropical Marine Ecosystems Management Symposium (R. Kenchington, personal communication.), and a summary document for the Global Coral Reef Monitoring Network states that "we know sufficient about the biology, geology and physics of coral reefs to implement sustainable management." How can this be true, when, for example, we cannot reliably discriminate coral species, estimate the dispersal distances of their larvae, calculate the densities needed for successful spawning, or identify their important pathogens? Coral reefs will be the real losers if cross-fertilization between science and management falls victim to short-sighted rivalry between research and other needs.

Acknowledgments

Marea Hatziolos, Anthony Hooten, and Jeremy Jackson made many helpful suggestions, and the Smithsonian Institution has supported my research on coral reefs for many years.

References

1. Taylor, D. L., ed. 1977. *Proceedings: Third International Coral Reef Symposium*, Miami. Rosenstiel School of Marine and Atmospheric Science.

2. Lessios, H. A., and I. G. Macintyre.1997. *Proceedings of the Eighth International Coral Reef Symposium*, Balboa, Panama: Smithsonian Tropical Research Institute.

3. Wilkinson, C. R. 1992. "Coral Reefs Are Facing Widespread Devastation: Can We Prevent This through Sustainable Management Practices?" *Proceedings of the Seventh International Coral Reef Symposium*, 1: 11-21. Ginsburg, R. N., ed. 1994. *Proceedings of the Colloquium on Global Aspects of Coral Reefs: Health, Hazards and History*, 1993. Miami: Rosenstiel School of Marine and Atmospheric Science.

4. Meffe, G., and C. R. Carroll. 1994. *Principles of Conservation Biology*. Sunderland, Mass.: Sinauer Press.

5. Cesar, Herman. 1996. "Economic Analysis of Indonesian Coral Reefs." World Bank Environmental Department Paper, Environmental Economic Series. Agricultural Operations, Country Department III, East Asia and Pacific Region and Environment Department, Washington, D.C.

6. May, R. M. 1977. "Thresholds and Breakpoints in Ecosystems with a Multiplicity of Stable States." *Nature* 269: 471–77. Knowlton, N. 1992. "Thresholds and Multiple Stable States in Coral Reef Community Dynamics. *American Zoology* 32: 674–82.

7. Jackson, J. B. C. 1997. "Reefs since Columbus." *Proceedings of the Eighth International Coral Reef Symposium* 1: 97–105.

8. Hughes, T. P . 1994. "Catastrophes, Phase Shifts, and Large-Scale Degradation of a Caribbean Coral Reef." *Science* 265: 1547–51.

9. Lessios, H. A. 1995. "Diadema antillarum 10 Years after Mass Mortality: Still Rare, Despite Help from a Competitor." *Proceedings of the Royal Society, London* B 259: 331–7.

10. Jackson, J. B. C. 1997. cited above.

11. Freestone, David, and Ellen Hey, 1995. *The Precautionary Principle and International Law : The Challenge of Implementation* (International Environmental Law and Policy Series, vol. 31.) Kluwer Law International.

12. Roberts, C. M. 1997. "Connectivity and Management of Caribbean Coral Reefs." *Science* 278: 1454–7.

13. Nee, S., and R. M. May. 1992. "Dynamics of Metapopulations: Habitat Destruction and Competitive Coexistence." *Journal of Animal Ecology* 61: 37–40.

14. Tilman, D., R. M. May, C. L. Lehman, and M. A. Nowak.1994. "Habitat Destruction and the Extinction Debt." *Nature* 371: 65–6.

15. UNEP (United Nations Environment Programme). 1996. *Handbook for the International Treaties for the Protection of the Ozone Layer: The Vienna Convention (1985), The Montreal Protocol (1987)*. Nariobi, Kenya: Ozone Secretariat, United Nations Environmental Programme.

16. ———. 1996. *Handbook for the International Treaties for the Protection of the Ozone Layer: The Vienna Convention (1985)*. Cited above.

17. Maby, N., S. Hall, C. Smith, and S. Gupta. 1997. *Argument in the Greenhouse: The International Economics of Controlling Global Warning*. Global Environment Change Series. New York: Routledge.

18. Schmidt, K. F. 1997. " 'No-take' Zones Spark Fisheries Debate." *Science* 277: 489–91.

19. Ogden, J. C. 1997. "Marine Managers Look Upstream for Connections." *Science* 278: 1414–5.

20. Jackson, J. B. C. 1995. "The Role of Science in Coral Reef Conservation and Management." In *Partnership Building and Framework Development: Report of the ICRI Workshop*. Dumaguete City, Philippines.

21. Wilkinson, C., and Salvat, B. 1998. "The Global Coral Reef Monitoring Network: Reversing the Decline of the World's Reefs." In M. E. Hatziolos and others, eds., *Coral Reefs: Challenges and Opportunities for Sustainable Management*. Washington, D.C.: World Bank.

Summary and Recommendations

Marea E. Hatziolos
World Bank

From the papers and discussions presented at the two and one half day conference and recorded in these proceedings, several key points emerge. These are listed below and form the basis for the recommendations that follow, which were adopted by the plenary.

- Coral reefs are under increasing stress around the world.
- In many cases, the sources of stress and impacts on reefs are known.
- However, the etiology of a growing number of diseases and pathologies now being reported in corals is not widely understood, highlighting the need for more research to unravel the complex interactive effects between natural and anthropogenic forms of stress and their effects on coral reefs.
- The tight recycling of nutrients and low net primary productivity of reef ecosystems limits the biomass available for harvesting and sustained fishery yields.
- The inability of scientists to predict with any certainty where the critical thresholds of resilience to stress lie along the continuum of human-induced and natural disturbances, make it inherently difficult to manage reefs sustainably.
- This calls for a conservative approach and application of the precautionary principle in developing management plans for coral reefs. Options for consumptive use are increasingly limited in the context of growing dependent coastal populations.
- Alternative uses that are low-impact, productivity enhancing, and nonpolluting or disruptive of complex food webs and species interactions need to be identified.
- Conditions contributing to environmental degradation, overharvesting, and the decline of reefs worldwide will be difficult to control under scenarios of growing demand for reef products and habitat loss fueled by increasing population growth and development activity in coastal areas, and rapid expansion of tourism and its associated impacts on coastal and marine environments.
- Solutions to these conservation and management problems will need to incorporate effective science, robust economic analysis, and sound policies and laws. Participatory actions grounded in the cultural and social reality of local people who depend on and benefit directly from coral reefs must be part of the solution. Creating political will, through communication and environmental education, will be essential in mobilizing and sustaining conservation efforts.

The overall consensus of the meeting is that time is running out. Tremendous challenges lie ahead, yet the problems are not intractable. In the course of our deliberations, concrete actions were identified in each of the major themes we addressed. Because of the large number of specific recommended actions and issues, conference recommendations are presented in their entirety in appendix A; however, a summary of the recommendations are grouped thematically below.

Destructive Fishing Practices

• Step up enforcement by governments, aided by external organizations, in areas affected by illegal practices
• Inventory key spawning habitat and fish aggregation sites
• Incorporate these into the design of marine protected areas
• Introduce seasonal closing of sites (MPAs) coupled with seasonal bans at markets
• Form alliances with the private sector for sustainable alternatives to reef-destructive practices, including mariculture and marine ecotourism [involve NGOs, private sector, donor agencies]
• Invest in technology for mariculture of high-demand species (Napoleon wrasse, coral trout)
• Catalog sustainable mariculture options and best practices for coral reef areas
• Actively support legislative reform and infrastructure for cyanide-free certification programs and other destructive forms of fishing
• Emphasize community-based education and training
• Promote the recognition or establishment of users' rights by governments, and the awareness of those rights.

Illegal and Sustainable Trade in Reef Products versus Certified Trade and Sustainable Bioprospecting

• Support independent certification linked to market incentives, best management practices, and conservation of coral reefs
• Assist with marketing of environmentally sound products
• Facilitate participation of all stakeholders including local community monitoring of coral reef ecosystem health, and strengthen incentives for all participants to adopt best practices

• Develop a portfolio of environmentally sound enterprises linked to coral reef organisms (such as food fish, aquarium fish, corals, invertebrates, bioprospecting, tourism)
• Maintain options open to bioprospecting to complement near-term income generation, and identify benefit arrangements for national and local communities at the outset.

MPAs

• Incorporate no-take fishery reserves into protected area planning and management as standard practice in the design of MPA sites and networks
• Provide for the local capture of entry and user fees for MPA management through trust funds or other arrangements for cost recovery (specifically, no general funds)
• Small to medium MPAs should be designed and developed within the context of larger ICZM programs when possible
• In MPA design, zoning should also be considered with the following approaches:
  • Relief mechanisms (rotation) for areas experiencing heavy use should be incorporated into zoning patterns for reef use
  • Ensure remote protection of spawning aggregation sites
• Ensure benefits or alternative compensation for fishers who participate in no-take reserves or MPA establishment
• Promote education programs for fishers and tourists. Promote shared conservation efforts with full involvement of local people, private sector, and NGOs.

Marine Information and Education

• Expose decisionmakers to coral reef experiences
• Target youth education
• Build environmental education into project planning and execution
• Convene a group to determine state of the knowledge of coral reefs—in other words, pointed fact finding for coral reefs
• Inventory and link with various resources

to coordinate funding opportunities to advance education in coral reefs

- Target messages to specific audiences, and factor the media into projects and events.

Economic Valuation

- Expand economic analysis for coral reefs, based on pilot studies in Indonesia, to other regions of the world
- Improve the incorporation of use and non-use values into economic arguments. Economics captures only a part of the reality. Enhance global concern for long-term future and intrinsic values that are difficult to express in economic terms
- Interpret and disseminate scientific information to a wide audience; incorporate it into GIS and other data management systems
- Improve access to existing studies and knowledge for informed management decisions
- Employ a dual-track approach, that is, incorporate immediate concern of local constituencies (governments, local people) with justifiable economic arguments
- Improve educational outreach to influence behavior of policymakers and consumers.

These recommendations highlight many of the actions that we need to take to slow and reverse our negative human impacts, and effectively manage those we accurately identify as sustainable. If implemented, these actions can have profound effects on the way we perceive and interact with the marine environment, and the fundamental dependence of humanity on the health of our blue planet. The challenge before us lies in turning these recommendations into specific actions and, through partnerships, maximizing effectiveness in their implementation.

Epilogue

Ismail Serageldin
World Bank

All good things must come to an end. So be it with this conference that has gathered so many from different parts of the world, united by a common concern for coral reefs and by a common intent to act in defense of the wondrous habitats and all the beautiful, exotic, and even strange creatures that inhabit them. So what will we say we have accomplished? What will we dedicate ourselves to achieve?

The scientific evidence is in. There are no pristine reefs anywhere. The unsustainable harvesting of fish is destroying marine fisheries and reefs. The condition is becoming critical. By the year 2008—only 10 years from now—the world population will have exceeded 6 billion people, with 4.5 billion, 75 percent—living in coastal areas, many of whom have few options for their health and welfare. As our population continues to grow and move into the coastal zone, we can no longer afford to only observe, define the problems facing coral reefs, and prescribe their solutions. We must act. We must issue a call to arms, to alert the world of the monstrous condition of the world's reefs and the frightening pace of degradation.

The recommendations of this conference stress the need for effective action. As a collective group—managers, scientists, economists, lawyers, entrepreneurs, and businesses—we now have a responsibility to establish partnerships, to set concrete goals for each of the most pressing thematic challenges, and to systematically work toward their achievement. Action is needed on three broad fronts: public education, scientific monitoring, and projects to change the destructive patterns of socioeconomic activities in coastal zones and to extend and affirm protected zones and marine parks. Above all, such actions must involve the local communities and respond to their needs, in an alternative and environmentally benign way. The combination of science, economics, law, and participatory actions grounded in the cultural and social reality of peoples is the way for this sustainable development to take place—development that will meet the aspirations of the poor and the destitute around the world, and maintain ecological integrity of coral reefs, their associated marine habitats, and the complex ecosystems they represent.

As a partner to ICRI, and as a leader in addressing issues of sustainable development, the World Bank must play an important role in meeting this challenge. So, on behalf of the World Bank, I pledge to you that my colleagues and I will do our utmost to incorporate the following 10 actions into our operations:

1. Develop a portfolio of environmentally sound enterprises linked to coral reef organisms (such as food fish, aquarium fish, corals, invertebrates, bioprospecting, and tourism), and build environmental education into project planning and execution.

2. Expose decisionmakers to coral reef experiences. Through the World Bank's new project-related activities, a concerted effort will be made

to ensure that the decisionmakers involved will be exposed—either first-hand or through specific educational materials relevant to them—in clearly understanding coral reef resources and the issues surrounding them. Furthermore, the media will, to the extent possible, be invited into these project activities and events. We will try to develop a series of contributions to case studies of global interest.

3. Reinforce partnerships with governments, NGOs, and local communities (through initiatives like the Critical Ecosystem Partnership Fund, the Global 200 Ecoregions, and debt for nature swaps) in developing action plans for the protection of critical marine ecosystems in each major coral reef region of the world.

4. Facilitate the establishment of three new MPAs as part of project-related activity in World Bank-financed efforts in the coming 18 months. Selection and management of these sites would take into account the best available information on fish spawning and aggregation sites and the productivity of reefs within a region to ensure that critical habitats are included and protected in MPA designation. We would also encourage that user fees for MPAs should go to trust funds for the management of those MPAs specifically, and not to general funds. The Bank would also work with its partners to try to ensure that benefits or alternative compensation is established for fishers who participate in no-take reserves or MPA establishment.

5. Facilitate participation of all stakeholders, including local community monitoring of coral reef ecosystem health, and strengthen incentives for all participants to adopt best practices.

6. Invest in technology for mariculture of species in high demand (for example, grouper and coral trout) working in collaboration with others, such as donor agencies, universities, and research organizations, to develop an appropriate list of such species. And working with its partners, the World Bank will support legislative reform and capacity building for cyanide-free certification programs.

7. Develop an alliance with the private sector for sustainable options to destructive practices, such as mariculture and ecotourism that channels consumer willingness to pay into effective marine conservation programs. We would try to pilot one or two such efforts within the next 18 months, including support for research and monitoring to ensure that conservation objectives are being met along with revenue generation.

8. Build on and expand efforts now under way in the Bank's "Marine Market Transformation Initiative" to create the necessary policy environment and incentive structure for greater markets in nondestructive reef-based goods and services.

9. Support the continuation of ICRI with assistance for development at the regional levels.

10. Continue support of scientific research through CoralBase and its contribution to the Global Coral Reef Monitoring Network.

There are many other recommendations that require action and coordination. Thus, a challenge is before all partners to take up these recommendations and to act. Furthermore, it is incumbent upon us to support and encourage our actions collectively and to keep track of our progress toward sustainability and effective management of these critical resources. These and other actions, in tandem with the ICRI Framework for Action, should be presented in the form of a scorecard that can be used as a means to measure our progress toward the goals we espouse. These proceedings represent a first step toward that end. Let us continue the challenge at the next international forum, the International Tropical Marine Ecosystems Management Symposium (ITMEMS), as we work toward achieving our goal in the next millennium and on behalf of our children. Coral reefs, with their beauty, splendor, and the richness they bestow upon us, deserve no less.

APPENDIXES

Appendix A
Conference Recommendations

The following recommendations were developed during the breakout sessions on Friday, October 10, 1997, by each of the thematic working groups.

Destructive Fishing Practices

Key Recommendations

1. Inventory key spawning habitat sites.
2. Regional organizations/governments incorporate into marine protected sites seasonal closing of sites coupled with seasonal bans at markets. Catalog of sustainable mariculture options for coral reef areas.
3. Criteria for site selection:
   i. Social, technical, and ecological feasibilities
   ii. Regional organizations [SPC, SEAFDEC, ICLARM].
4. Promote the recognition or establishment of users' rights by governments, and the awareness of those rights.
5. Community-based education and training [NGOs]. Monitor harmful trade of coral reefs by country.
6. Donor agencies to support legislative reform and infrastructure for cyanide-free certification programs.

Other Recommended Measures Noted

1. Need for governments in areas affected by illegal practices to step up enforcement [aided by external organizations].

2. Alliance with private sector for sustainable options to destructive practices, such as mariculture and ecotourism [NGOs, private sector, donor agencies].
3. Invest in technology for mariculture of high demand species (Napoleon wrasse, coral trout) [donor agencies, universities, research organizations].

Illegal and Sustainable Trade in Reef Products versus Certified Trade and Sustainable Bioprospecting

Comprehensive Ecosystem Management

1. Develop portfolio of environmentally sound enterprises linked to coral reef organisms (for example, food fish, aquarium fish, corals, invertebrates, bioprospecting, tourism)
2. Facilitate participation of all stakeholders, including local community monitoring of coral reef ecosystem health, and strengthen incentives for all participants to adopt best practices
3. Assist with marketing of environmentally sound products
4. Support independent certification linked to market incentives, best management practices, and conservation coral reef ecosystems.

Marine Protected Areas

1. In designing a network of protected areas, no-take zones should be considered stan-

dard in any preliminary MPA proposal.

2. Fishers should be off-set for not fishing—system of MPAs preferable.
3. The integrated approach to implement a wider context of MPA (ICZM) design is the preferred approach.
4. Opportunistic approach acceptable; in MPA design, zoning should also be considered with the following approach:

    i. Relief mechanisms for areas experiencing constant use should be provided (rotation)

    ii. Remote protection of spawning aggregation sites

    iii. Education programs for fishers and tourists

    iv. Promote shared conservation efforts with private sector, NGOs, full involvement of local people

    v. Fees for MPAs should go to trust funds for management of those MPAs (that is, no general funds).

Marine Information and Education

1. Issues/challenges

    i. Inability to network on a global basis

    ii. Uneven technological capability worldwide

    iii. No global constituency for coral reefs

    iv. No way to coordinate costs for media coverage and dissemination

2. Information Gathering

    i. Processes in place such as ReefBase, GCRMN, and ReefCheck to specifically gather data on coral in good shape

    ii. Community-based ecological monitoring

    iii. Information archaeology and coordination of past and disparate data sources on coral reefs

3. Information Dessimination

    i. Integrate ecological information with economic information for decisionmakers

    ii. Training teachers

    iii. Partnering with religions worldwide in forwarding education for coral reefs

    iv. Target youth education

    v. No clearinghouse—10 to 20 years for attitude change; loose leaf binders are useful tools for updating educational materials

    vi. Add education as an equal partner (in addition to science, economics and law)

    vii. Simple methods for information dessimination to developing countries (for example, posters, banners—such as the Smithsonian display in the exhibit area)

    viii. Match medium with technological capacity in information dissemination

4. Recommendations

    i. *Short term*

    a. Expose decisionmakers to coral reef experiences

    b. Endorse congressional legislation for specific conservation of coral reefs

    c. Convene a group to determine state of the knowledge of coral reefs—in other words, pointed fact finding for coral reefs

    d. Inventory and link with various resources to coordinate funding opportunities to forward education in coral reefs

    ii. *Intermediate*

    a. Improved audience research to target messages to specific audiences

    b. Illuminate consumer options (for example, consuming aquaculture-raised fish as opposed to reef fishes)

    iii. *Longer-term actions*

    a. Target youth education

    b. Integrated and Interdisciplinary approaches in education

    c. Media factored into projects and events for tools in contributing to case studies

    d. Incorporate coral reef monitoring into NASA's Mission to Planet Earth (in particular water penetration and high-resolution capability for remote sensing)

    e. International role/project for an education network

    f. Keeping ecotourism as an important media tool

    g. Build environmental education into project planning and execution.

Economic Valuation

1. More effective education and information dissemination

    i. More of educational outreach to influence behavior of policymakers and consumers (Jacques-Yves Cousteau and Rachel Carlson) *ii.* Translate research results into common language and disseminate scientific information, GIS

2. Develop management systems

i. Better use of existing studies and knowledge in management decisions

ii. Approach coral reefs as systems, not as individual sites. Not all reefs are created equal

iii. Sacrificial lamb system—allow for cross-transfers

iv. Most of the most destructive uses are managerially preventable

3. Tailor economic information to users

i. Immediate concern to local groups (governments, local people)—justifiable economic arguments

ii. Global concern for long-term future and intrinsic values that are difficult to express in economic terms

iii. Economics captures only a part of the total reality—more in the case of a eucalyptus plantation than of a rain forest; more in the case of aquaculture than a pristine coral reef.

Appendix B
International Coral Reef Initiative
Regional Summaries

Washington, D.C.
October 9-11, 1997

South Pacific

ICRI activities in the South Pacific have centred on the Pacific Year of the Coral Reef (PYOCR) campaign.

PYCOR focuses on outreach and awareness activities geared to the local community and cultural needs of the countries involved in the campaign with a "Pacific Way" theme.

PYCOR has been coordinated by the South Pacific Environment Programme (SPREP) based in Apia, Western Samoa, with activities including:
- art and poster competitions
- video production
- a youth music CD
- curriculum development
- a major protected areas conference.

South Asia

Focal point for coordination of action is the South Asia Cooperative Environment Programme (SACEP) based in Colombo, Sri Lanka.

Focus for activities includes:
- revision of existing environmental legislation
- capacity building including the development of training program outlines
- monitoring including the establishment of a presence by the Global Coral Reef Monitoring Network (GCRMN) with training and database linkages to ReefBase.

A coastal management handbook for Sri Lanka, the Maldives, and India is close to completion. Management of tourism and mariculture for sustainable use of coral reefs is a priority in the region. Issues of inadequate coordination of coastal management coral mining, overfishing, and, to a lesser extent, destructive fishing practices are still evident in the area.

Western Indian Ocean

ICRI activities growing in number and importance—now nine countries actively involved in ICRI in the region.

Coordination of activities is through the UNEP office in Nairobi. A heavy focus is on monitoring with activities including:
- the establishment of two monitoring nodes in Kenya and Tanzania
- implementation of a pilot project in coral reef rapid assessment technology (both biophysical and socioeconomic) developed by UNEP/UNDP
- preparation for a remote sensing imagery workshop for reefs and mangroves
- the preparation of a report on the status of reefs in the region.

Middle East

Impetus for ICRI action has been the regional coordinating meeting held in Aqaba, Jordan, in September 1997. Attended by Israel, Jordan, the

Arab Republic of Egypt, Djibouti, Yemen, and Oman with facilitation from Australia and the United States.

Major focuses for ICRI activity in the region are:

- ICZM, particularly in terms of coastal development and tourism issues
- Capacity building centering on the development of an ICRI coordination system and training in coastal and marine protected area management
- Monitoring with emphasis on the establishment of nodes for the Global Coral Reef Monitoring Network.

Latin America and the Caribbean

Regional coordination is through the Jamaica office of the UNEP Regional Seas Program. The major focuses for action relate to:

- Coordination among the many countries, political and administrative systems, and differing languages of the region.
- Actions arising from the Cartegena Convention including:
  - land-based sources of pollution
  - oil pollution
  - protection of wildlife

Integrated coastal management guidelines have been developed but are yet to be widely implemented. UNEP is working with CARICOMP to develop a monitoring manual. Coordination of monitoring activity also involves the GCRMN. Species recovery and management programs have been developed for:

- Turtles
- Manatees
- Conch and spiny lobsters

The field of capacity building offers challenges and opportunities. Particular effort is being applied to multilingual presentation of materials, information technology systems, and school curriculum development.

East Asian Seas

The effort is coordinated from the UNEP office in Bangkok. An ICRI action plan has been developed but it lacks an overarching protocol to bind it to the participating 10 countries. Existing arrangements for ratification of projects and programs hinder timely implementation of strategies. A major emphasis has been placed on land-based sources of marine pollution issues, with a major workshop held this year in Australia. Training manuals for coral reef protected area management have been developed but require revision.

Appendix C
Selected Educational Materials Pertaining to Coral Reefs

(as of November 1997)

Barbara J. Ornitz, compiler

Australian Institute of Marine Science. 1997. *Survey Manual for Tropical Marine Resources,* 2nd edition. Townsville, Australia.

Bortesch, James, and Brenda Maxwell. 1997. *Coral Reef Systems and Ecology Lecture Notes.* Florida Science Institute. Palm Bay, Florida.

Coral Forest. 1996. *The Coral Forest: Diversity of Life on the Coral Reef: Teacher's Guide.* San Francisco.

Great Barrier Reef Aquarium Volunteers Association of Townsville, Inc. 1996. *Sea Works: Resources for Primary Schools.* Townsville, QLD, Australia: March.

Great Barrier Reef Marine Park Authority. 1988. *Project Reef-Ed.* Townsville, QLD, Australia.

Great Barrier Reef Marine Park Authority. 1996. *Seaworks, Resources for Primary Schools.* Townsville, QLD, Australia.

Maxwell, Brenda. Undated. *Environmental Problem Solving through Water Quality Monitoring Curriculum,* third edition. Florida Science Institute. Palm Bay, Florida (Video and CD available as well).

Moffat, Bob. 1993. *WaterWise: Water Resource Management and Conservation.* DPI and Wet Paper. Ashmore, Queensland.

Moffat, Bob. 1995. *Marine Environment Students Manual.* Wet Paper Publications. Queensland, Australia.

Rogers, Caroline, and others. 1994. *Coral Reef Monitoring Manual for the Caribbean and Western Atlantic.* Virgin Islands National Park. St. John, USVI: June.

Ryan, Tim. 1990. *Issues in Conservation Pollution.* Wet Paper. Ashmore, Australia.

Texts for Use in Spanish-Speaking Countries/Commonwealths

Autoridad de Desperdicios Solidos. Undated. *La naturaleza recicla y maneja correctamente lo gue genera.* La Comision Estatal de Elecciones. San Juan, Puerto Rico.

Colegio Sea Grant & Colegio Universitario de Humacao. 1991–92. *Centro De Educacion Marina.* Humacao, Puerto Rico.

Departamento de Recursos Naturales. Undated. *Aquatic project WILD, en espanol y adaptado para Puerto Rico.* Programa Educacion en Recursos Acuaticos. Puerta de Tierra, San Juan.

NOAA Office of Sea Grant. 1983. *Estuary: an Ecosystem and a Resource—A Reading Guide for Grades 9–12.* South Slough Sanctuary.

Procter & Gamble. 1993. *Planet Patrol.* The Procter & Gamble Company. Cincinnati, Ohio.

Programa Sea Grant De la Universidad de Puerto Rico. 1988. Los Quitones de Puerto Rico. Regime de Humacao. UPR-E1-33.

Programa de Colegio Sea Grant. 1994. *Un Mar de Creaciones.* UPR-RUM. Mayaguez, Puerto Rico. UPRSG E-58.

United States Environmental Protection Agency. 1993. *Usted Puede Ayudar a Detener la Marea de Basura, Guia.* Office of Water. EPA842-B-93-003

World Wildlife Fund. 1987. *Guia Para El Profeso–Manual De Los Arrecifes Coralinos.* Washington, D.C.

World Wildlife Fund and RARE, Inc. 1986. *Coral Reefs/Arrecifes Coralinos.*

Films/Videos

Brevard Community College. *Living Rock in Crystal Seas.* Palm Bay, Florida.

Earth Communications Office. 1997. *Hidden City and Other Spots.* Van Nuys, California.

Appendix D
World Wildlife Fund
and Coral Reef Conservation

Sue Wells
World Wildlife Fund

The World Wildlife Fund (WWF) has had a long history of involvement in coral reef conservation work. A review in 1992 (Wells and Price 1992) revealed that it was then involved with, or had recently completed, some 40 coral reef projects. Since then many other projects have been supported and developed. Other WWF activities also indirectly benefit reefs, such as the promotion of policies and international treaties relating to the marine environment and the encouragement of sustainable fisheries management. Three of WWF's major regional programs (Latin America/Caribbean, Asia/ Pacific, and Africa/Madagascar) have played major roles, as have the efforts of many of the WWF national organizations and associate organizations.

WWF's coral reef work is carried out as part of its overall marine program, which is aimed at maintaining the biodiversity and productivity of marine and coastal systems. Five closely linked objectives have been identified as the basis of the program:

- The establishment of a global network of ecologically representative, well-managed marine protected areas (MPAs) designed to conserve critical ecosystems and areas of high biological diversity
- The protection of threatened marine species and those of special conservation concern
- The introduction of measures to ensure that fishing is carried out in a sustainable manner, in order to conserve genetic, species, and ecosystem diversity

- The reduction—and elimination where feasible—of marine pollution from land, atmospheric, and marine sources
- The introduction of integrated coastal management (ICM) as an underlying principle in all marine and coastal conservation activities worldwide.

Guiding principles for meeting the five objectives include:

- Developing and promoting sustainable practices that will both meet human needs and conserve biodiversity and ecological processes
- Fostering the concept of stewardship for both coastal waters and the open oceans
- Building local capacity and empowering communities to protect and manage their marine and coastal resources
- Creating social and economic incentives for conservation and sustainable use
- Implementing a precautionary approach.

The five objectives are being achieved through a diverse range of activities, including site-based projects (for example, assistance with the establishment and management of MPAs, education and public awareness work, policy initiatives, and lobbying efforts through regional and international agreements (such as the, United Nations Law of the Sea Convention, the Regional Seas Convention, the Convention on Biological Diversity, and various fisheries agreements). To coordinate these activities, a WWF Marine Advisory Group was formed in 1990, comprising about 50 individuals from around the network involved in marine work. This group meets annually to review progress, identify priorities for future work, and develop ideas and plans for increasing the marine program's effectiveness. Its current priority is to revise the WWF Marine Strategy, which will be published as a joint policy booklet with the World Conservation Union (IUCN) in June 1998, as part of a series of activities to be undertaken during the United Nations International Year of the Ocean.

WWF's Current Involvement in Reef Conservation

Information on WWF's current reef-related projects is summarized in Annex 1. Countries in which one or more major WWF-supported coral reef projects are under way include Kenya, Tanzania, Mozambique, the Philippines, Indonesia, Malaysia, Hong Kong (China), Japan, Mexico, Nicaragua, Belize, and Ecuador. The majority of these projects are carried out in association with local NGOs and government agencies, and often in collaboration with other international agencies.

Marine Protected Areas

There is considerable variety in both the type of MPA that WWF is working with (in terms of size, budget, and objectives) and in the role that it plays (such as funding, research, education, or management). A recent WWF workshop on MPAs, however, revealed common issues and problems, and these will be reviewed in a WWF discussion document being prepared for publication in March 1998. This will include a summary of WWF's current work with MPAs, a review of current topical issues relating to MPAs, including consideration of the application of the IUCN protected area categories in the marine environment, and case studies of WWF projects. Part of the project will be to identify targets for MPA work for the marine program in general, and more specifically for the next phase of the Endangered Seas Campaign (see below), where the use of "no-fishing areas" will be promoted as a fishery management tool.

Management of Reef Fisheries

The WWF Endangered Seas Campaign, established in 1995 specifically to address WWF's fisheries concerns, provides leadership and direction for fisheries management work throughout the network. The campaign has three specific targets, all of which relate to reef fisheries:

- The development of effective recovery plans for key threatened species (such as sharks)
- The creation of social and economic incentives for sustainable fishing (certification schemes such as the Marine Stewardship Council and the Marine Aquarium Fish Council (the latter being supported through WWF-US), and environmentally appropriate subsidies)
- The elimination of destructive fishing practices (such as the South-east Asia anti-cyanide fishing campaign) and reduction in by-catch.

Integrated Coastal Management

The WWF Marine Program is currently considering how it can further promote ICM as an essential management framework, building on its existing MPA and coastal management projects. The ICM approach will be used to address climate change issues (in collaboration with WWF's Climate Change Campaign) and tourism (in collaboration with WWF offices currently developing a new initiative on this topic), both of which have a bearing on coral reefs. The WWF Climate Change Campaign has already commissioned a report, and subsequently prepared an issue paper, on the effect of climate change on coral reefs. ICM work carried out through WWF will be assessed, and it is hoped that existing projects can be strengthened and new ones developed that will demonstrate ICM in practice.

Pollution

Pollution work that relates to coral reefs includes the work of WWF-UK, WWF-Australia, and several other national organizations with the shipping and oil and gas industries, and with the International Maritime Organization, to reduce and eliminate pollution from oil and hydrocarbons from shipping, and to promote the establishment of Particularly Sensitive Sea Areas.

Public Awareness and Education

WWF-Malaysia has prepared a marine education kit in collaboration with the Department of Fisheries and the Ministry of Education as a teaching resource for use in primary and secondary schools. The kit has four units (coral reefs, managroves, seashores, and oceans and seas), and includes fact sheets, indoor and outdoor activities, a poster, and worksheets. Ten thousand copies have been produced in Malay and 2,000 in English. Regional workshops are being held to train teachers in the use of the kit, and to explain how to incorporate it into the school syllabus. A public awareness kit on the marine environment has also been produced by WWF-Indonesia, including a variety of items relating to coral reefs, such as booklets for children in Bahasa, Indonesia.

Survey and Research Work

Several WWF projects carried out in coral reef regions involve survey work and monitoring (for example, production of a monitoring manual in Spanish for the Caribbean). Research work has also been supported, such as WWF-UK's funding of the Chagos Expedition in 1996.

Direct Involvement in the International Year of the Reef (IYOR)

Several publications have been produced carrying the IYOR logo, including a Marine Update on coral reefs by WWF-UK (1997), and an issue paper and summary on climate change and coral reefs by the WWF Climate Change Campaign (1997). WWF-Japan and WWF-Indonesia played an active role in Reef Check, and other WWF staff have participated in national IYOR committees (such as those in WWF-Malaysia and WWF-Tanzania). The Marine Program Coordinator at WWF International has worked on the promotion of IYOR globally in association with IUCN, the Coral Reef Alliance,

and Dr. Robert Ginsburg, and has participated in IYOR activities in Germany and Switzerland.

Future Reef-Related Work

WWF's regional programs and many of its country offices have identified marine conservation as an emerging issue of high priority, and new marine staff posts have been created in many offices. The marine strategy will continue to provide the direction for this work. Since all five components of the strategy are essential for the sustainable management of coral reefs, a separate campaign on coral reefs is unlikely to be launched in the immediate future. However, it is hoped that reef-related activities can be increased and that there will be growing collaboration with other regional and international reef initiatives.

One way in which reef conservation and management efforts could be strengthened is through the WWF 2000 Living Planet Campaign, a new campaign to mark the last 1,000 days of this century and to encourage worldwide action for conservation. One of its goals has direct relevance to coral reefs: the conservation of a representative selection of the world's most outstanding and distinctive biological regions, or ecoregions, (referred to as the Global 200). About 60 of these ecoregions are marine, and of these 25 contain coral reefs.

WWF has projects under way in over half of these areas, and many other organizations are involved in the others. The WWF marine program will be promoting further work in these areas, both directly and indirectly.

The International Year of the Oceans (IYO) will be a major focus of WWF's work in 1998, and will provide a further vehicle for promotion of coral reef activities. Two IYO events are planned in association with IUCN: an IYO launch in January, and publication of a joint WWF/IUCN marine policy booklet. Many of the activities will be spearheaded by the Endangered Seas Campaign and the Living Planet Campaign, and the potential for linking some of these events with EXPO '98 is currently being investigated.

References

Wells, S. M., and A. R. G. Price., 1992. "Coral Reefs—Valuable but Vulnerable." A WWF International Discussion Paper, WWF International, Gland, Switzerland.

WWF Climate Change Campaign. 1997. "Issue Summary of Coral Reefs and Climate Change." Washington, D.C.

WWF-UK 1997. "Coral Reefs: Valuable but Vulnerable." Marine Update (IYOR special). WWF-UK, Godalming.

Appendix E
World Wildlife Fund Projects
Involving Coral Reefs

International/Endangered Seas Campaign

Marine Aquarium Fish Council—WWF-US and other organizations

Marine Stewardship Council—WWF Endangered Seas Campaign

Impact of climate change on reefs—issue summary put out by WWF

Climate Change Campaign
  Asia/Pacific Program

SE Asia Campaign for Coral Reef Protection and Sustainable Fishing
  Project on live reef fish trade and cyanide fishing with WWF-Hong Kong, WWF-Indonesia, TRAFFIC Southeast Asia, KKP-Philippines, The Nature Conservancy (TNC), and other regional collaborators.

WWF-Indochina program office (Vietnam)

Collaborative project on Coastal and Marine Environmental Management in the South China Sea; phase 2 of an Asian Development Bank-funded program will be starting shortly and will cover the coastal areas from Cambodia to Vietnam, following on from earlier survey work in this region, supported by WWF. WWF's role in phase 2 will involve providing technical advice for the establishment of MPAs within an ICM framework.

WWF-Malaysia

Active member of Malaysia's IYOR committee, Marine Education Kit prepared for schools (see above). Preparation of "Marine Park Island Conceptual Plan for Peninsular Malaysia," and assistance with its implementation, has involved work related to tourism, reef survey, pollution, and carrying capacity in marine parks (P. Pulau, P. Redang, P. Tioman).

WWF-Japan

Shiraho project: 1997 coral reef campaign to raise funds for a research and education center; work with the local community to build local efforts to protect this reef.

WWF-Hong Kong

Hoi Ha Wan Marine Park—establishment of a marine studies and visitor center.

WWF-Indonesia

Kepulauan Seribu Marine National Park—environmental education and awareness raising, establishment of an information and training center, support to home-based business.

Take Bone Rate National Park—preparation of draft management plan, funding for giant clam hatchery.

Aru Tenggara Marine Reserve—research on traditional *sasi* system, public awareness, turtle protection.

Teluk Cenderawasih National Marine Park—assistance with management plan development and implementation, research and survey work. Review of status of marine aquarium fish, corals, and curio trade in Indonesia, in collaboration with TNC.

WWF-Philippines

National Marine Conservation and Education Programme KKP, Philippines.

Tubbataha National Marine Park—training of dive masters, photo exhibition.

El Nido Marine Park.

Turtle Islands transboundary marine park.

Anti-cyanide fishing work—training in non-damaging methods.

Training in Geographic Information Systems at Subic Bay facility.

WWF-South Pacific

Involvement in Fiji's Pacific Year of the Reef activities (public awareness and workshops on coral exploitation—funding needed to continue coral exploitation work).

Program outline in preparation for coral reef and lagoon complexes of the southwest Pacific proposal for European Union-funded program on ICM and community-based management.

Africa and Madagascar

WWF-Africa and Madagascar

Bazaruto National Park, Mozambique—establishment and management of park.

Mafia Island Marine Park, Tanzania—establishment and management of park, including community work, controls on dynamite fishing, provision of equipment, and so forth.

Menai Bay community-based project, Zanzibar—local community work (provision of radios, establishment of village committees), training of government staff.

Kiunga Marine Reserve, Kenya—involvement of local communities in reserve management.

Madagascar—some support for conservation work at Toliara, identification of marine conservation priorities.

Proposal for European Union-funded regional program on ICM and community-based management.

WWF-UK

Support to 1996 Chagos Expedition.

Latin America/Caribbean

WWF-LAC program (WWF-US)

Utria Sound National Park, Colombia.

ENCORE project, Eastern Caribbean (with USAID): community-based coastal management projects in Dominica and St. Lucia, including MPA management and training, and public awareness.

PROARCA, Central America: WWF-US, with TNC, University of Rhode Island, funded by US-AID; includes coral reef sites in Nicaragua (Miskitia Cayes), Honduras, Guatemala and Belize (Gulf of Honduras), and Panama. (Bocas del Chico).

Caribbean Coral Reef Initiative: projects in the Dominican Republic (volunteer coral reef monitoring and trainer's guide prepared in Spanish) and Haiti (Les Arcadins Marine Park).

WWF- Mexico Program Office

Banco Chinchorro Biosphere Reserve—community work to help implement reserve.

Sian Ka'an Biosphere Reserve—establishment and management (input from WWF finished).

FUDENA, Venezuela

Contributing to national IYOR activities.

Identification of regional priorities for marine ecosystems, including reefs in the Southern Caribbean.

Coral reef monitoring program.

Fundacion Natura, Ecuador

Galapagos Marine Park.

WWF-UK

Support to projects in British dependent territories (Anguilla, Montserrat, Turks, and Caicos).

Technical assistance provided for the designation of a particularly sensitive sea area in Cuba.

WWF- Canada

Development of a marine program in Cuba with several reef-related activities.

TRAFFIC

TRAFFIC East Asia: survey of pet shops for live corals and turtles in Japan.

TRAFFIC Southeast Asia: analysis of hard coral trade in Indonesia.

TRAFFIC India: study of trade in marine species, focusing on sharks and turtles but including other species.

TRAFFIC Oceania: monitoring and investigating vertebrate and invertebrate fisheries in the South Pacific and Australia.

TRAFFIC USA: study of the U.S. role in international trade in hard corals, in cooperation with U.S. National Marine Fisheries Service.

TRAFFIC Europe: study of Indonesian marine products imported into the European Union.

Appendix F

Coral Reef Conservation in the Wider Caribbean through Integrated Coastal Area Management, Marine Protected Areas, and Partnerships with the Tourism Sector

Alessandra Vanzella-Khouri
United Nations Environment Programme, Kingston, Jamaica

Having recognized the need for cooperation in the protection and management of coastal and marine resources, the governments of the wider Caribbean established the Caribbean Environment Program (CEP), one of the Regional Seas Programs of the United Nations Environment Program (UNEP) more than two decades ago.

In 1983, the governments adopted the legal framework for CEP, the Convention for the Protection and Development of the Marine Environment of the Wider Caribbean (Cartagena Convention), which has been in force since 1986 and is currently supported by two protocols: the Cooperation to Combat Oil Spills (1983) and the Specially Protected Areas and Wildlife (SPAW 1990). A third protocol on land-based sources and activities of marine pollution is currently under negotiation and is expected to be adopted by the end of 1998.

The SPAW protocol is arguably the most comprehensive regional wildlife protection treaty in the world and certainly the most comprehensive of its kind (Freestone 1990). In addition to the formal annexing requirements, which include ecosystems and groups of species, and the institutional structure that it establishes, the SPAW provisions on environmental impact assessment, planning and management regimes, and buffer zones, as well as the range of protection measures it envisages (including species recovery plans), reflect much of the best modern thinking on wildlife protection and management.

The mission of the SPAW protocol is to protect, preserve, and manage in a sustainable way:
- Areas that require protection to safeguard their special value
- Threatened or endangered species of flora and fauna
- Species—with the objective of preventing them from becoming endangered or threatened.

The SPAW protocol stresses the importance of protecting habitat as an effective method of protecting listed species. Protection is focused on fragile and vulnerable ecosystems as a whole, rather than on individual species.

The governments of the region identified the Catagena Convention and its SPAW Protocol as a vehicle to assist with the implementation of the Convention on Biological Diversity (CBD) and requested that the CEP develop a cooperation program with the CBD to coordinate and support activities of mutual interest and avoid any duplication. As a result, a memorandum of cooperation was recently signed by both secretariats.

The CBD, the Cartagena Convention, and its two protocols are comprehensive in scope and congruent in most of their provisions. The few elements unique to each instrument are nevertheless mutually supporting as they contribute towards the overall common objectives of both treaties. The Cartagena Convention and its protocols provide, in many instances, more concrete and specific guidance to implement the strong and broader obligations of the CBD at the regional level. In particular, the obligations contained in the SPAW Protocol:

- Manage the components of biodiversity on an ecosystem basis
- Establish and manage protected areas
- Establish protection programs for endangered and threatened species of wildlife
- Manage wildlife to prevent species from becoming threatened or endangered with extinction.

To address the common coastal and marine environmental problems in the region in an integrated way—through the application of the Cartagena Convention and its protocols—the CEP's major activities provide assistance to garments in the following areas:

- Establishment and enforcement of measures necessary to prevent, reduce, and control marine pollution and implementation of the Global Program of Action (GPA) for the Protection of the Marine Environment from Land-based Activities. Inventories of land-based sources of marine pollution have been completed in 26 countries of the wider Caribbean, and activities on pollution control are being developed, as well as promotion of best management practices.
- Development of integrated planning and management of coastal and marine areas. Common guidelines for the region on integrated coastal area management have been developed, and assistance is being provided systematically to countries with the development of integrated coastal area management plans.

3) Establishment and management of protected areas. Some 250 marine protected areas (MPAs) have been established or proposed in the wider Caribbean. Regional guidelines for the selection, identification, establishment, and management of protected areas have been developed, and assistance is provided to countries for their application. A comprehensive training program for trainers and managers of protected areas has been developed, as well as a database of marine protected areas. The process of development of a network of marine pro-

tected areas has been initiated, and technical assistance will be provided to specific MPAs.

- Regional guidelines and national recovery plans for sea turtles, manatees, and other species of regional concerns have been developed, and assistance is provided for implementation.
- Common methods for coral reef monitoring are currently under development, and assistance will be provided to countries for implementation, as well as for participation and coordination with the Global Coral Reef Monitoring Network.
- Strengthening of information management systems for coastal and marine environmental resources among the countries of the region, including global databases and information systems.

In addition, as a followup to the Regional Agenda for Action of the International Coral Reef Initiative (ICRI) adopted in Montego Bay, Jamaica, in August 1995 and as the ICRI contact point for the wider Caribbean, the CEP is implementing a USAID/UNEP-funded regional project to address coastal degradation resulting from tourism. This regional project is promoting best management practices for coastal tourism through the implementation of pilot demonstration projects and the development of a regional plan of action outlining recommended policies for sustainable tourism in the region. Furthermore, a training program is being implemented for the private and public sectors to reduce the negative impacts of tourism activities on coastal ecosystems, particularly concerning solid and wastewater management, design and siting of tourist facilities, and integrated coastal management practices. This initiative was developed in an effort to involve all relevant sectors related to tourism (private, public, and nongovernmental organizations) in the sustainable management of the natural environment on which tourism is based in the wider Caribbean.

A literature review and report was recently conducted as part of the project to determine the nature and causes of coastal degradation resulting from tourism. Based on an analysis of factors such as the significance, scale, and frequency of impact, ecosystem linkages, and cost (such as lost revenue or rehabilitation costs), the report listed the most detrimental practices related to tourism in the coastal zone as physical changes or damage to habitats, sewage disposal, and solid waste disposal.

However, a third major source of impact is the nonconstruction element of the industry, such as recreational activities, which are often linked with major facilities like hotels or marinas, but may also occur apart from such fixed operational bases. The recreational activities include:

- Scuba diving and snorkeling
- Yachting
- Motorboating, water skiing, jet skiing
- Sport fishing
- Mountain biking.

While the above practices are directly attributable to the tourist industry, there are a number of sectors and activities that are indirectly linked to the tourist industry that also contribute to coastal resource degradation. These include overfishing, harvest of reef materials for curio items, overharvest of trees and plants (such as thatch palm or *Lignum vitae*) for craft and construction purposes, and speculative land development.

Tourism impacts on coastal resources are far from uniform. First, the coastal zone is a complex of interlinked ecosystems, with different sensitivities and vulnerabilites, and therefore different abilities to withstand stress. Second, the stresses produced by tourism are not exerted uniformly across systems, or even over the lifetime of projects, facilities, or activities.

Any framework to promote best management practices in tourism should be able to address the systemic problems (public sector planning, inadequacy of essential services, and social issues) as well as the more direct issues of site design, management, and regulation. As such, any effort to develop a coordinated approach to deal with coastal zone management must access resources from—and coordinate the actions of—nontourism interests in the public sector.

In the area of facility operations, and the provision of services (including recreation), the application of best management practices should be supported by the development of the related management systems; that is, environmental policies, appropriate purchasing policies, and environmental management and monitoring systems, staff training, and assigning the responsibility of the program to a senior member. Areas of operation for which past practices have been identified include waste management, water usage, energy usage, facilities maintenance, recreation, and public/social interaction.

A number of best management practices have been tried in many hotels and operations in the wider Caribbean. The most widely most practices include:

- Erosion and sediment control (U.S. Virgin Islands, British Virgin Islands, Jamaica, Dominican Republic, and Barbados)
- Selective purchasing to reduce packaging (several countries)
- Low-flush toilets and low-flow shower heads (several countries)
- Reuse of gray water for irrigation (several countries)
- Energy conservation (most countries).

To achieve environmental best management practices for tourism requires coordinated approaches, information sharing, available instruction materials, and incentives for the sector to invest in the idea. Several regional and international organizations have embarked on programs to improve the environmental practices in hotels. It is the goal of the USAID/UNEP project to contribute to these efforts in support of rational use and conservation of coastal zone and resources in the wider Caribbean region.

Reference

1. Freestone. 1990. *International Journal of Estuarine and Coastal Law,* vol. 5(4).

Appendix G
Conference Participants

Walter Adey
Museum of Natural History
Smithsonian Institution
Washington, DC   USA
Tel: (202) 357-1860
Fax: (202) 357-3037
Email: Adey.Walter@nmnh.si.edu

Tundi Agardy
Senior Director
Conservation International
2501 M Street, NW
Washington, DC 20037 USA
Tel: (202) 973-2203
Fax: (202) 887-0193
Email: t.agardy@conservation.org

Daniel Akaka
U.S. Senator
United States Senate
Washington, DC 20510 USA
Tel: (202) 224-6361
Fax: (202) 22402126

James Armstrong
Deputy Secretary General
Convention on International Trade in
  Endangered Species of Wild Fauna and Flora
Tel: (41 22) 979-9127
Fax: (41 22) 979-9061
Email: armstroj@unep.ch

Eric-Invald Ask
FMC Food Ingredients Division
c/o FMC Marine Colloids Inc.
Mandaue City, Cebu   Philippines
Tel: (63 32) 345-0196
Fax: (63 32) 346-1182

John Baldwin, ICRI Secretariat
Great Barrier Reef Marine Park Authority
PO Box 1379
Townsville, Queensland 4812 Australia
Tel: 61-77-500743
Fax: 61-77-242264
E-mail: J.Baldwin@gbrmpa.gov.au

Celso S. Barrientos
Supervisory Physical Scientist
National Oceanic and Atmospheric
  Administration
NOAA/NESDIS - E/RA3
Camp Springs, MD 20746 USA
Tel: (301) 763-8102
Fax: (301) 763-8020

Lisa Barnett
Development Officer
Smithsonian Tropical Research Institute
900 Jefferson Drive
Suite 2207 MRC 435
Washington, DC 20560 USA
Tel: 202-633-9473
Fax: 202-786-2819
E-mail: lbarnett.stridc@si.edu

Steven Bartimo
Student
University of Maryland
P.O. Box 18
Solomons, MD 20688 USA
Tel: 410-326-6632
E-mail: bartimo@cbl-umces.edu

Heather Benway
National Sea Grant Fellow
NOAA Office of Global Programs
1100 Wayne Avenue
Suite 1210
Silver Spring, MD 20910 USA
Tel: 301-427-2089 ext. 504
Fax: 301-427-2082
E-mail: benway@ogp.noaa.gov

Barbara Best
AAAS Science Diplomacy Fellow
US Agency for International Development
1300 Pennsylvania Avenue
Washington, DC 20523-3800 USA
Tel: (202) 712-0553
Fax: (202) 216-3174

Sofia U. Bettencourt
Natural Resources Economist
World Bank
1818 H Street, NW
Washington, DC 20433 USA
Tel: (202) 458-2554
Fax: (202) 522-1674
Email: sbettencourt@worldbank.org

Juan Bezaury
Amigos de Sian Ka'an
Tel: (52 98) 87 30 80
Fax: (52 98) 84 95 83
Email: sian@cancun.rce.com.mx

Jerry Bisson
Biodiversity Team Leader
USAID
1300 Pennsylvania Ave.
Washington, DC, USA
Tel: 202-712-4178
Fax: 202-216-3174
E-mail: JBisson@USAID.gov

Jennifer Bossard
Research Assistant, ENVGC
World Bank
1818 H Street, NW
Washington, DC 20433 USA
Tel: 202-458-2685
E-mail: JBossard@Worldbank.org

Kay Briggs
Marine Biologist
QuanTech
1911 N. Fort Myer Drive
Arlington, VA 22201 USA
Tel: (703) 312-7800

Lauretta Burke
Environmental and GIS Analyst
World Resources Institute
1709 New York Avenue, NW
Washington, DC 20006 USA
Tel: 202-662-2593
E-mail: Lauretta@wri.org

Kerstin Canby
ENVDR
World Bank
1818 H Street, NW
Washington, DC 20433 USA
Tel: (202) 473-1407
Fax: (202) 477-0565
Email: kcanby@worldbank.org

Eduardo O. Castro
Ataché, Economic Section
Embassy of the Philippines
1600 Massachusetts Avenue, NW
Washington, DC 20036 USA
Tel: 202-467-9317
Fax: 202-467-9417

Herman Cesar
Environmental Economist
World Bank
1818 H Street, NW
Washington, DC 20433 USA
Tel: (202) 458-5759
Fax: (202) 522-1664
Email: hcesar@worldbank.org

Candace Coen
George Washington University
1010 25th Street, NW, #801
Washington, DC 20037 USA
Tel: 202-337-6851
E-mail: Candace@gwis2.circ.gwu.edu

Patric L. Colin
Coral Reef Research Foundation
P.O. Box 1765
Koror, Palay 96940
Tel: (680) 488-5255
Fax: (680) 488-5513
Email: crrf@palaunet.com

Stephen Colwell
Executive Director
Coral Reef Alliance
64 Shattuck Square, Suite 220
Berkeley, CA 94704 USA
Tel: (510) 848-0110
Fax: 510) 848-3720
Email: CoralReefA@aol.com

David Craven
Geographic Information Specialist
Development Alternatives, Inc.
7250 Woodmont Avenue
Suite 200
Bethesda, MD 20814 USA
Tel: 301 215 7028
Fax: 301 718 7968
E-mail: david_craven@dai.com

Michael Crosby
National Research Coordinator
National Oceanic and Atmospheric
  Administration
SSMC-4, Rm 10541
Silver Spring, MD 20910 USA
Tel: (301) 713-3155
Fax: (301) 713-4012
Email: mcrosby@coasts.nos.noaa.gov

Richard Curry
Science Coordinator
Biscayne National Park/ National Park Service
P.O. Box 1369
Homestead, Fl 33090-1369 USA
Tel: (305)230-1144
Fax: (305)230-1190
E-mail: BISC_Science@nps.gov

Ariel Cuschnir
Consultant
Unigroup International-Environmental Consultants
4365 Farm House Lane
Fairfax, VA 22032 USA
Tel: (703) 425-8260

Albert Daley
Executive Director
Environmental Foundation of Jamaica
7 Trinidad Terrace
Kingston, 20 Jamaica
Tel: 876-960-1732/3
Fax: 876-960-1731
E-mail: efjja.@toj.com

Jonathan C. Day
Regional Manager
Northern Region
Queensland Department of Environment
P.O. Box 5391
Townsville, Queensland 4810 Australia
Tel: (61 77) 225-310
Fax: (61 77) 225-311

Michael DeAlessi
Coordinator
Center for Private Conservation
1001 Connecticut Ave, NW
Suite 1250
Washington, DC 20036 USA
Tel: 202-331-1010
Fax: 202-785-7815
E-mail: dealessi@cei.org

Caras Dean
Intern
Coast Alliance
Washington, DC 20016 USA
Tel: (202) 895-4585

Jan DeJarnette
Research Scientist
University of Maryland
Dept. of Microbiology
8380 Greensboro Drive #2
McLean, VA 22102 USA
Tel: 703-356-3116
E-mail: JD89@umail.umd.edu

Yula Del Gallo
Student
The George Washington University
Washington, DC 20004 USA
Tel: (202) 728-9037

Katherine C. Delhotal
Economist
USAID (Contractor)
1331 Pennsylvania Ave. NW
1425
Washington, DC 20004 USA
Tel: 202-661-5808
Fax: 202-661-5890
E-mail: kdelhota@esds.cdie.org

John Dixon
Principal Environmental Economist
World Bank
1818 H Street, NW
Washington, DC 20433 USA
Tel: (202) 473-8594
Fax: (202) 477-0565
Email: jdixon@worldbank.org

Rili Djohani
Deputy Director
Coastal and Marine Program, Asia/Pacific
Director, Coastal and Marine Program, Indonesia
The Nature Conservancy
Jl.Radio IV/5
Kebayoran Baru
Jakarta 12001   Indonesia
Tel: (62 21) 720-6484
Fax: (62 21) 724-5092

James Dobbin
Dobbin International, Inc.
527 Maple Ave, East
Vienna, VA 22180 USA
Tel: (703) 255-1170
Fax: (703) 255-0754

Nancy Dobbin
Dobbin & Associates
304 Springwood Court, NE
Suite 100
Vienna, VA 22180 USA
Tel: 703-255-1170

Philip Dustan
Department of Biology
University of Charleston
Charleston D.C. 29424 USA
Tel: (803) 953-8086
Fax: (803) 953-5453
Email: PDustan@zeus.cofc.edu

Sylvia Earle
President
Deep Ocean Research and Exploration
Oakland, CA 94619 USA
Tel: (510) 530-9388
Fax: (301) 530-3660

Sheila Einsweiler
Senior Wildlife Inspector
U.S. Fish & Wildlife Service
4401 N. Fairfax Drive, Rm 500
Arlington, VA 22203 USA
Tel: (703) 358-1949
Fax: (703) 358-2271

Habib EL-Habr
Interim Coordinator
UNEP
UN Building
Bankok, 10200 Thailand
Tel: 66-2-2881860
Fax: 66-2-267-8008
E-mail: habr.unesacp@un.org

Peter Espeut
Executive Director
South Coast Conservation Foundation
91 A Old Hope Road
Kingston 6   Jamaica
Tel: (876) 927-4047
Fax: (876) 927-3754
Email: pespeut@infochan.com

Bill Faries
Consultant
GEF Secretariat
2111 Jeff Davis Highway
#1013-5
Arlington, VA 22202 USA
Tel: 202-458-9274
E-mail: wfaries@worldbank.org

Martin Fodor
Environmental Specialist
World Bank
1818 H Street, NW
Washington, DC 20433 USA
Tel: (202) 473-9131
Fax: (202) 477-0568
Email: MFodor@worldbank.org

Karen Font
Editorial Staff, Environment
National Geographic Society
1145 17th Street, NW
Washington, DC 20008 USA
Tel: 202-857-7196
Fax: 202-828-6695
E-mail: Kfont@ngs.org

Maureen Flynn
Senior Edit Cartographer
National Geographic Society
Washington, DC 20036 USA
Tel: (202) 775-7855
Fax: (202) 429-5704

Anna Marija Frankic
Office of Senator Akata
US Senate
Washington, DC 20510 USA
Tel: (202) 224-6361
Fax: (202) 22402126

Rex Garcia
Statistical Assistant
United Nations - ECLAC
1825 K Street NW
Washington, DC 20006 USA
Tel: (202) 955-5613
Fax: (202) 296-0826

Janet Gibson
National Project Advisor
UNDP/GEF CZM Project Belize
United Nations Development Programme
Belize City   Belize
Tel: (501 2) 357 39
Fax: (501 2) 357 38

Steve Gittings
Sanctuary Manager
Flower Gardens Banks National Marine
  Sanctuary
NOAA/FGBNMS
216 W. 26th Street, Suite 104
Bryan, TX 77803 USA
Tel: 409-779-2705
Fax: 409-779-2334
E-mail: sgittings@ocean.nos.noaa.gov

Edmund Green
Marine Programme Development Officer
World Conservation Monitoring Centre
219 Huntingdon Road
Cambridge, CB3 0DL UK
Tel: 44 1223 277314
Fax: 44 1223 277136
E-mail: ed.green@wcmc.org.uk

Juan C. Godoy
Co-Director
PFA/CCAD-UE
Los Angeles Calle 62 Oeste 12   Panama
Tel: (507) 236-8186
Fax: (507) 236-3966

Gina Green
Director, Caribbean Region
The Nature Conservancy
1815 N. Lynn St.
Arlington, VA USA
Tel: (703) 841-4865
Fax: (703) 841-4880

George Grice
Senior Assistant Secretary
Ocean Sciences and Living Marine Resources
Intergovernmental Oceanographic Commission
UNESCO
1 Rue Miollis
Paris, CEDEX 15 France
Tel: 33.1.4568.4189
Fax: 33.1.4568.5812
E-mail: GGrice@unesco.org

Gracia Gu-Fang
George Washington University
Tourism and Hospitality Management
Washington, DC 20052 USA
Tel: (202) 887-5251

Lynne Zeitlin Hale
Associate Director
Coastal Resources Center
Graduate School of Oceanography
University of Rhode Island
Narragansett, RI 02882 USA
Tel: 401-792-6112
Fax: 401-789-4670
E-mail: lzhale@gsosun1.gso.uri.edu

Marea E. Hatziolos
Coastal/Wetland Specialist
World Bank
1818 H Street, NW
Washington, DC 20433 USA
Tel: (202) 478-5779
Fax: (202) 477-0568
Email: mhatziolos@worldbank.org

Donald Hawkins
Director
International Institute of Tourism Studies,
George Washington University
School of Business and Public Management
710 21st Street, NW
Washington, DC 20052 USA
Tel: (202) 994-7087
Fax: (202) 994-1420
E-mail: dhawk@gwis2.circ.gwu.edu

Indu Hewawasam
Environmental Specialist
World Bank
1818 H. Street, NW- J-3097
Washington, DC 20433 USA
Tel: 202-473-5559
E-mail: IHewawasam@Worldbank.org

Carolyn Hill
EcoSource
814 W. Diamond Ave
Gaithersburg, MD 20878 USA
Tel: (410) 263-2128
Fax: (410) 268-0923
Email: ecosource@podi.com

Don Hinrichsen
Consultant
United Nations
235 East 53rd Street
Apt. 3C
New York, NY 10022 USA
Tel: 212-223-5842
Fax: 212-207-3888

Gene Holder
Munson Foundation
2900 M Street, NW
Washington, DC 20007 USA
Tel: (202) 298-7874

David Holtz
Director
Florida Keys Field Office
Center for Marine Conservation
513 Fleming Street #14
Key West, FL 33040 USA
Tel: 305-295-3370
Fax: 305-295-3371
E-mail: DHoltz@cenmarine.com

Anthony J. Hooten
Consultant
AJH Environmental Services
4005 Glenridge Street
Kensington, MD 20895-3708 USA
Tel: (301) 942-8839
Fax: (301) 942-8839
E-mail:
Environmental_Services@Compuserve.com

Akemi Horiguchi
Policy Analyst
NAC International/PCI
1101 Connecticut Ave., NW
Suite 1200
Washington, DC USA
Tel: 202-828-2435
Fax: 202-828-2324
E-mail: akemi-horiguchi@nacintl.com

Richard M. Huber
Environmental Economist
World Bank
1818 H Street, NW
Washington, DC 20433 USA
Tel: (202) 473-8581
Fax: (202) 696-7393
Email: rhuber1@worldbank.org

Eliot Hurwitz
National Oceanic and Atmospheric
   Administration
14th & Constitution, NW
Washington, DC 20230 USA
Tel: 202-482-1846
Fax: 202-482-2663
E-mail: ehurwitz@noaa.gov

Bob Johannes
R.E. Johannes Pty Ltd.
8 Tyndall Court
Bonnet Hill, Tasmania 7053   Australia
Tel: (62 36) 229-8064
Fax: (61 36) 229-8066
Email: bobjoh@netspace.net.au

Ken Kassem
University of Alabama
Department of Geography
Tuscaloosa, AL 35401 USA
Tel: (205)366-9743

Richard Kenchington
Executive Director
Great Barrier Reef Marine Park Authority
PO Box 791
Canbera , ACT 2601 Australia
Tel: 61-262-247-02
Fax: 61-6-247-5761
E-mail: r.kenchington@gbrmpa.gov.au

Sunil K. Khanna
Vice President
Tata Energy and Resources Institute
1600 Wilson Blvd.
Arlington, VA 22209 USA
Tel: (703) 841-1136

William Kiene
Coordinator
Year of the Ocean
National Museum of Natural History
EG-13 MRC-125
Washington, DC 20560 USA
Tel: 202-357-2309
Fax: 202-786-2832
E-mail: kiene@nmnh.si.edu

Maritta Koch-Weser
Chief
Environment and Natural Resources Division
Latin America and the Caribbean Region
World Bank
1818 H Street, NW
Washington, DC 20433 USA
Tel: (202) 473-3286
Fax: (202) 522-1664
Email: mkochweser@worldbank.org

Nancy Knowlton
Smithsonian Tropical Research Institute
Naos Island Marine Laboratory
APO-AA, 34002-0948
Tel: 011-507-228-4303
Fax: 011-507-228-0516
Email: KNOWLTON@naos.si.edu

Rhonda Kranz
Program Manager
Ecological Society of America
2010 Massachusetts Ave, N.W.
Washington, D.C. 20036 USA
Tel: (202) 833-8748
Fax: (202) 833-8775

Coalter Lathrop
NOAA/MNFS
1206 T Street, NW
Washington, DC 20009 USA
Tel: 301-713-2319 ext. 133
Fax: 301-713-0376
E-mail: coalter.lathrop@noaa.gov

Michael Leuthner
Embassy of the Marshall Islands
4400 Massachusetts Avenue, NW
Washington, DC 20016
Tel: 202-865-4619
E-mail: kickin@rocketmail.com

Michele Lemay
Inter-American Development Bank
1300 New York Avenue, NW
Washington, DC 20577 USA
Tel: (202) 623-1838
Fax: (202) 623-1315
E-mail: MicheleL@IADB.org

Olof Linden
Coordinator
SAREC
Department of Zoology
Stockholm Sweden
Tel: (46 8) 16 40 29
Fax: (46 8) 16 77 15

Stephen Lintner
Prinicipal Environmental Specialist
World Bank
1818 H Street, N.W.
Washington, DC 20433 USA
Tel: (202) 473-2508
Fax: (202) 477-0568
E-mail: SLintner@Worldbank.org

Engelke Lynn-Steven
Education Consultant
Smithsonian Institute
Smithsonian Office of Education
A-I Building 1163 MRC 402
Washington, DC 20560 USA
Tel: 202-357-3050
Fax: 202-357-4908
E-mail: Engelkel@SOE.si.edu

Nancy MacKinnon
The Nature Conservancy
1 Sutter Street #308
San Francisco, CA 94104 USA
Tel: (415) 362-2011
Fax: (415) 902-9930
Email: 71134.2772@compuserve.com

Solomon Makoloweka
Program Coordinator
Tanga Coastal Zone Conservation and
 Development Programme
P.O. Box 5036
Tanga   Tanzania
Tel: (255 53) 47463
Fax: (255-53) 47465
Email: tangacoast@twiga.com

Sergio Marchisio
Professor
National Research Council
Corso Vittorio Emanuele II, 251
Rome, 00186 Italy
Tel: 0039.6.6893009
Fax: 0039.6.68308307
E-mail: marchisio@iasi.rm.cnr.it

Robin G. Marinos
Marine Specialist
c/o Munson Foundation
Tegelberg Str. 4
Stadtbergen, 86391 Germany
Tel: (202) 298-7879
Fax: (202) 625-6204

Teri Marsh
Sea Grant Fellow
Office of Protected Resources
NOAA/NMFS
1315 East-West Highway
Silver Spring, MD 20910 USA
Tel: 301-713-2319 x. 140
Fax: 301-713-0376
E-mail: Teri.Marsh@NOAA.gov

Amy Matthews-Amos
Program Director
Marine Conservation Biology Institute
205 N. Edgewood Street
Arlington, VA 22201 USA
Tel: (703) 276-1434
Fax: (703) 276-1528

Christopher Mattia
President, Innovative Cyber Solutions
P.O. Box 18
Solomons, MD 20688 USA
Tel: 301-510-6925
Fax: 410-721-5247
E-mail: mattia@smbcinc.com

John W. McManus
Reefbase Project Leader
International Center for Living Aquatic
  Resources Management
MCPO Box 2631,
0718 Makati City Philippines
Tel: (63 2) 818-0466
Fax: (63 2) 816-3183
Email: J.McManus@cgnet.com

Yolanda Membreno
Third Secretary, Embassy of Honduras
3007 Tilden Street, NW
POD 4-M
Washington, DC 20008 USA
Tel: 202-966-7702/08
Fax: 202-966-9751
E-mail: embhondu@ix.netcom.com

Marshall Meyers
Pet Industry Joint Advisory Council
1220 19th Street, NW
Washington, DC 20036 USA
Tel: (202) 466-8270
Fax: (202) 293-4377

Jon Moore
President
Chesapeake Marine Aquaria Society
5187 B Bennett
Andrews AFB, MD 20762 USA
Tel: 301-599-1756
E-mail: JMoore@Digizen.net

Judith Moore
World Bank
1818 H Street, N.W.
Washington, DC 20433 USA
Tel: (202) 458-4578
jmoore1@worldbank.org

Sitoo Mukerji
Director
Office of Science and Technology
Organization of American States
1889 F Street, NW , Office 270-J
Washington, DC 20006 USA
Tel: 202-458-3368
Fax: 202-458-3167
E-mail: smukerji@oas.org

Peter Mumby
Research Fellow Geography
University of Sheffield
Sheffield, S102TW UK
Tel: (44 114) 222-7970
Fax: (44 114) 279-7912

Richard Murphy
Jean Michel Cousteau Institute
Email: RMurphy000@aol.com

Abdulla Naseer
Marine Researcher
Ministry of Fisheries and Agriculture
White Waves/H
Male
Republic of Maldives
Tel: (960) 323 28
Fax: (960) 32 25 09

Ken Newcomb
ENVDR
World Bank
1818 H Street, NW
Washington, DC 20433 USA
Tel: (202) 473-6010
Fax: (202) 477-0565
E-mail: KNewcomb@Worldbank.org

David Newman
National Cancer Institute
Bethesda, MD 20814 USA
Tel: (301) 846-5387
Fax: (301) 846-6178
Email: Newman@dtpax2.ncifcrf.gov

Jennifer Newton
Sea Grant Fellow
Congressman Sam Farr
1117 Longworth House Office Building
Washington, DC 20515 USA
Tel: 202-225-2861
Fax: 202-225-6791
E-mail: jen.newton@mail.house.gov

Agneta Nilsson
United Nations Environment Programme
Water Branch
P.O. Box 30552
Nairobi   Kenya
Tel: (254 2) 62 23 09
Fax: (254-2) 62 27 88

John C. Ogden
Director
Florida Institute of Oceanography
University of South Florida
830 First Street South
St. Petersburg, FL 33701 USA
Tel: 813-893-9100
Fax: 813-893-9109
E-mail: jogden@seas.marine.usf.edu

David Orrukem
Minister (DCM)
Palaun Embassy
1150 18th Street, NW
Washington, DC 20036 USA
Tel: (202) 452-6814
Fax: (202) 452-6281

Daniel Pelicier
Flic en Flac
Morcellement Anna Mauritius
Tel/Fax: (230) 453-8109

Michael Philley
Team Leader
Water and Coastal Resources
US Agency for International Development
Ronald Regan Building
Washington, DC 20523-3801 USA
Tel: (202) 712-1679
Fax: (202) 216-3174

Brady Phillips
Constituent Affairs Officer
Sanctuary and Reserves Division
NOAA
1305 East-West Highway, N/ORM-2
Silver Spring, MD 20910 USA
Tel: 301-713-3141 ext. 169
Fax: 301-713-0404
E-mail: bphillips@ocean.nos.noaa.gov

Eleanor Phillips
Fisheries Officer
Department of Fisheries
Nassau   Bahamas
Tel: (242) 393-2965
Fax: (242) 393-2751

Jan Post
Senior Environmental Affairs Specialist
World Bank
1818 H Street, NW
Washington, DC 20433 USA
Tel: (202) 473-3400
Fax: (202) 477-0568
Email: jpost@worldbank.org

Vaughan R. Pratt
President
International Marinelife Alliance - Philippines
36 Sta. Catalina cor. Stella Maris St.
Bo. Kapitolyo, Pasig City, Metro Manila
Philippines 1600
Tel: (63 2) 633-5687, 631-4940
Fax: (63 2) 631-9251
Email: Imaphil@mnl.sequel.net

Ernesto Quintero
Research Scientist, Oceanix Biosciences
7170 Standard Drive
Hanover, MD 21076 USA
Tel: 410-712-4410
Fax: 410-712-4412
E-mail: EQI@umail.umd.edu

Raymond A. Rasamoelina
Counselor
Embassy of Madagascar
2374 Massachusetts Avenue, NW
Washington, DC 20008 USA
Tel: (202) 265-5525
Fax: (202) 265-3034

Devin Reese
AAAS Science, Engineering, Diplomacy Fellow
USAID
USAID/G/ENV
Ronald Reagan Building, Room 3.08
Washington, DC 20523-3800 USA
Tel: 202 712-0546
Fax: 202 216-3174
E-mail: dereese@usaid.gov

Ralf Reichert
Founding CEO
Hope For Tomorrow Foundation
12000 Bobwhite Drive
Catharpin, VA 20143 USA
Tel: (703) 754-4871
Fax: (703) 754-2976

Jamie Resor
World Wildlife Fund
1250 24th Street, NW
Washington, D.C. 20037 USA
Tel: (202)778-9766
Fax: (202) 861-8324
Email: Jamie.Resor@wwfus.org

Thomas Rhodes
Water Resources Advisor
Global Environment Center, USAID
USAID/G/ENV/ENR, Ronald Reagan Building
Washington, DC 20523-3800 USA
Tel: (202) 712-5373
Fax: (202) 216-3174

Callum Roberts
University of York
York, Y01 SDD UK
Tel: (44 19) 04 434 066
Fax: (44 19) 04 432 998
Email: cr10@york.ac.uk

Michael Rubino
Project Officer
International Finance Corporation
2121 Pennsylvania Avenue, NW
Washington, DC 20433 USA
Tel: (202) 473-2891
Fax: (202) 974-4349
Email: mrubino@ifc.org

Bernard Salvat
Professor
E.P.M.E. Perpignan France Université
Perpignan, 66860 France
Tel: 33-4-68662055

Francine Salvat
Biologist
E.P.M.E. Perpignan France Université
Perpignan, 66860 France
Tel: 33-4-68662055

Richard Schwabacher
The Cousteau Society
2104 Pickwick Lane
Alexandria, VA 22307 USA
Tel: (703) 660-8683
Fax: (703) 660-6239

Kenneth P. Sebens
University of Maryland
Department of Zoology
1200 Zoology-Psychology Building
College Park, MD 207412-4415 USA
Tel: 301-405-7978
Fax: 301-314-9358

Janine Selendy
Chairperson and Executive Producer
Horizon Communications
Yale University Department of Biology
New Haven, CT 06520-8103 USA
Tel: (203) 432-6266, (617) 547-8932
Fax: (203) 432-6161
Email: jselendy@aol.com

Ismail Serageldin
Vice President, ESSD
World Bank
1818 H Street, NW
Washington, DC 20433 USA
Tel: 202-473-5690
Fax: 202-473-3112
E-mail: ISerageldin@Worldbank.org

Ivar Serejski
Senior Agricultural Extension Specialist
World Bank
1818 H Street, NW
Washington, DC 20433 USA
Tel: (202) 458-1278
Fax: (202) 522-1778
iserejski@worldbank.org

Brooke Shearer
Special Advisor
Dept. of Interior, USG
1849 C Street, NW
Washington, DC USA
Tel: 202-208-3724
Fax: 202-208-1873

David Slade
Law Offices of David C. Slade, Esq.
1221 Roundtree Lane
Bowie, MD 20715 USA
Tel: (301) 464-6473

Jack Sobel
Director
Ecosystem Protection
Center for Marine Conservation
1725 DeSales Street, NW, Suite 600
Washington, DC 20036 USA
Tel: (202) 429-5609
Fax: (202) 872-0619
Email: jsobel@cenmarine.com

Jay Steine
Verner Liipfert
701 13th Street, NW
Washington, DC 20005 USA
Tel: (202) 371-6176
Fax: (202) 371-6279

Alexander Stone
Director
Reefkeeper International
2809 Bird Avenue
Suite 162
Miami, FL 33133   175 USA
Tel: 305-358-4600
Fax: 305-358-3030
E-mail: Reefkeeper@earthlink.net

Alan Strong
Oceanographer
National Oceanic and Atmospheric
   Administration/NESDIS/ORAD
NOAA Science Center
Suitland, MD 20233 USA
Tel: (301) 763-8102
Fax: (301) 763-8108

Carolina Suau
Local Agenda 21 Coordinator
Calvia City Council, Mallorca-Spain
   Government
Can Vich 29
Calvia, 07184 Spain
Tel: 34-71-139100
Fax: 34-71-139148
E-mail: calvia@bitel.es

Boyce Thorne-Miller
Senior Scientist
SeaWeb
1731 Connecticut Ave., NW
Washington, DC 20009 USA
Tel: 202-483-9570
E-mail: oceans@igc.apc.org

Asamnew G. Tzada
Economic Officer
Embassy of Eritrea
1708 New Hampshire Ave, NW
Washington, DC 20009 USA
Tel: 202-319-1991
Fax: 202-319-1304
E-mail: Asamnew@eritreaembassy.org

Mark Valentine
Program Officer
David and Lucile Packard Foundation
300 Second Street
Suite 200
Los Altos , CA 94022 USA
Tel: 650-948-7658
Fax: 650-948-5793
E-mail: m.valentine@packfound.org

Shiela Vergara
Research Associate
ICLARM
Bloomindale Building 205 Salcedo Street
Makati, 1229 Philippines
Tel: 63-281-80466
Fax: 632-8163183
E-mail: S.vergara@cgnet.com

John Walch
The Aquatic Wildlife Company
15042 N. Moon Valley Dr.
Phoenix, AZ 85022 USA
Tel: (602) 548-8697
Fax: (602) 862-9061
Email: AquaWildAZ@aol.com

Clive R. Wilkinson
Coordinator
Global Coral Reef Monitoring Network
Australian Institute of Marine Science
Townsville MC, QLD 4810 Australia
Tel: (61 77) 78 93 72
Fax: (61 77) 72 58 52
Email: C.Wilkinson@aims.gov.au

Henry Wolcott
President
The Henry Foundation
2900 M Street, NW
Suite 200
Washington, DC 20007 USA
Tel: 202-298-7879
Fax: 202-298-7874
E-mail: CWHReef@aol.com

Matthew Wright
Post-Graduate
Cambridge University
1 Great House Mews
Kingston, 6 Jamaica
Tel: 809-977-2832
E-mail: rwright@colis.com

David Younkman
Vice President, Resources,
Latin America and Caribbean Region
The Nature Conservancy
1815 North Lynn Street
Arlington, VA 22209 USA
Tel: 703-841-4867
Fax: 703-841-4100
E-mail: DYounkman@TNC.org

Michele Zador
Environmental Specialist
Development Alternatives
2032 Belmont Road, NW
Washington, DC 20009 USA
E-mail: Michele_Zador@dai.com

Jose Zertuche
Universidad Autonoma de Baja California
Instituto de Investigaciones Oceanologicas
Km. 103 Carr. Tijuana Ensenada
Ensenada, B.C., Mexico C.P. 22800 Mexico
Tel: (52 61) 74 46 01 ext. 113
Fax: (52 61) 74 49 43
Email: 74054.1065@compuserve.com

Laura Zertuche
Food Engineer
SEP
Km. 103 Carr. Tijuana_Ensenada
Ensenada, B.C., Mexico C.P. 22860 Mexico
Tel: 52 (61) 74 49-56

Distributors of World Bank Publications

Prices and credit terms vary from country to country. Consult your local distributor before placing an order.

ARGENTINA
Oficina del Libro Internacional
Av. Córdoba 1877
1120 Buenos Aires
Tel: (54 1) 815-8354
Fax: (54 1) 815-8156
E-mail: olilibro@satlink.com

AUSTRALIA, FIJI, PAPUA NEW GUINEA, SOLOMON ISLANDS, VANUATU, AND SAMOA
D.A. Information Services
648 Whitehorse Road
Mitcham 3132
Victoria
Tel: (61) 3 9210 7777
Fax: (61) 3 9210 7788
E-mail: service@dadirect.com.au

AUSTRIA
Gerold and Co.
Weihburggasse 26
A-1011 Wien
Tel: (43 1) 512-47-31-0
Fax: (43 1) 512-47-31-29

BANGLADESH
Micro Industries Development
Assistance Society (MIDAS)
House 5, Road 16
Dhanmondi R/Area
Dhaka 1209
Tel: (880 2) 326427
Fax: (880 2) 811188

BELGIUM
Jean De Lannoy
Av. du Roi 202
1060 Brussels
Tel: (32 2) 538-5169
Fax: (32 2) 538-0841

BRAZIL
Publicações Tecnicas Internacionais Ltda.
Rua Peixoto Gomide, 209
01409 Sao Paulo, SP.
Tel: (55 11) 259-6644
Fax: (55 11) 258-6990
E-mail: postmaster@pti.uol.br

CANADA
Renouf Publishing Co. Ltd.
5369 Canotek Road
Ottawa, Ontario K1J 9J3
Tel: (613) 745-2665
Fax: (613) 745-7660
E-mail: order.dept@renoufbooks.com

CHINA
China Financial & Economic
Publishing House
8, Da Fo Si Dong Jie
Beijing
Tel: (86 10) 6333-8257
Fax: (86 10) 6401-7365

China Book Import Centre
P.O. Box 2825
Beijing

COLOMBIA
Infoenlace Ltda.
Carrera 6 No. 51-21
Apartado Aereo 34270
Santafé de Bogotá, D.C.
Tel: (57 1) 285-2798
Fax: (57 1) 285-2798

COTE D'IVOIRE
Center d'Edition et de Diffusion Africaines
(CEDA)
04 B.P. 541
Abidjan 04
Tel: (225) 24 6510;24 6511
Fax: (225) 25 0567

CYPRUS
Center for Applied Research
Cyprus College
6, Diogenes Street, Engomi
P.O. Box 2006
Nicosia
Tel: (357 2) 44-1730
Fax: (357 2) 46-2051

CZECH REPUBLIC
USIS, NIS Prodejna
Havelkova 22
130 00 Prague 3
Tel: (420 2) 2423 1486
Fax: (420 2) 2423 1114

DENMARK
SamfundsLitteratur
Rosenoerns Allé 11
DK-1970 Frederiksberg C
Tel: (45 31) 351942
Fax: (45 31) 357822

ECUADOR
Libri Mundi
Libreria Internacional
P.O. Box 17-01-3029
Juan Leon Mera 851
Quito
Tel/Fax: (593 2) 521-606; (593 2) 544-185
Fax: (593 2) 504-209
E-mail: librimu1@librimundi.com.ec

CODEU
Ruiz de Castilla 763, Edif. Expocolor
Primer piso, Of. #2
Quito
Tel/Fax: (593 2) 507-383; 253-091
E-mail: codeu@impsat.net.ec

EGYPT, ARAB REPUBLIC OF
Al Ahram Distribution Agency
Al Galaa Street
Cairo
Tel: (20 2) 578-6083
Fax: (20 2) 578-6833

The Middle East Observer
41, Sherif Street
Cairo
Tel: (20 2) 393-9732
Fax: (20 2) 393-9732

FINLAND
Akateeminen Kirjakauppa
P.O. Box 128
FIN-00101 Helsinki
Tel: (358 0) 121 4418
Fax: (358 0) 121-4435
E-mail: akatilaus@stockmann.fi

FRANCE
World Bank Publications
66, avenue d'Iéna
75116 Paris
Tel: (33 1) 40-69-30-56/57
Fax: (33 1) 40-69-30-68

GERMANY
UNO-Verlag
Poppelsdorfer Allee 55
53115 Bonn
Tel: (49 228) 949020
Fax: (49 228) 217492
E-mail: unoverlag@aol.com

GHANA
Epp Books Services
P.O. Box 44
TUC
Accra

GREECE
Papasotiriou S.A.
35, Stoumara Str.
106 82 Athens
Tel: (30 1) 364-1826
Fax: (30 1) 364-8254

HAITI
Culture Diffusion
5, Rue Capois
C.P. 257
Port-au-Prince
Tel: (509) 23 9260
Fax: (509) 23 4858

HONG KONG, CHINA; MACAO
Asia 2000 Ltd.
Sales & Circulation Department
302 Seabird House
22-28 Wyndham Street, Central
Hong Kong
Tel: (852) 2530-1409
Fax: (852) 2526-1107
E-mail: sales@asia2000.com.hk

HUNGARY
Euro Info Service
Margitszgeti Europa Haz
H-1138 Budapest
Tel: (36 1) 350 80 24, 350 80 25
Fax: (36 1) 350 90 32
E-mail: euroinfo@mail.matav.hu

INDIA
Allied Publishers Ltd.
751 Mount Road
Madras - 600 002
Tel: (91 44) 852-3938
Fax: (91 44) 852-0649

INDONESIA
Pt. Indira Limited
Jalan Borobudur 20
P.O. Box 181
Jakarta 10320
Tel: (62 21) 390-4290
Fax: (62 21) 390-4289

IRAN
Ketab Sara Co. Publishers
Khaled Eslamboli Ave., 6th Street
Delafrooz Alley No. 8
P.O. Box 15745-733
Tehran 15117
Tel: (98 21) 8717819; 8716104
Fax: (98 21) 8712479
E-mail: ketab-sara@neda.net.ir

Kowkab Publishers
P.O. Box 19575-511
Tehran
Tel: (98 21) 258-3723
Fax: (98 21) 258-3723

IRELAND
Government Supplies Agency
Oifig an tSoláthair
4-5 Harcourt Road
Dublin 2
Tel: (353 1) 661-3111
Fax: (353 1) 475-2670

ISRAEL
Yozmot Literature Ltd.
P.O. Box 56055
3 Yohanan Hasandlar Street
Tel Aviv 61560
Tel: (972 3) 5285-397
Fax: (972 3) 5285-397

R.O.Y. International
PO Box 13056
Tel Aviv 61130
Tel: (972 3) 649 9469
Fax: (972 3) 648 6039
E-mail: royil@netvision.net.il

Palestinian Authority/Middle East
Index Information Services
P.O.B. 19502 Jerusalem
Tel: (972 2) 6271219
Fax: (972 2) 6271634

ITALY
Licosa Commissionaria Sansoni SPA
Via Duca Di Calabria, 1/1
Casella Postale 552
50125 Firenze
Tel: (55) 645-415
Fax: (55) 641-257
E-mail: licosa@ftbcc.it

JAMAICA
Ian Randle Publishers Ltd.
206 Old Hope Road, Kingston 6
Tel: 876-927-2085
Fax: 876-977-0243
E-mail: irpl@colis.com

JAPAN
Eastern Book Service
3-13, Hongo 3-chome, Bunkyo-ku
Tokyo 113
Tel: (81 3) 3818-0861
Fax: (81 3) 3818-0864
E-mail: orders@svt-ebs.co.jp

KENYA
Africa Book Service (E.A.) Ltd.
Quaran House, Mfangano Street
P.O. Box 45245
Nairobi
Tel: (254 2) 223 641
Fax: (254 2) 330 272

KOREA, REPUBLIC OF
Daejon Trading Co. Ltd.
P.O. Box 34, Youida, 706 Seoun Bldg
44-6 Youido-Dong, Yeongchengpo-Ku
Seoul
Tel: (82 2) 785-1631/4
Fax: (82 2) 784-0315

LEBANON
Librairie du Liban
P.O. Box 11-9232
Beirut
Tel: (961 9) 217 944
Fax: (961 9) 217 434

MALAYSIA
University of Malaya Cooperative
Bookshop, Limited
P.O. Box 1127
Jalan Pantai Baru
59700 Kuala Lumpur
Tel: (60 3) 756-5000
Fax: (60 3) 755-4424

MEXICO
INFOTEC
Av. San Fernando No. 37
Col. Toriello Guerra
14050 Mexico, D.F.
Tel: (52 5) 624-2800
Fax: (52 5) 624-2822
E-mail: infotec@rtn.net.mx

Mundi-Prensa Mexico S.A. de C.V.
c/Rio Panuco, 141-Colonia Cuauhtemoc
06500 Mexico, D.F
Tel: (52 5) 533-5658
Fax: (52 5) 514-6799

NEPAL
Everest Media International Services (P) Ltd.
GPO Box 5443
Kathmandu
Tel: (977 1) 472 152
Fax: (977 1) 224 431

NETHERLANDS
De Lindeboom/InOr-Publikaties
P.O. Box 202, 7480 AE Haaksbergen
Tel: (31 53) 574-0004
Fax: (31 53) 572-9296
E-mail: lindeboo@worldonline.nl

NEW ZEALAND
EBSCO NZ Ltd.
Private Mail Bag 99914
New Market
Auckland
Tel: (64 9) 524-8119
Fax: (64 9) 524-8067

NIGERIA
University Press Limited
Three Crowns Building Jericho
Private Mail Bag 5095
Ibadan
Tel: (234 22) 41-1356
Fax: (234 22) 41-2056

NORWAY
NIC Info A/S
Book Department, Postboks 6512 Etterstad
N-0606 Oslo
Tel: (47 22) 97-4500
Fax: (47 22) 97-4545

PAKISTAN
Mirza Book Agency
65, Shahrah-e-Quaid-e-Azam
Lahore 54000
Tel: (92 42) 735 3601
Fax: (92 42) 576 3714

Oxford University Press
5 Bangalore Town
Sharae Faisal
PO Box 13033
Karachi-75350
Tel: (92 21) 446307
Fax: (92 21) 4547640
E-mail: ouppak@TheOffice.net

Pak Book Corporation
Aziz Chambers 21, Queen's Road
Lahore
Tel: (92 42) 636 3222; 636 0885
Fax: (92 42) 636 2328
E-mail: pbc@brain.net.pk

PERU
Editorial Desarrollo SA
Apartado 3824, Lima 1
Tel: (51 14) 285380
Fax: (51 14) 286628

PHILIPPINES
International Booksource Center Inc.
1127-A Antipolo St, Barangay, Venezuela
Makati City
Tel: (63 2) 896 6501; 6505; 6507
Fax: (63 2) 896 1741

POLAND
International Publishing Service
Ul. Piekna 31/37
00-677 Warzawa
Tel: (48 2) 628-6089
Fax: (48 2) 621-7255
E-mail: books%ips@ikp.atm.com.pl

PORTUGAL
Livraria Portugal
Apartado 2681, Rua Do Carmo 70-74
1200 Lisbon
Tel: (1) 347-4982
Fax: (1) 347-0264

ROMANIA
Compani De Librarii Bucuresti S.A.
Str. Lipscani no. 26, sector 3
Bucharest
Tel: (40 1) 613 9645
Fax: (40 1) 312 4000

RUSSIAN FEDERATION
Isdatelstvo <Ves Mir>
9a, Kolpachniy Pereulok
Moscow 101831
Tel: (7 095) 917 87 49
Fax: (7 095) 917 92 59

SINGAPORE; TAIWAN, CHINA; MYANMAR; BRUNEI
Hemisphere Publication Services
41 Kallang Pudding Road #04-03
Golden Wheel Building
Singapore 349316
Tel: (65) 741-5166
Fax: (65) 742-9356
E-mail: ashgate@asianconnect.com

SLOVENIA
Gospodarski Vestnik Publishing Group
Dunajska cesta 5
1000 Ljubljana
Tel: (386 61) 133 83 47; 132 12 30
Fax: (386 61) 133 80 30
E-mail: repansekj@gvestnik.si

SOUTH AFRICA, BOTSWANA
For single titles:
Oxford University Press Southern Africa
Vasco Boulevard, Goodwood
P.O. Box 12119, N1 City 7463
Cape Town
Tel: (27 21) 595 4400
Fax: (27 21) 595 4430
E-mail: oxford@oup.co.za

For subscription orders:
International Subscription Service
P.O. Box 41095
Craighall
Johannesburg 2024
Tel: (27 11) 880-1448
Fax: (27 11) 880-6248
E-mail: iss@is.co.za

SPAIN
Mundi-Prensa Libros, S.A.
Castello 37
28001 Madrid
Tel: (34 1) 431-3399
Fax: (34 1) 575-3998
E-mail: libreria@mundiprensa.es

Mundi-Prensa Barcelona
Consell de Cent, 391
08009 Barcelona
Tel: (34 3) 488-3492
Fax: (34 3) 487-7659
E-mail: barcelona@mundiprensa.es

SRI LANKA, THE MALDIVES
Lake House Bookshop
100, Sir Chittampalam Gardiner Mawatha
Colombo 2
Tel: (94 1) 32105

Fax: (94 1) 432104
E-mail: LHL@sri.lanka.net

SWEDEN
Wennergren-Williams AB
P. O. Box 1305
S-171 25 Solna
Tel: (46 8) 705-97-50
Fax: (46 8) 27-00-71
E-mail: mail@wwi.se

SWITZERLAND
Librairie Payot Service Institutionnel
Côtes-de-Montbenon 30
1002 Lausanne
Tel: (41 21) 341-3229
Fax: (41 21) 341-3235

ADECO Van Diemen EditionsTechniques
Ch. de Lacuez 41
CH1807 Blonay
Tel: (41 21) 943 2673
Fax: (41 21) 943 3605

THAILAND
Central Books Distribution
306 Silom Road
Bangkok 10500
Tel: (66 2) 235-5400
Fax: (66 2) 237-8321

TRINIDAD & TOBAGO AND THE CARRIBBEAN
Systematics Studies Ltd.
St. Augustine Shopping Center
Eastern Main Road, St. Augustine
Trinidad & Tobago, West Indies
Tel: (868) 645-8466
Fax: (868) 645-8467
E-mail: tobe@trinidad.net

UGANDA
Gustro Ltd.
PO Box 9997, Madhvani Building
Plot 16/4 Jinja Rd.
Kampala
Tel: (256 41) 251 467
Fax: (256 41) 251 468

UNITED KINGDOM
Microinfo Ltd.
P.O. Box 3, Omega Park, Alton,
Hampshire GU34 2PG
England
Tel: (44 1420) 86848
Fax: (44 1420) 89889
E-mail: gus@swiftuganda.com

The Stationery Office
51 Nine Elms Lane
London SW8 5DR
Tel: (44 171) 873-8400
Fax: (44 171) 873-8242

VENEZUELA
Tecni-Ciencia Libros, S.A.
Centro Cuidad Comercial Tamanco
Nivel C2, Caracas
Tel: (58 2) 959 5547; 5035; 0016
Fax: (58 2) 959 5636

ZAMBIA
University Bookshop, University of Zambia
Great East Road Campus
P.O. Box 32379
Lusaka
Tel: (260 1) 252 576
Fax: (260 1) 253 952

ZIMBABWE
Academic and Baobab Books (Pvt.) Ltd.
4 Conald Road, Graniteside
P.O. Box 567
Harare
Tel: 263 4 755035
Fax: 263 4 781913